BibleWorld

Series Editor: Philip R. Davies and James G. Crossley, University of Sheffield

BibleWorld shares the fruits of modern (and postmodern) biblical scholarship not only among practitioners and students, but also with anyone interested in what academic study of the Bible means in the twenty-first century. It explores our ever-increasing knowledge and understanding of the social world that produced the biblical texts, but also analyses aspects of the bible's role in the history of our civilization and the many perspectives – not just religious and theological, but also cultural, political and aesthetic – which drive modern biblical scholarship.

Recently Published:

SIMULATING JESUS
REALITY EFFECTS IN THE GOSPELS

George Aichele

LONDON   OAKVILLE

Published by Equinox Publishing Ltd.
UK: 1 Chelsea Manor Studios, Flood Street, London SW3 5SR
USA: DBBC, 28 Main Street, Oakville, CT 06779

www.equinoxpub.com

First published 2011

British Library Cataloguing-in-Publication Data

A catalogue record for this book is available from the British Library.

ISBN-13 978 1 84553 680 0 (hardback)
         978 1 84553 681 7 (paperback)

Library of Congress Cataloging-in-Publication Data

Aichele, George.
   Simulating Jesus : reality effects in the Gospels / George Aichele.
      p. cm.
   Includes bibliographical references (p.   ) and indexes.
   ISBN 978-1-84553-680-0 (hb)—ISBN 978-1-84553-681-7 (pb) 1. Jesus Christ—Person
and offices. 2. Bible. N.T. Gospels—Criticism, interpretation, etc. I. Title.

BT203.A52 2011
232'.8—dc22

                          2010031023

Typeset by S.J.I. Services, New Delhi
Printed and bound in Great Britain by Lightning Source UK Ltd, Milton Keynes

For Connie

CONTENTS

ACKNOWLEDGMENTS

Unless otherwise noted, English quotations from the Bible in this book are from the Revised Standard Version (1971). The Greek text of the New Testament is from Nestle and Aland (1979) and that of the Septuagint is from Rahlfs (1979).

Parts of many of these chapters have been previously published, but all of this material has been edited, expanded, or revised to fit into the larger argument of this book. An earlier version of Chapter 1 appears in Roland Boer and Fernando Segovia, eds, *The Future of the Biblical Past* (Semeia Studies, SBL Press, 2011). A much shorter version of Chapter 2 appears in Roberta Sabbath, ed., *Sacred Tropes: Tanakh, New Testament, Qur'an as Literary Works* (Brill, 2009), and parts of Chapter 3 appear in *Cross Currents*, Winter, 2002. Chapter 4 was written especially for this book. An earlier version of Chapter 5 appears in George Aichele and Richard Walsh, eds, *Those Outside: Noncanonical Readings of Canonical Gospels* (Continuum/ T & T Clark International, 2005), and a shorter version of Chapter 6 appears in *Biblical Interpretation* 12(4), 2004. Parts of Chapter 7 appear in *Biblical Interpretation* 14(1–2), 2006, and this double issue was also published as J. Cheryl Exum, ed., *The Bible in Film – the Bible and Film* (Brill, 2006). Chapter 8 was written especially for this book, and parts of Chapter 9 appear in *The Bible and Critical Theory* 4(1), 2008. Chapter 10 was written especially for this book.

I am deeply indebted to many friends who have spent time and effort reading drafts of these writings and sharing their thoughts with me. They help me to see problems and opportunities in the texts that I would have otherwise missed. Others have provided helpful expert answers to my questions. I take full responsibility for the contents of this book and any errors it may contain, but without the help of these friends any value that may be found here would be seriously diminished. These friends and advisers include Fred Burnett, Elizabeth Castelli, Kevin Hart, Peter Miscall, Raj Nadella, Adele Reinhartz, Yvonne Sherwood, Jeffrey Staley, and Richard Walsh, as well as my former students, Carli Dice and Krystal Bedtelyon.

PREFACE

> Scripture ... is a privileged domain for this problem [of meaning], because, on the one hand, theologically, it is certain that a final signified is postulated: the metaphysical definition or the semantic definition of theology is to postulate the Last Signified; and because, on the other hand, the very notion of Scripture, the fact that the Bible is called Scripture, Writing, would orient us toward a more ambiguous comprehension of the problems, as if effectively, and theologically too, the base, the *princeps*, were still a Writing, and always a Writing. (Barthes 1988: 242)

> The characteristic of the signifier is to be a *departure* (for other signifiers); and the signifying point of departure ... is the [alphabetic] Letter. (Barthes 1985: 114)

Reading is inherently anachronistic. We always read, as we always live, in the present moment, even though that moment is itself always "non-present," divided but also constituted by temporal difference (Derrida 1973: 63; Deleuze 1994: 70–128). A text comes to us from what we call "the past," marked by a quality of already having been written, but we hold it in our hands and perhaps smell and most importantly read it right now. We are tempted to think of it as the "voice" of another, even though there is neither sound nor the living presence of a speaker, and we can at best only imagine the moment of its writing.[1] Each reader "hears" each text as though it "spoke" with a distinct voice, even texts that we know were written by the same author, and this is sufficient to tell us that there is no simple identity between the voice that the reader "hears" (the implied author) and any actual author in the past.

However, reading is also necessarily a struggle with the passive and yet resistant inertia of a text, an attempt which always fails to transform silent letters into the effects of a living voice, to make the text come alive right now, to make it speak for itself. The reader "produces" the text, recognizing

---

1. I refer to reading and writing because that is the primary focus of this book, but these comments also apply more generally to any technology of decoding and encoding. I use "text" to describe any sequence of more or less durable phenomena that are considered to be signifiers.

it to be a significant object and transforming it into the meaningful work (making it "speak"). This is what both Socrates and the apostle Paul acknowledged and feared (Plato 1973, section 275; 2 Cor. 3:1–8), and what the gospels of Mark and Thomas both particularly exemplify. We all were most aware of that reading struggle when we were children, just learning to master the technologies of reading and of writing (before any text had a "voice"), but we still engage in it even now, no matter how transparent or alive the text may seem to us.

Less perceptible perhaps even than the inert materiality of text with which the reader struggles is a second layer of textuality. The illusory voice of the written text is not just talking to the reader, but it is saying something, and that something is a message about something else, something outside of the text. In this book, I call this layer the level of simulation, following Gilles Deleuze and others. Simulation is the field of what Roland Barthes calls the "effect of the real" (1986: 141–148), and it occurs when a story takes on a "life" of its own, seeming to be a window through which the reader encounters reality, no matter how familiar or bizarre that reality may be. The novelist Kim Stanley Robinson says, "what we call history has at least two meanings to it: first, simply what happened in the past, which no one can know, as it disappears in time, and then second, all the stories we tell about what happened" (Robinson 2002: 635).[2] However, the reality effect is not only a matter of history. Stories about ghosts or fairies, or about life on other planets or in the far future, or about the gods, may also produce the effect of the real, even though the realities that they simulate are not actual. Stories and their effects are the only reality that we have, whether they be stories of science or mythology, of religion or politics, of literary classics or everyday life.

There are reality effects in every meaningful narrative. However, a reality effect is not something that is produced within the text alone as a mere string of signifiers, but rather it is something that is negotiated between the reader and the text (and other texts). Like the "voice" of the implied author, it must be produced. The words never speak for themselves, no matter how hard we might wish that they could – indeed, they cannot speak at all without readers to make them come alive, and it is those readers who are always here and now. The realities that are simulated in stories are constructed out of virtual objects, to borrow another term from Deleuze. A virtuality is a concept in relation to which readers understand reality or

2. Compare Deleuze 1989: 66–94, especially 76–78. Robinson's own stories illustrate this point very well.

truth. Virtuality contributes in important ways to the reality effect, and some of these ways will be detailed in the following.

In the Bible's gospels, the texts that are my primary focus in this book, the words of these texts tell stories that present worlds, characters, events, and dialogue to the reader as though they all were real – that is, as virtualities. However, the Bible itself is also a virtuality, not within its own stories, but within the stories that people tell about it. As a result, there is yet a third layer of textuality that concerns me in this book, and perhaps it should be the most evident of the three, but despite that, it too remains largely unrecognized, perhaps especially in relation to the books of the Bible. An actual Bible is a bunch of books that are themselves like any other books: it is a text composed of other texts. Despite this evident fact, for a very long time now, and still often today, the Bible has been widely regarded as more than just a catalog or collection of old writings. Instead it is believed to be the "Word of God," a single thing that purportedly conveys an eternal and absolute message of truth. This virtual Bible is more than just another book. As a result, people – Christians, to be sure, but sometimes even nonbelievers and those of other religions – often read the Bible as a single unit, and the various books within it become in effect its chapters.

The virtuality of the Bible is the reader's tendency to think of it as a unified book, the one and only word of the one and only God, regardless of whether or not that reader actually believes that there is a God or that He speaks a Word. As the single Word of God, the Bible must be all or nothing. As a result, readers tend to expect that all of the Bible's component texts must mean the same thing, or at least contribute to some single over-arching meaning. These readers do not read four different gospels telling stories of four distinct Jesus simulacra, but instead they read one Gospel (the capitalization is significant) "according to" four different "evangelists," in which a single coherent story of salvation through the one, unique Jesus Christ is narrated. The virtuality of the Gospel is closely related to that of the Bible. As different texts, the various gospels tell of distinct Jesus simulacra, but the virtuality of the Bible unites these multiple Jesuses into a single simulacrum, the Jesus Christ of the Gospel, and of Christian faith.

In this book, my primary focus is on the second layer of effects, the distinct Jesus simulacra that appear among the reality effects produced by the differing texts of the gospels of Matthew, Mark, Luke, and John. I play with the divergent multiplicity of these gospel texts without assuming any unity, historical or theological, among them. I also play with four different and inconsistent Jesus simulacra, exploring the differences and similarities between these simulacra without in any way trying to resolve them into some consistent singular entity or larger story. In other words, I explore each of the gospels' Jesuses as a distinct reality effect.

While distinctions between the Jesuses of the gospels are implicit in much New Testament scholarship, they are rarely if ever foregrounded, as they are here, and the nearly universal assumption is that the gospels' various Jesuses all have some relation to one historical or theological archetype. These Jesuses are regarded as more or less accurate copies of a single prior model. In contrast, I do not arrange the gospel texts in a hierarchy of priority and secondarity, along coherent trajectories that originate in a single unique "historical Jesus" or at least in the beliefs of very early Christian communities. I make no claims about what the "historical Jesus" actually said or did, nor about any similarity or other relationship between the gospels' Jesus simulacra and anyone who actually existed. Nor do I say anything about the intentions of the gospels' historical authors or how early readers might have understood those texts. I do not reject the value of historical study of the Bible, but I do not place great weight on its conclusions, either.

However, I do not read the gospel texts independently of any other text (including each other), for that would be impossible. No text is ever read strictly on its own. Meaning is not found "in" texts, much less "behind" them; instead, meaning always appears "between" texts. In other words, reading is always intertextual. This does not mean that "anything goes," and every reading must stay at least somewhat responsive to the materiality of the text, just as every reading is inevitably controlled by the reader's ideology. Every reading is situated: some actual person reading some specific text using some particular set of codes (see Barthes 1974). However, if each gospel narrative is freed from the larger virtuality of the Bible and allowed to signify in other intertextual networks, then its own peculiarities may become more apparent, and its characters, actions, and settings may be more readily understood to be simulacra – that is, virtual entities or events. I read the gospels with particular attention to significant differences between them and between each of them and other texts, both biblical and otherwise, and including especially products of contemporary popular culture, such as films and novels. In such contexts, the gospels are four distinct stories and their Jesus simulacra are four distinct characters.

One consequence of this approach is that I must keep a vigilant eye also on the third layer of textuality, the virtuality of the Bible, and I must willfully read each gospel as independent not only from its New Testament context but also from the virtuality of the Gospel and of the Bible. I do not avoid the inevitable intertextuality of reading (indeed, I celebrate it), but I also do not read each gospel as part of some larger canonical whole that eventually consumes all of their differences. In order to separate out the various simulacra, to maintain their differences and to explore their respective reality effects, I read as though there were no canon.

This reading practice results in radically different understandings not only of these books, but also of the Christian canon. When the gospels are freed from canonical control, the reader not only becomes aware of important and finally unresolvable differences between their four Jesuses (as well as other New Testament Jesuses, especially Paul's "Christ Jesus"), but also of new ways to think about what/who the Jesus of each gospel is, and what his actions and words might mean in intertextual contexts beyond the canon. As a result, for any reader for whom any or all of the gospels remain unquestionably encased within the Christian canon of scriptures and thus the single "Word of God," the readings presented in this book will be implausible at best.

Therefore these readings of the gospels are post-canonical ones. I do not pretend to read the gospels in some pristine non-canonical way, as though the New Testament had never existed, but rather I try to read them as though they have been liberated from the biblical canon. It is my view that they are indeed already on the way to some form of liberation. However, I have found that the virtuality of the Bible still exerts a very powerful effect, even in today's increasingly post-canonical world, and the habits of my education and of years of thinking and writing in a certain style are very hard to break. For many years now, biblical scholars have referred to the gospels as though they were variants on each other (or at least on Mark, which is probably the oldest one), and likewise they have described the Jesus simulacra as though they were different versions of one Jesus, whether "the historical Jesus" or "the Christ of faith." I resist the temptation to contribute to this discourse, but sometimes I fail, or my struggles become apparent in what seem (to me, anyway) to be strange linguistic effects.

One example of this temptation appears in the concept and terminology of textual "parallels" or "versions," which remains almost indispensable to my analyses here, but which is quite problematic to me because it strongly suggests a relationship that extends beyond mere coincidence of wording. Readers often see parallels between two or more texts even where there is no exact coincidence of words, and this may imply a coincidence of thought – that is, a rather strong relationship. And indeed, maybe there is something more to that relationship between the texts, but to assume as much would be to beg the question of this book. Even an exact coincidence of words may not imply a relationship between the texts. My argument requires that I avoid such assumptions, and I would really like to, but the language that results from my efforts sometimes seems stilted and awkward, and there are probably points where I slip and return to forms of discourse that are inconsistent with my argument. I do not deny that there are historical relationships between the gospels, but I do not presume them, either.

Because of this, it may also seem at times that I am making historical or theological claims about multiple Jesuses. To be sure, everyone has her own ideological biases, and I'm sure that mine have deeply influenced this book. In addition, it is sometimes impossible to talk about some of the matters discussed here without making some historical assumptions. However, I am not claiming that multiple Jesuses in ancient Palestine, each one with his own disciples, crowds, and opponents, actually performed miracles and spoke in parables and eventually got themselves crucified and then were resurrected. Indeed, I am not making any claims at all here about actual persons who lived two thousand years ago.

Instead, my concern is with the effects produced by these four biblical stories as they are read, and one of those effects is the illusion of reality. One large part of the question that I am addressing here is the deep desire of modern readers to read these texts as all pointing into the past, and indeed all pointing (whether correctly or not) to the exact same set of actual people and events. This desire both contributes to and is a product of the virtuality of the Bible.

Outline of the Book

This book extends explorations that I began in my books, *The Control of Biblical Meaning* and *The Phantom Messiah*. However, it is not a direct sequel to either of those books, and its reader need not have read either one of them. Instead, this book dovetails with extended arguments that I have made in those and other writings, some of which will be summarized or referenced again here. Like those writings, this book pursues critical postmodern semiotic approaches to biblical texts, with particular emphasis on concepts developed by Barthes and Deleuze, but also drawing upon a wide range of other scholars.

Part One lays out the concepts of virtuality, the simulacrum, and the reality effect, and it sketches out in general how these concepts relate to the Bible as a canonical whole as well as to the various texts of which it is composed and especially to the Jesuses of the four gospels. Chapter 1 focuses on the general concept of virtuality, but it also develops the concept of the Bible as a virtuality. This chapter reviews the argument regarding the semiotic control function of the biblical canon that I developed in detail in *The Control of Biblical Meaning*, but with specific reference to the topic of this volume. "Canon" and "virtuality" do not mean the same thing, but they are closely related. Chapter 2 develops the related concepts of the simulacrum and the reality effect. In addition, it surveys in broad outline the four Jesus simulacra of the gospels, and it introduces the important distinction between the gospels as books and the theological concept of "the Gospel."

Part Two explores each gospel in turn, following the canonical sequence for convenience's sake. I should have probably followed Barthes's lead (1975) at this point and arranged the chapters alphabetically according to the gospels' accepted titles, or in some other non-significant order, but the gains in methodological purity might be offset by losses in reader confusion, and so I have not. Each gospel's Jesus simulacrum is examined in terms of selected distinctive features, which impact in various ways on larger structures of the respective stories, but not in complete detail. Chapter 3 explores distinctive features of the gospel of Matthew's Jesus simulacrum in intertextual tension with that gospel's cinematic "translation" in Pier Paolo Pasolini's film, *The Gospel According to Saint Matthew* (1964). That controversial film in effect produces a post-canonical "version" of Matthew. Chapter 4 approaches distinctive features of Mark's Jesus through his use of child language to refer to adults, and the relation in the gospel of Mark between this language and Jesus's sayings about the kingdom of God and about the son of man, which in turn "unsettle" theological connotations that are often ascribed to this language. Chapter 5 examines Luke's Jesus simulacrum through an intertextual reading with China Miéville's urban fantasy novel, *King Rat* (1998), which emphasizes disturbing aspects of Luke's birth narrative and of the relations of Luke's Jesus simulacrum to his two fathers, God and Joseph. Chapter 6 describes John's Jesus simulacrum through his peculiar act of writing in the problematic text of the woman taken in adultery (7:53–8:11), which is often regarded as out of place in John but which has important repercussions for the reading of John, especially its multiple and self-referential endings.

Part Three examines the gospels in their canonical relations to one another, and in mutual tension with the virtuality of the Bible. Chapter 7 examines Mark's role as the "minority report" in contrast to the other two synoptic gospels, Matthew and Luke, in an intertextual reading with Steven Spielberg's movie, *Minority Report* (2002), and the Philip K. Dick story on which that movie is based. Chapter 8 tackles the synoptic problem from a different angle, examining how the "minor agreements" between Matthew and Luke against Mark contribute to differences between their various Jesus simulacra, and conversely, how the concept of distinct Jesus simulacra addresses and critiques recent historical-critical solutions of the synoptic problem, especially the Q hypothesis. Chapter 9 considers a rather different synoptic problem, the curious agreements of language and thought between the gospels of Luke and John against either Matthew or Mark. With strong canonical support from the letters of Paul, this synopsis functions in the New Testament virtuality and in Christian discourse generally to produce the single theological simulacrum of "Jesus Christ," the unique object of Christian belief. Finally, Chapter 10 is hardly a "conclusion" but rather a question and anticipation of the future of the gospels in a world beyond the Christian canon.

Part I

VIRTUAL BIBLE, VIRTUAL GOSPEL

Chapter 1

Virtuality and the Bible

Within every book there lies concealed a book of nothing. Don't you sense it when you read a page brimming with words? The vast gulf of emptiness lying beneath the frail net of letters. The ghostliness of the letters themselves. (Wharton 2001: 75–76)

Simulation is precisely this irresistible unfolding, this linkage of things as if they had a meaning, so that they are no longer controlled or regulated except by artificial montage and non-sense. (Baudrillard 1992)

Virtual, Actual, Real

The Bible has always been virtual. This does not mean that the Bible is somehow unreal or incomplete, nor does it describe another Bible, a Bible that is somehow "other" than the one that people read. The virtual Bible is the only Bible that we know, and the virtuality of the Bible is perhaps its most important feature. This virtuality is not at all unique – we live in a world composed of many virtualities – but the relation of the Bible's virtuality to anything actual is very specific and rich with ideological overtones. In addition, since the Bible has had and continues to have a huge impact upon the world by way of its virtuality, the Bible's virtuality is more important than are many other virtualities.

I am writing here about the Christian Bible, the Old and New Testaments. There is also a virtual Bible in Judaism, but it is quite different from the Christian one, and not merely because of the evident canonical differences. In Judaism, the physical texts of the scriptures tend to be valued more highly than they are in Christianity, which generally treats the physical text itself as a dispensable channel through which an important message is transmitted.[1] For Christians, the Bible's virtuality is more important than its actuality. As a result, there are significant differences of belief between

1. I discuss this further in Aichele 2001: 28–37.

Christians and Jews concerning questions of translation, interpretation, and canon, among other matters. The impact of these differences on the virtual Bibles of Judaism and Christianity deserves study, but that is not the topic of this book.

According to Katherine Hayles, "Virtuality is the cultural perception that material objects are interpenetrated by information patterns" (1999: 13–14). Hayles claims that "we participate in the cultural perception that information and materiality are conceptually distinct and that information is in some sense more essential, more important, and more fundamental than materiality" (1999: 18, see further her discussion on 248–251). In other words, virtuality entails what Jacques Derrida calls logocentrism, which is the idea that the meaning (or signified) of any sign is more important than its physical form and material signifier (1976: 12–15). This does not mean that the virtual is unreal or merely mental. Gilles Deleuze argues that the virtual object corresponds to a desire for reality which "governs and compensates for the progresses and failures of … real activity" (1994: 99).[2] Thus the virtual is neither unreal nor optional; on the contrary, "The virtual … is the characteristic state of Ideas: *it is on the basis of its reality that existence is produced*, in accordance with a time and a space immanent in the Idea" (Deleuze 1994: 211, emphasis added).[3] For Deleuze, the "Idea" is neither a Platonic form nor an object of consciousness. Instead it is the theater or scene in which reality is staged. Virtuality is a relation to wholeness or totality – that is, a relation to sense, or connotation. Apart from its virtuality, the Bible has (or makes) no sense.

In other words, existence or reality insofar as we know it at all is not simply anything or everything that is actual. Our knowledge of reality is derived from empirical sensation, but there can be no sensation, at least at the human level, that is not informed by virtual structures of consciousness.[4] The newborn infant may experience William James's "blooming, buzzing confusion" of unfiltered sensation, but that is not

2. Deleuze's discussion of virtuality runs throughout *Difference and Repetition*, especially 103–105 and 205–214. See also Deleuze and Parnet (2007: 148–152) and Williams (2003: 7–11, 164, 198–200).

3. See also Deleuze (1994: 279); Deleuze and Guattari (1994: 140, 157); and Eco (1979: 23, 29).

4. Although Deleuze's insistence on the "univocity of being" and his rejection of the "analogy of being" might support a pantheistic understanding of his views, his insistence on the priority of multiplicity and difference and his radical, "transcendental" empiricism of the Idea are contrary to ontological monism (1994: 278). As Deleuze repeatedly states, the univocity of being is a matter of "sense" – that is, connotation. In other words, it belongs to the virtual.

understood as reality. Virtuality is the means and the meaning through which we encounter the real, and without which there is no "real." "A different, virtual mental image would correspond to a different description, and vice versa. ... [E]ach time description has obliterated the object, at the same time as the mental image has created a different one" (Deleuze, 1989: 44, see also 66–67). According to Deleuze, your idea of reality and the only reality that you know at any given moment is reciprocally determined by the virtual and the actual. The virtual is "real without being actual, ideal without being abstract" (1994: 208, quoting Proust). Virtuality belongs to the realm of ideology because it creates the illusion of reality. It makes the meaning of things and events seem obvious and "natural" (Barthes 1974: 206).

For Deleuze, there is no option of escape from virtuality into a direct encounter with actuality. Virtuality is indispensible. Still, we do best when we pursue what Deleuze calls "lines of flight," by which we break free – but only temporarily and relatively – from our ideological entrapments. Lines of flight are the ways by which we escape for a moment from the order of a cosmos and of our separate selves, or indeed from anything (any virtuality) that "makes sense." They offer a kind of liberating schizophrenia.[5] Yet even lines of flight do not lead to direct encounters with actuality.

Suppose that we are each reading a text. What makes the text that I am reading the same as, or different from, the one that you are reading? Is it physical qualities of the signifiers, or less tangible qualities of the signified meaning? If the latter, are you reading the same book today that you read yesterday, or last year, if the same physical text now means more (or other) than it did then, as it almost always does? If the former, what entitles two readers who disagree about the meaning of a text to think that they are discussing "the same text," even if they are both reading, side by side, from a single copy? In addition, if letter for letter equivalence of the signifiers makes two texts "the same," then you still must trust in the reliability of your memory and the stability and finally the sanity of the physical world – that is, that reality as you know it is not like that of *Alice in Wonderland*, and that signifiers cannot change in the blink of an eye once they are written. Perhaps that is not so difficult for you, but you cannot do even that much without virtualities (the strength of personal memory, the laws of logic and physics, and finally the semiotic values of the signifiers). However, if

---

5. Friedrich Nietzsche expresses similar ideas in many of his writings, and Nietzsche's thought plays a large role in Deleuze's writings. See especially Deleuze (1983).

neither the signifier nor the signified provides an entirely satisfactory answer to the question, then perhaps you need to consider a third possibility: that the "identity" of a text is nothing other than its virtuality.

Suppose that you find a book lying in the street. Its covers and title page are missing. How do you identify it? The reader gets her idea or concept of the Bible from having seen Bibles, perhaps in bookstores or churches, or from having read one or more Bibles, or maybe just from having heard people talk about the Bible. Nevertheless, apart from the virtual Bible, the reader would have no concept of "the Bible," and then she would not know what to look for in order to identify a Bible. She would have no idea of the difference between Bible and non-Bible. This may seem paradoxical or even contradictory (you cannot perceive something unless you already know it), but indeed this is how we learn any concept (or Idea, as Deleuze would say). As a baby you entered a world that was for you a blooming, buzzing confusion but was itself already organized by others as a virtuality or system of ideas, and through your experiences you have gained some mastery of those ideas.

Writing, Canon, and the Bible

Digital and perhaps especially online versions of the Bible make readers particularly aware of its virtuality today, but the virtuality of the Bible is not limited to such texts. Instead, the Bible's virtuality is closely bound to the fact that the Bible has always been a writing. As Edmund Husserl says: "The important function of written, documenting linguistic expression is that it makes communications possible without immediate or mediate personal address; it is, so to speak, communication become *virtual*" (1978: 164, emphasis added). Writing makes possible the formation of ideal objects that remain the same across time and space, but as Derrida notes, commenting on Husserl's words, "That *virtuality* ... is an ambiguous value: it simultaneously makes passivity, forgetfulness, and all the phenomena of *crisis* possible" (1978: 87, Derrida's emphases).

As Walter Benjamin says, discussing the writings of Franz Kafka, "Reversal is the direction of learning which transforms existence into writing" (1968: 138). No text can speak for itself, but written text inevitably escapes its author's control and falls into the hands of a reader, who may be anyone, as Socrates recognized long ago in the *Phaedrus* (1973: 95–99).[6] Ancient

---

6. See further Derrida (1981: 61–171). Something very much like Socrates's fears about writing also appears in 2 Cor. 3:1–8.

peoples knew that once oral stories were written down, they had been profoundly changed. Socrates says that "The productions of painting look like living beings, but if you ask them a question they maintain a solemn silence. The same holds true of written words; you might suppose that they understand what they are saying, but if you ask them what they mean by anything they simply return the same answer over and over again" (Plato 1973: 97 [sec. 275]).

Written text especially indicates a loss or transformation of reality, and it compensates with its own virtual objects. Writing offers a surrogate for memory, and thus even when it preserves the formulas, images, or sequences typical of oral culture, it threatens a loss of cultural self-identity and challenges the very order of the universe. Socrates attacks writing as a "conceit of wisdom" that results in ignorance. The oral text exists only in the living presence of its speaker, but a written text cannot provide its own explanation. Writing removes the text from memory, and it leaves the reader with the task of deciphering inert letters, signifiers that are in themselves meaningless. Socrates argues that the written text cannot speak for itself and must be "rescued" by its "parent," the spoken word.

Any text (oral, written, or electronic) is a machine that makes meaning, or rather, it is part of an intertextual machine through which readers or hearers or viewers make whatever meanings they can. However, unlike oral communication, writing/reading inevitably produces virtualities, which in turn produce the crisis that both Socrates and Derrida talk about. As Roland Barthes says of the alphabetic letter, "a letter, at one and the same time, *means* and *means nothing*, imitates nothing and yet symbolizes, dismisses both the alibi of realism and that of aestheticism" (1985: 116, his emphases). All writing is copied and therefore false.

In writing, semiosis is less tightly controlled than in oral language. "[T]he letters which form a word, though each of them is *rationally* insignificant ..., keep searching, in us, for their freedom, which is to signify *something else*" (Barthes 1985: 117, his emphases).[7] The meaningful connection between signifier and signified is neither tight nor exclusive, and it is always artificial. This connection must itself be explained, or in other words, it must be established. The message is not simply received; it must be understood – that is, it must become virtual – and this inevitably requires yet other signs which themselves must also be explained, and so on. The realm of meaning is divided into signifiers and signifieds, but this division

---

7. See also Barthes (1985: 98–124); Kelber (1983: 92, 114); and Derrida (1973, 1976).

is constantly collapsing, for every signifier may also be signified, and every signified may be itself the signifier of yet another signified. The semiotic channel is deconstructed, and instead of a well-controlled flow of meaning there is a flood. Semiosis flows without limit, in both the direction of the signifier and that of the signified, and both the First Signifier and the Last Signified of any utterance become illusions hovering over semiotic abysses. Umberto Eco, following C. S. Peirce, notes that

> signification ... by means of continual shiftings which refer a sign back to another sign or string of signs, circumscribes cultural units in an asymptotic fashion, without ever allowing one to touch them directly, though making them accessible through other units. (1976: 71)

As a result, meaning is elusive and fluid, and connotation runs wild (de Man 1979: 208). There is no absolute signifying anchor to which a proper meaning could be attached.

This unlimited semiosis characterizes every text, but it is particularly problematic in relation to written texts, and it becomes an especially serious challenge to any text that is desired to have a definite and authoritative meaning – that is, any scripture, any text that is believed to transmit the "Word of God." The value of writing as a means to communicate leads to the need to authenticate and stabilize that same writing. The semiotic function of the biblical canon is to control the understanding of the included texts, to establish an authoritative structure that defines for its Christian readers a single, coherent message. As Yvonne Sherwood says:

> A deeply ingrained cultural sense of the Bible as the "Word of God," or at the very least a homogeneous canon, means that we expect that separate textual voices will be gathered into a single consciousness ... This book, of all books, is expected to process life into a gigantic metanarrative, to frame the world in a Great, all-encompassing Code. (2000: 217)

Although individual written texts cannot speak at all by themselves, the canon of scriptures forms an authorized and complete set of texts that is supposed to speak for itself, at least in the hands of the faithful. For Christian readers, all of the biblical books "speak" clearly together, expressing "a single consciousness." Readers either accept that consciousness, or they reject it.

In other words, the Bible is not simply a collection of sacred writings, but it is a powerful intertextual mechanism. According to Julia Kristeva, "The term *inter-textuality* denotes this transposition of one (or several) sign system(s) into another ... its 'place' of enunciation and its denoted 'object' are never single, complete, and identical to themselves, but always plural, shattered, capable of being tabulated" (1984: 59–60, her emphasis).

Meaning is never neatly packaged in any text, to be unwrapped and displayed by careful *exe*-gesis, but rather meaning is stretched between texts, as they are brought together in the various understandings of actual readers – that is, through *eise*-gesis.

Intertextuality presents another form of the paradox of virtuality that was noted above: you cannot read the text unless you have already understood it, or in more traditional language, there is no understanding without pre-understanding. Every reading is intertextual: every text is always read in the light of other texts, which themselves were read in the light of yet other texts, and so on.[8] As Roland Barthes says, "as it turns out in any true inter-textuality ... what is henceforth displaced is the work's responsibility: it is no longer consecrated by a narrow ownership (that of its immediate creator), it journeys in a cultural space which is open, without limits, without partitions, without hierarchies" (1985: 153–154). In contrast to the oral text, as Socrates noted, the written text cannot be controlled by its original "owner," the author.

Intertextuality and unlimited semiosis stand in a peculiar tension with one another. Although Deleuze and Félix Guattari do not use these terms, the tension between these concepts appears again and again in their writings. Deleuze and Guattari describe this tension as a machine:

> A machine may be defined as a *system of interruptions* or breaks. ... Far from being the opposite of continuity, the break or interruption conditions this continuity; it presupposes what it defines or cuts into as an ideal continuity. The machine produces an interruption of the flow only insofar as it is connected to another machine that supposedly produces this flow. And doubtless this second machine in turn is really an interruption or break, too. ... In a word, every machine functions as a break in the flow in relation to the machine to which it is connected, but at the same time is also a flow itself, or the production of a flow, in relation to the machine connected to it. (1983: 36, their emphasis)

There are only breaks and flows of semiosis. Unlimited semiosis produces and disperses texts, and therefore it makes intertextuality possible. In turn, intertextuality breaks or interrupts the potentially endless flows of semiosis. Intertextuality provokes and directs semiosis, elaborating but also confining the significance of each text through its interplay with other texts. Nevertheless, there is always the possibility that semiosis will break free along "lines of flight."

8. This concept of intertextuality is quite distinct from the notion of historical sources or influences that still dominates biblical studies, even though that notion is also sometimes confusingly called "intertextuality."

Both unlimited semiosis and intertextuality imply that meaning is not "in" the text, to be dredged out by careful exegesis, but rather it only appears *between* texts, as they are brought together in the various understandings of readers. Reading inevitably and arbitrarily limits semiotic unfolding by drawing upon intertextuality to break the flow of signification – that is, to fix and determine meaning. As Timothy Beal says: "The interpreter makes a de-cision, a cut, which cuts off other possible relations, positions roadblocks against other intersections" (2000: 129). Meaning is attached to the text through the process of reading, when an intertext "breaks" the flow of semiosis and establishes an ideological field in which acceptable, "natural" readings can occur. By the same stroke, as Beal suggests, this interpretive decision inevitably excludes or omits other possibilities for meaning, which produces or is produced by a kind of blindness (see further Chapter 7).

The intertextuality of the biblical canon "displaces" the semiosis of its component texts by curtailing their meanings, making them appear familiar and normal, naturalizing them. It makes it so that these texts seem to belong together. However, unlike Barthes's open "cultural space," the Bible's intertextuality is exclusive: only these texts are believed to belong together, and only in this way, and their true "owner" is identified as God. In this way the canon frames and limits the flows of semiosis. It carves these particular texts out of the larger intertextual cultural space, and it establishes a new set of partitions and hierarchies. It draws upon conventional codes that allow the reader to recognize the Bible's texts as meaningful works, to identify their structures and how they fit together, and to make sense out of their messages and how they belong to the message of the Bible as a whole (the Word of God).

In the terminology of Deleuze and Guattari, the biblical canon reflects a "paranoid signifying regime" (1983, 1987). As an intertextual machine, the Bible stands opposed to the unrestrained "schizophrenic" flows of semiosis that arise from any written text, and particularly the scriptures.[9] The restricted intertextuality of the biblical canon is virtuality at work, containing and directing semiosis, breaking its flows and bringing it decisively to an end, thereby allowing the return of the Last Signified. Ideology shapes the Bible through the intertextuality of the canon. Every intertext is ideological, but as the Word of God, the Bible is exclusively and therefore profoundly ideological.

---

9. For Deleuze and Guattari, there is no third option, no position that is neither paranoid nor schizophrenic.

Like unlimited semiosis, intertextuality locates the meaning of a text firmly in the reader. Intertextuality lies in spaces between texts that are formed by similarities and differences between signifiers and occupied by readers. Each reader is a living repository of texts, a network of potential connections, and thus each reader is herself both the product and the event of intertextuality, the point at which an intertextual network comes to bear upon a text. She is the site where the negotiation between actual and virtual takes place, the means through which actual text (physical signifiers) encounters virtual idea and thus becomes meaningfully real. The biblical canon limits the reader's intertextual network, bringing together precisely *these* texts in precisely *this* sequence in order to control the way that she reads the Bible's texts, and insofar as it succeeds, it shapes her thoughts and her life, her understanding of herself and the world.

In other words, the canonical control of meaning does not appear in the individual biblical texts themselves but rather in the ways in which those texts are juxtaposed with one another in the interpretive practice of faithful readers. The Bible's virtual story, Sherwood's "gigantic metanarrative," grounds reality for such a reader, both describing and forming her world (compare Barthes 1974: 76). The canon responds to the "crisis" inherent in the "chaotic literalness" (Derrida 1978: 88) of the written texts by obscuring their diversities and assimilating them into the theological unity of the "Word of God." It shapes a virtuality. The actual collection of biblical texts can itself only be an "artificial montage," as Jean Baudrillard says in the second epigraph to this chapter, but as a canon, it is a "linkage of things as if they had a meaning."

According to Jon Berquist, "The canonical text is not a unified whole; it is not a body of literature at all. Instead, it is an assemblage held together only by the imperialist power that first created it" (1996: 28). Berquist is referring to the Jewish scriptures in the Persian period, but the point remains true for the Bible. The Christian canon was formed by Constantinian Christianity to deter the pursuit of heretical connotations (unlimited semiosis) of the "scriptures" and to justify the emerging imperial church's own claim to be the "new Israel," the chosen people of God. Furthermore, the "imperialist power" that forms the canon is not merely confined to its initiatory moments, like the dynamite charges that compress fissionable material in a nuclear bomb, but instead it is a dynamic intrinsic to the canon itself and closely related to the long imperial history of Christianity. The canon holds sway only as long as the imperial dream continues.

The canon of the scriptures could not have been developed without the availability of two technologies. These technological factors are: 1. the invention of writing itself; and 2. the invention of the codex, which occurred shortly prior to the beginnings of Christianity. The single codex of the Christian Bible connotes to many people that the Bible is one single book with a proper sequence, and it assembles that canonical, intertextual network in a format that can be easily used as such. "The codex is an existential code unto itself, a unifying factor of a culture" (Debray 1996: 141). The singularity of the biblical codex is not essential to the concept of canon, but it nevertheless plays an important role in signifying the Bible's single, coherent message for a united, universal Church – or in other words, in the Bible's virtuality.

The biblical canon obscures and replaces the component texts themselves with something else, a signified or at least a signifying potential that far surpasses any of the included texts. *This is the virtuality of the Bible.* However, the canon is not the same thing as the virtual Bible, nor is the codex; indeed, the distinctions between these concepts are important. The Christian Bible appears in various different canons and different physical forms (as well as differing languages, translations, and manuscripts), but despite these differences, we usually talk as though there is just one Bible. The virtual Bible is the dream of coherence and identity that the canon seeks to realize. The virtual Bible does not tell the truth, but rather it produces truth.

Indeed, the Bible as an actual book would never have come into existence if it had not already existed as a virtuality in the thoughts and desires of Christians as early as the second century. The Bible as a canon of texts *cannot exist* apart from its virtuality, and the actual Bible cannot be read apart from the virtual Bible. Nevertheless, the canon is precisely that which makes the Bible the Bible, for without the canon there is no Bible, but merely a more or less fluid assortment of more or less unrelated texts, which may or may not be "scriptures." If there were no canon, but merely a collection of texts or even of scriptures, a quite different virtuality would appear. This is elementary semiotics: when you change the signifier, the signified also changes.

However, this must be qualified at two points. First, the intertextual context of any text, even the most ancient or authoritative ones, is always finally the *here* and *now* of the living reader (a unity that is always riven by difference, as Deleuze among others has made clear). In other words, the act of reading is always partial. There is no neutral, objective, scientific, or comprehensive reading of any text. Readers today may have some sense of historical conditions under which the biblical canon was produced or how other readers understood or understand biblical texts, but our awareness of such circumstances and other readings is itself always conditioned by our own contexts, interests, and commitments. Ancient or foreign readings always stand at an inherent disadvantage to the contemporary, local readings through which they are inevitably filtered, thanks to virtuality and especially the virtual Bible. The ideology "in" the canon is always refracted through the reader's own ideology, even when it challenges or is rejected by that ideology.

Second, just as no single text can explain itself, so no collection of texts can explain itself. Although the canon is a powerful intertextual mechanism, it is never entirely successful. It deeply influences the deciphering of its component texts, but its control over those texts is inevitably loose and incomplete. That the Christian biblical canon has never worked very well has been made clear by a long history of theological disputes, heresy trials, and religious wars. Lively and significant disagreement over the meaning of the Bible, or the extent of the canon (or which are the best translations or manuscripts), will always occur. Thus the virtual Bible is a somewhat fuzzy concept (as are perhaps all virtualities). Even binding the canon into a single physical codex cannot guarantee that the reader will assemble the various texts in the "proper" way, and so additional assistance, in the form of extra-canonical commentaries, introductions, sermons, catechisms, and other guides on "how to read the Bible," is continually required.

Challenges to Canonical Control

The canon of the Bible could not have come into existence apart from the ideological and technological factors noted above.[10] As those ideological factors change and the technological factors are replaced by new ones, the need for a canon fades away. Prior to the invention of the movable type printing press at the end of the fifteenth century, nearly all written texts were hand-written copies, and both the care taken by copyists and the freedom that they exercised in the copies that they produced varied widely. In manuscript culture there is no fixed text that would be analogous to a printed book. The fluidity of these manuscripts is evident in the many differences between the ones that have survived to the

10. See further Aichele (2001: 15–104).

present.[11] In such a world, the virtuality of the Bible would be crucial to its function as the Word of God.

The biblical canon was formed in part to stabilize the hand-copying of its component texts, as well as to produce a uniform collection of scriptures for use throughout the newly-imperial Christian church. Scribes would be less willing to modify the "Word of God." However, with the appearance of print technology, control over reproduction of the Bible passed into the hands of commercial printing shops and publishing houses, freeing the dissemination of texts from control by the churches. The need to secure the physical limits of the individual books and of the canonical list as a whole is from then on addressed by circumstances arising from the mechanical reproduction of the texts. The printing press produces many identical copies of the Bible, word for word and page for page, and the variations that are inevitable with hand-copying disappear. Printing diminishes the need for a canon, because the semiotic control function of the canon is weakened.

In addition, the dangers of unlimited semiosis are exacerbated when formerly hand-written texts are mass (re)produced by means of the printing press. The printing of the Bible and other books plays a role in the emergence of the important modernist distinction between model and copy, for the printed Bible is a copy of manuscript Bibles. To be sure, all of the known manuscripts of biblical texts are also copies, but as hand-written books they share in what Walter Benjamin calls the "aura" of the "authentic" work of art (1968: 220–222). Benjamin compares printed texts to photographed paintings, and he argues that once it has been mechanically reproduced through photography or printing, the painting or writing loses its authenticity.[12] Benjamin compares the painter and the cameraman to the magician and the surgeon, respectively: "The magician heals a sick person by the laying on of hands; the surgeon cuts into the patient's body" (1968: 233). The magician addresses the patient face to face, but the surgeon avoids dealing with the patient as a human being. Both painter and cameraman generate illusions of reality, but the cameraman does so by

11. Approximately 5000 pre-print culture manuscripts of biblical texts, ranging from tiny fragments to complete Bibles, are known today. No two are verbally identical. On the instability of text in manuscript culture, see Gamble (1995), Ehrman (1993), and Aland and Aland (1987: 55–64).

12. This point is developed further in Benjamin (1968: 83–109). For a similar judgment in regard to geometry and science, see Husserl (1978: 168–170). As Eisenstein makes clear, modern science would be impossible without print technology (1979).

utilizing machinery. The painter respects the integrity of the artwork, but the cameraman impersonally invades and dismembers it. The picture produced by the painter "is a total one, [but] that of the cameraman consists of multiple fragments which are assembled under a new law" (1968: 234).

Because every printed book is always a "copy," each printed Bible then becomes a copy of the virtual Bible. Benjamin argues that "within the phenomenon which we are here examining, from the perspective of world history, print is … [a] particularly important … case" (1968: 219). The painter corresponds to the scribe, and the cameraman corresponds to the typesetter and printing press operator. Like the photographed painting, and perhaps even more so, the relation of printed text to a hand-made "original" is highly problematic (see further Eisenstein 1979). As a result, the reader's relation to the text changes. Each "copy" of the Bible, even the ancient manuscripts, becomes itself a simulacrum, part of a system, a "site for the actualisation of Ideas" (Deleuze 1994: 278) – that is, a site of the virtual Bible. As a result of the act of printing it, the virtuality of the Bible itself shifts, from the Bible as transitory manifestation of eternal, universal truth in a manuscript culture dominated by allegorical interpretation, to the Bible as historically reliable reproduction of "original" texts produced by the Bible's writers.[13]

Yet paradoxically, print culture also accelerates the postmodern erosion of the model/copy binarism. Since the print revolution, the Bible has functioned less and less as the communal property of Christian churches, and more and more as the private property of individual readers, and therefore as a commodity to be bought and sold. As a mass-produced text, the printed Bible makes the reader more aware of the Bible's virtuality, even as the printing process replaces ecclesiastical, canonical assurances of the Bible's authority. Likewise, ever since the Protestant Reformation – which began at the same time as the print revolution, and surely not by coincidence – we have become more and more aware of the multiplicity of the Bible: multiple canons and multiple translations and multiple interpretations, as well as the multiplicity of texts that has always been there within the Bible. The virtual Bible has become even fuzzier.

The transformations that occur between manuscript and printed text are just as important as the transformations that occur between oral and written text, but we are only now beginning to become aware of them, even as yet another important transformation of text is beginning. Today the

---

13.   This shift within biblical scholarship during this time period is well documented, albeit in rather different terms, in Sandys-Wunsch (2005).

Bible appears on numerous World Wide Web pages as well as in other electronically mediated versions and contexts, and the effects of the mechanical reproduction of text are amplified greatly. Indeed, the digital biblical text is often a mechanical reproduction of a mechanical reproduction – that is, a scanned copy of a printed text. The dissemination of digital texts via the Internet is quick and global, and it is out of anyone's control. The Bible on a computer screen is not a printed Bible, even if it is a copy of one, just as printed Bibles are not the same as manuscript Bibles.[14] The digitized Bible is not a discrete object like a codex or scroll that the reader can hold in her hand and read with her eyes. Its physical form derives from countless invisible bits and bytes – Benjamin's "multiple fragments … assembled under a new law" – which are recorded in arcane storage media and accessible for reading only through complex networks of sophisticated electronic technology.

The canon has no significant impact on digital access to biblical texts. For example, the digital files that contain the Bible's books (usually one book per file) are most often named along lines suggested by the traditional biblical names, but the computer automatically arranges these files in alphabetic or numeric order, not the traditional sequence that plays a significant role in the canon. Genesis is not the first book, and Revelation is not the last one, and Old and New Testament books are often jumbled together. First Corinthians comes immediately "after" 1 Chronicles, and both "precede" (by several books) 1 Kings.

"The canon," once separated from the materiality of the codex, ceases to be something that you can hold in your hands and becomes once more an abstract idea. Text display software may create the illusion of a canon – for example, ordering the books in their "proper" sequence – and perhaps one could argue that the canon itself is simply an early version of such software, but that would diminish the concept of canon. Stored in databases that make the texts easier to retrieve, but which also decontextualize them and make them available for uncontrolled recontextualizations, the texts are fragmented to the level of what Barthes calls the lexia[15] and beyond – but a database is not a canon.

---

14. See further Nunberg (1996).
15. "The [Bible] verse is an excellent working unit of meaning; since it is a question of *creaming* (or skimming) the text … For us, a verse is a lexia" (Barthes 1988: 229, his emphasis). In *S/Z* Barthes uses the division into lexias to analyze a non-biblical text, Balzac's novella, *Sarrazine* (1974).

In some ways, the electronic media revolution suggests a return to earlier cultural stages. As has been widely noted, email is in some respects more "oral" than "written." Perhaps more important, the reader "scrolls" through digital text, page numbers and indexes are becoming anachronistic and unnecessary, and the text can be easily modified by the reader, who then becomes in effect a scribe. However, the new medium combines a rich mixture of technologies: the World Wide Web site is in effect a digital scriptorium, but the digital nature of the text means that each copy is an exact duplicate of the source text, as in printed text (but even more so). Even though the digital image is composed of numerous pixels arrayed along lines of resolution on a screen – unlike both speech and print[16] – texts prepared on a computer usually resemble printed texts in the computer display, and they can be easily printed out. Digital alphanumeric text is closer to print than it is to handwriting.

With the advent of electronic culture, the reader becomes even more aware of the physical stuff of text and of the tenuous connections between text and meaning. The number of technological stages between the sender and the receiver of a digital message adds to the reader's consciousness of the frailty of the connecting media, reminding her that reading and writing are themselves artificial technologies. Readers become more conscious both of their own need for meaning and of the constructed character of meaning. At the same time, digitization gives the reader greater control both over the individual text, which can easily be rewritten, and over the extent and structure of the textual collection, for whole texts can easily be added to or deleted from the directory. Texts become "fluid" again, and something like Thomas Jefferson's famous "cut and paste" Bible can now be assembled by anyone with a computer. In this electronic culture we are all increasingly aware that every text is a "hybrid" and that the search for "the [uncorrupted] original text" arises from misunderstanding, as D. C. Parker suggests (2003: 401).[17]

The digitized Bible makes it more evident than before that the Bible is and has always been virtual. Electronic, digital text simulates printed text, which in turn simulates hand-written text. However, no written text can ever simulate an oral text; instead, it is the canon itself as an intertextual mechanism that attempts to simulate living, oral text. The Christian Old Testament simulates the "written Torah" of Judaism, and the New

16. See Deleuze (1989: 321, n. 8).
17. For the relevance of this claim to ancient manuscripts, see Ehrman (1993) and Gamble (1985).

Testament simulates Christian "oral Torah," without which the written Torah makes no sense to Christians. (The Old Testament has always been a Christian virtuality, as opposed to the Jewish Tanakh. Likewise, the New Testament is a Christian virtuality, regardless of who the historical authors or original audiences of the books might have been.) Just as the mass-produced media of print and digital publication simulate the canon of the Bible, developed to accommodate a culture that knew only manuscripts, even so the Christian Bible itself has always simulated the unique, living Word of God – the powerful, authoritative, oral word of prophet, psalmist, messiah, or even deity. The virtuality of the Bible shifts again, and the remaining chapters of this book will explore some aspects of that shift.

Consequences of Virtuality

The conditions of human existence have once again changed. This change is comparable in its effect on the virtual Bible to other great transformations of human life, such as the Babylonian exile of Judah and the Constantinian triumph of Christianity, in which fundamental structures of human action and thought were challenged and forever altered. The dream of Christian empire came to an end with the birth of Protestantism and the growth of humanistic consciousness during the Renaissance, both of which are strongly associated with the emergence of print culture. The Bible is no longer the scripture of an imperial, universal church. Likewise, the text of the Bible is no longer the vehicle of an eternal, apostolic message.

Just as writing has made us aware of semiosis in ways that pure orality could not, so also the technologies of mechanical and digital reproduction and the mass media associated with them now make us aware of virtuality in ways that we were not previously. We are beginning to be in a position to appreciate the virtuality of the Bible, and to understand some of its consequences. As a virtuality, the Bible is the clear, ideal object of a united community of understanding, the Christian church. The meaning of the Bible may not be clear to everyone, but the idea and value of "the Bible" is. The virtual Bible is always the same in every translation and edition; its message, the "Word of God," never changes. It is a global, eternal Bible, transcending every history and culture. This ideal of universality, changelessness, homogeneity, and singularity defines the ideological concept of "the Bible" as the canon of Christian scriptures. In contrast, actual Bibles are multiple, local, ephemeral, and polysemic, and their many truths and values are disputed and often obscure.

Like all cultural products, the Bible has become a commodity to be sold in competition with a wide array of other products in a global market. As Robert Carroll says, "When the market drives, there are no limits to human folly or to the production of what will sell, and … bibles will continue to be produced in whatever forms are dictated by the consumerism of a commodity culture" (1998: 60). The Bible is now available in reader-friendly "dynamic" translations in comic book or magazine formats, as well as special editions addressed to particular markets.[18] In its many consumer-oriented forms, the Bible stands on market shelves beside fashion and hot rod magazines, as well as Beanie Babies, mp3 players, video games, and countless other "entertainment" items, competing for the buyer's attention. The Bible's status as popular commodity transforms its authority, shifting its virtuality.

Electronic culture is a global phenomenon. The old colonial empires are increasingly replaced by multinational corporate "empires" such as Microsoft, Disney, Shell, McDonald's, or Sony. The divisions between rich and poor, strong and weak, will be realigned but not eliminated. Those who have access to digital technologies are already privileged in this new imperial order, just as those who have access to books and print technology have long been privileged and still are, even as the world of print culture fades away. Hayles reminds us that "70 percent of the world's population has never made a telephone call" (1999: 20). As she says, the "experience of virtuality" is "exotic." Much of the world's population remains in effect isolated in circumstances typical of print or even oral culture, and in many of these communities the canonical authority of the Bible is still a strong cultural force. Yet today's global, electronic culture shapes the lives of people in the most remote villages just as much as it does the inhabitants of New York or Tokyo, even though that shaping may be far less obvious. Both the relative isolation of these communities and the apparent vigor of the Bible within them are also dependent upon electronic culture.

Additional millions of people in less isolated circumstances continue to believe that the Bible is the authoritative Word of God, but for these people, the Bible no longer signifies *as a canon*. The loudness of believing communities' protests on behalf of the canon is itself a symptom of the withering of canonical control, for if the canon's authority is not self-evident, then it is not doing its job. Althought the virtual Bible remains active

18. See further Beal (2010) and Carroll (1998: 58–61). Michael Carden's blog <http://michaelcardensjottings.blogspot.com/> contains numerous postings of relevance to this topic.

today within the discourse of both believers and non-believers, it is increasingly only as a talisman: a sign of Christian identity, and a symbol of cultural superiority, moral righteousness, and personal salvation.[19] In such contexts the virtual Bible has become a husk, an unopened codex, the illusion of a book. It is no longer valued for what its various texts actually say, but for what "we all know" that it says, even if what we all know is completely wrong. Preachers and politicians, as well as bumper stickers and billboards, can dogmatically assert that "the Bible says ...," without ever having to justify their claims, and they get away with it. The virtual Bible today does not convey a universal, apostolic message, but it has itself become the message.

In today's globalized, digitized world, when the Bible signifies, it does so in increasingly non-canonical ways. As the canon increasingly fails to control the meaning of the biblical texts, different sorts of cultural play with or upon those texts take its place. Many forms of such intertextual play with the Bible are readily to be found among competing cultural products, including novels, movies, music and video recordings, comic books, and electronic games. In many cases, this interplay simply reflects prevailing ideological positions and thus reinforces dominant understandings of the Bible. One recent example is Mel Gibson's hugely popular and controversial movie, *The Passion of the Christ* (2004).

Gibson's film draws upon venerable Hollywood traditions of sentimental "Jesus movies," and like most other "Bible movies," it transforms the biblical stories in ways that go far beyond the liberties of artistic imagination or the necessities of translation between media. Nevertheless, both its harmonizations of different written stories into one story, and its back-translation of dialogue into Aramaic and Latin, create an illusion of historical authenticity and suggest that this is the one true story, the story that really happened. The further transformation of the resulting story from written screenplay into full-color, non-silent film translates it from a medium that always requires a fair amount of work on the part of the reader – written text – to a medium that often requires almost no work on the part of the viewer. Although some scenes have a dream-like or surreal quality, the film never provokes that "suspension of the world" through which, according to Deleuze, thought "is brought face to face with its own impossibility, and yet draws from this a higher power of birth" (1989: 163).

There is no attempt in this movie to transmit the hermeneutic questions that are addressed in the various gospels, such as the identity of Jesus and

---

19. Some remarkable examples are surveyed in Sugirtharajah (2003).

his relation to God, the way of the disciple and the paradox of repentance, or the parabolic secret of the kingdom of God. Instead, Gibson's movie demonstrates how deficient the passion stories are as narratives if they are removed from the larger frames of the respective gospels, contrary to the claims of biblical scholars that the gospels are simply passion stories with prologues. In this film, the biblical passion stories are transformed into a prolonged orgy of gore, and the movie's skimpy flashbacks provide little context for the death of Jesus. As a result, the ample blood and suffering must signify in a context provided either by the viewer's prior knowledge of Christian doctrine or biblical texts, or perhaps more likely, by the viewer's prior experience of other graphically violent movies. One commentator, David Edelstein, described the movie as "The Jesus Chainsaw Massacre." Edelstein also notes that:

> When Jesus is resurrected, his expression is hard, and, as he moves toward the entrance to his tomb, the camera lingers on a round hole in his hand that goes all the way through. Gibson's Jesus reminded me of the Terminator – he could be the Christianator – heading out into the world to spread the bloody news. Next stop: the Crusades. (2004)

However, it is the popularity of Gibson's film, not its graphic depictions of torn flesh, that may be its most noteworthy feature. The movie's popularity demonstrates the fragility of the Christian canon. For many of its viewers, devout Christians, the film itself has become "scripture," and to question its historical accuracy or its translation of biblical texts, or to note its anti-Semitism, is blasphemy to them. The film presumes that viewers already "know the story" of Christ, and also that they are agreed about its meaning and especially about the importance of Jesus's death – that is, that the viewers share the Christian ideology. The pre-release blessings of the movie by both Protestant and Catholic religious leaders authenticated the value of the movie for the faithful, and the Pope's later withdrawal of his blessing didn't hurt ticket sales any, either. At the same time, advance condemnations by biblical scholars who had seen preliminary screenplays, if they had any effect at all, only added to the movie's attraction for anti-intellectual fans. Its simultaneous release into thousands of movie theaters, timed to coincide with a major Christian holiday, resulted in the mass hysteria of Christian audience response, and perhaps also in the widespread applause of professional movie reviewers who might have been more critical of the film under different circumstances. Gibson's movie was eventually and ironically replaced as box office champion by a second rate horror film, although it did briefly "resurrect" its ticket sales in time for Easter.

The Passion of the Christ highlights the contemporary impotence of the canon of scriptures. By now this movie has effectively entered the canon and replaced the gospels, or perhaps even the entire Bible, for many of its functionally illiterate viewers. People leaving theaters after viewing the movie were quoted as saying, "now I want to read the Bible." Comparable viewer comments could be heard at the end of the Harry Potter movies or Peter Jackson's *The Lord of the Rings* films, and perhaps these films really have enticed more people to read the Bible or the novels of J. K. Rowling or J. R. R. Tolkien. Nevertheless, even if they become readers, these movie viewers may well end up judging Tolkien's character Eowyn by whether she lives up to Miranda Otto's performance in Jackson's movies, and not vice versa. Likewise, Gibson's film will be the "touchstone" by which these new Bible readers will judge the written texts. For them, at least, Gibson will have successfully rewritten the Bible.

In contrast, other instances of intertextual play offer radically different translations or contextualizations of biblical texts, provocative rewritings that in effect remove the text from the canon of the scriptures. In such cases, the biblical texts take on remarkably different meanings apart from the canon, as non-canonical intertexts channel the semiosis. A recent example is the transformation of both the Eden and Christ stories in Philip Pullman's controversial, and also quite popular, novel trilogy, *His Dark Materials* (1995, 1997, 2000), even though the novels never specifically mention those stories. Another controversial, and more obvious, instance is the movie, *Monty Python's Life of Brian* (Jones 1979), in which the British ensemble Monty Python "read" the gospels as slapstick comedy. In even more extreme cases, the relation between literature or film (or other popular media) and the gospels moves beyond any focus on christological themes or Christ-figures. Some of these will be discussed further in this book. In these narratives, whether they are clearly "biblical" or not, the biblical texts are recycled and recontextualized, and their semiotic potential is played out in a wide variety of ways. The multiplicity of the Bible is highlighted yet again as it is broken up, reassembled, and often de-canonized. This would not be possible if the virtual Bible were still strong.

There have always been serious tensions between biblical texts and the canon. As the canon fails more and more in the contemporary world, these tensions become more and more evident. The authority of the canon as a whole, the ideological illusion of a powerful and coherent Bible, slips away further with each passing year, and the various texts that once were thought to "speak" with one "voice" the Word of God are seen to transmit different messages, in different ways, to different people, and even from different deities. The old imperial forms of power and desire reflected in the canon become less and less viable. Will we continue to think the virtuality of the Bible at all in a world where the canon increasingly appears only as a list of titles, as in the writings of early Christians? By itself a list is not a canon, but merely (at most) an expression of desire (or nostalgia) for a canon. If the canonical totality of the Bible is no longer a factor in the way that the Bible's texts are read, then its exclusive juxtaposition of writings that guarantees that these texts (and only these) all speak together the authoritative and universal, coherent Word of God – that is, the virtual Bible – may even disappear altogether.

As the Bible's function as a canon of scriptures fades further away, the virtuality of the Bible will also disappear. But if that happens, can the actual Bible continue to exist? The individual texts will continue to exist as long as people continue to read them, but if those texts are no longer seen as part of a larger, authoritative whole, a virtuality, then in what ways will people continue to read them?

Chapter 2

THE SIMULATION OF JESUS AND THE VIRTUAL GOSPEL

Why is the writerly our value? Because the goal of literary work (of literature as work) is to make the reader no longer a consumer, but a producer of the text. (Barthes 1974: 4)

... even if we, or an angel from heaven, should preach to you a gospel contrary to that which we preached to you, let him be accursed. (Gal. 1:8)

... if some one comes and preaches another Jesus than the one we preached, ... or if you accept a different gospel from the one you accepted, you submit to it readily enough. (2 Cor. 11:4)

Four Jesuses

Let's suppose that you and I discover that we have a mutual friend, whom I will call A.B. We start to talk about her, comparing stories, and we soon discover that although we agree about her in many ways, each of us seems to know things about her that the other does not. Indeed, the longer we talk, the greater the differences grow, and we begin to question whether your friend A.B. is the same person as my friend A.B. To be sure, there are many similarities, and some disparities of detail may be easily dismissed; perhaps you know her better, or in a considerably different context, than I do. However, other differences simply cannot be reconciled. My friend A.B. is a Marxist and your friend A.B. is a Republican. My friend is a celibate Japanese Buddhist nun and yours is a happily married Scottish Presbyterian who has several children. My friend is 20 years old and yours is 60. At what point in our conversation do we conclude that there must be two different people, each one named A.B., who do strikingly but only coincidentally resemble each other?

Now let us suppose instead that two written stories each feature a character named E.F. These characters are described in similar ways, they each have friends and enemies with similar names, they do and say similar things, and they are caught up in similar activities that come to similar ends. The reader does not know who the writer or writers of these stories are. Is she entitled to conclude that the two E.F.s are the same character? Let us modify our supposition a bit: the reader learns that the stories were written by two writers who were completely ignorant of one another. Should this knowledge affect the reader's view about the identity of the two E.F.s? Would it make a difference if she knew without doubt that at least one of the E.F.s was fictional?[1]

What if instead of two entirely independent writers, we suppose that the two writers of these stories did know each other's work, or (supposing even further) that they sometimes worked together, or (further still) that there is only one person who wrote the two stories – should the reader's conclusion about the identity of the two E.F.s change as we intensify the supposition? Let us modify this supposition one last time: even though each of these two stories (whether both by just one writer or each by different writers) is "complete" in its own right, however we might define such completeness, nevertheless they are also both episodes in a single larger narrative, such as a television or comic book series which presents the ongoing adventures of E.F. Does the reader now have any reason to think that there are two different E.F.s?

The New Testament begins with four gospels, each of which tells a different story of Jesus. Or rather, each gospel tells a story of a different Jesus. Each of these four Jesuses has disciples named Peter, James, and John. Each gospel's Jesus speaks enigmatically but provocatively and also performs miracles, and each one of them is crucified by the Romans and resurrected from the dead. These are certainly striking similarities. Nevertheless, any careful reader of these books will note that their four Jesuses are deeply incompatible. Roland Barthes suggests that a story poses and then finally answers one or more questions (1974: 19). Each of the gospels asks a different question, to which it gives the answer, "Jesus." However, the four questions are so different from each other that the answers are too, even though the name is always the same.

The different gospels describe the identity of each Jesus in different ways. Both Matthew's and Luke's Jesuses appear in miraculous birth events,

---

1. Casteneda describes the "startling case" of two such stories, one from a novel and the other a newspaper account of an event that happened a year after that novel was published. In these stories not only are the names, street addresses, and feelings and activities of the fictional character of the novel and the non-fictional person mentioned in the newspaper story the same, but the stories are narrated in nearly identical words (1989: 176–177). On the relation of fact and fiction, see also Aichele (2005: 45–60).

and each of them clearly resists the devil's temptations. The gospel of Matthew's Jesus is a second Moses who emphasizes the law (5:17–20), but after his resurrection he receives "all authority in heaven and on earth" and is worshiped by his followers (28:9, 17–20, see also 14:33). Luke's Jesus is the "Lord" (1:76, 2:11, 7:13, etc.), who belongs from the story's beginning in his (divine) "Father's house" (2:49), and who is rather comfortable on the cross (23:43, 46). Luke's Jesus shares these features with John's Jesus (see 2:16, 14:2, 19:28–30),[2] but John's Jesus alone is the incarnate divine Word through whom all things were made, come from God and at one with God, to shine the light of truth in the dark world (1:1–14). He is never tempted. Mark's Jesus is an unchrist (8:30) who teaches about a secret kingdom (4:11). He may be possessed by Beelzebul (3:22), and after he dies in despair (15:34), his resurrection is announced paradoxically (16:1–8).

Some of the differences between these four Jesuses appear in chunks of narrative that are unique to or absent from one of the gospels, such as birth or childhood stories, resurrection appearances, lengthy discourses, or specific miracles or parables. Other differences appear in substantial disparities between the gospels' discussions of the relations of each Jesus to God, Israel, the gentiles, or his family or followers. Still other differences appear in significant variations in the language of each Jesus, such as his reply to Peter at Caesarea Philippi, or to the high priest at his trial, or his last words on the cross. Among other differences between them, the four gospels do not share the same view of Jesus as Christ. Not only does the Jesus of each story have a different relation to Christ, but "Christ" means something different in each story. The gospel of Matthew's Jesus is surely the Christ (16:16–17), but he is not referred to as "the Lord." In contrast, Luke's Jesus is clearly both Christ and Lord (2:11), as is John's Jesus (11:2, 27). However, it is uncertain whether Mark's Jesus is the Christ (8:27–30) or even what "Christ" is (11:27–33, 12:35–37), and Mark's Jesus is at best a puzzling and paradoxical Christ.

In each of the four gospels, Jesus speaks often about a "son of man," a common phrase in the Jewish scriptures. "The son of man" in Jesus's words is usually understood to connote Jesus himself, as a unique being with a special relation to God, but only John's Jesus explicitly identifies himself as the son of man (8:28, 9:35–37). In contrast, in Mark 3:28, "the sons of men [*tois huiois tōn anthrōpōn*]" are not only sinners and blasphemers,

---

2. A more detailed review of similarities between Luke and John appears in Chapter 9.

but also plural.[3] This is the only time that this plural "son of man" phrase appears in the New Testament. As a result, although the phrase "son of man" in each Jesus's words may refer uniquely to himself in Matthew, Luke, or John, it cannot do so in the gospel of Mark. Mark's Jesus speaks the words, "the sons of men," to the people crowded around him in a house, whom he then calls his "brother and sister and mother" (3:32–35). These sons of men may include Mark's Jesus among their number, but they are not innocent, unique saviors. They are ordinary human beings, which is what "son of man" usually connotes in the Jewish scriptures. The saying in Mt. 12:31 that corresponds to Mk 3:28 obliterates the plural, sinful sons of men, and in Mt. 12:48–49, it is Jesus's disciples, not the crowd, who are his "mother and brothers."

Each Jesus has a mother, whose name is Mary in Matthew, Mark, and Luke, but who is unnamed in John, although in that gospel her sister may be named Mary (19:25). Only Matthew and Luke narrate Christmas stories, and there are important differences between those two accounts. In both of these stories, Mary is a virgin and her husband is Joseph, but most of the other details vary. Matthew's discussion of Jesus's virginal conception leaves much unsaid, when compared to Luke's detailed account (see further Chapter 5). Jesus is born in a house (Mt. 2:11) or he is laid in a manger (Lk. 2:7). Joseph requires angelic intervention in Mt. (1:20–21), but it is Mary who talks to the angel in Luke (1:28–38). The gospel of John agrees with Matthew and Luke that Jesus's human father is Joseph, and John's mystical prologue (1:1–18) serves a theological function not unlike that of the Christmas stories, but it is far less "fleshy" and detailed than the other two stories. Despite their considerable differences, each of these three gospels makes it much clearer than Mark ever does that its Jesus really is "the son of God," clarifying the meaning of that phrase, although in different ways. Mark has no birth story, and Mark's reference to Jesus as the "son of Mary" (6:3, compare Lk. 4:22) suggests that Jesus's birth was not only quite natural but also illegitimate, and that his father was unknown.

In Matthew, Mark, and Luke, each Jesus preaches about the "kingdom of God" (or "heaven" in Matthew), often in parables that present that kingdom as a secret. In contrast, in the gospel of John, the phrase "kingdom of God" appears only in Jesus's dialogue with Nicodemus, where it is associated with being "born anew" (3:3, 5). Each of the Jesuses of the three synoptic gospels explains his use of parables by quoting Isa. 6:9–10, but

---

3. Unfortunately, many modern translations replace this phrase with inclusive language, obscuring its status as a "son of man" saying.

with significant differences. Mark 4:11–12 and Lk. 8:10 follow the Greek text of Isaiah closely, and according to each of them, Jesus speaks in parables *so that* (*hina*) "those outside" will not understand. The parables of these Jesuses are not invitations but obstacles to repentance and forgiveness. However, Paul's citation of the Isaiah passage in Acts 28:26–27 may clarify the words of Luke's Jesus, for Paul then says, "this salvation of God has been sent to the Gentiles; they will listen" (Acts 28:28). In contrast, Mt. 13:13 rewrites Isaiah and eliminates the harshness of the saying, and as a result, Matthew's Jesus tells parables *because* (*hoti*) the crowd does not understand. He wants the crowd to repent. John's Jesus has his own unique collection of richly symbolical "I am" sayings, but he speaks in "figures" instead of parables, and Jn 9:39 completely transforms the saying from Isaiah.

Jesus's relations with his disciples and his family are stormy throughout the gospel of Mark. Even though they are "insiders," the disciples often do not understand Jesus and are sometimes hostile (8:32–33), and his family thinks that he is crazy (3:21). Nevertheless, outsiders understand him rather well (12:12, 28–34). As a result, Mark's distinction between outsiders and insiders in 4:11–12 becomes paradoxical.[4] In contrast, the disciples have no difficulty understanding Jesus in Matthew, Luke, or John, and there is no suggestion in these gospels that Jesus's family thinks that he is crazy (however, see Jn 10:20).

No story of Jesus's time in the wilderness and his temptation by Satan appears in John's gospel, and Mark's temptation story occupies only a single verse, but nearly identical[5] temptation stories that emphasize each of their Jesuses' rejection of Satan's offers are narrated in great detail in both the gospels of Matthew and Luke. In contrast, Mark never states that Jesus did not succumb to temptation, and Mark's scribes claim that he is "possessed by Beelzebul, and by the prince of demons he casts out the demons" (3:22). John too suggests the possibility that Jesus has a "demon" (7:20, 8:52, 10:20), although John's Jesus explicitly denies that this is true (8:48, compare 10:21). Mark's Jesus does not.

Each of the gospels associates numerous miracles with its Jesus, but once again sometimes in the gospel of Mark it is not clear whether a miracle has been performed at all, or who controls the miraculous powers (5:22–43), or by whom the miracle has been performed (7:25–30). Often among the four biblical gospels it is Mark, not John, that is semiotically and

---

4. See further Kermode (1967: 23–47) and Aichele (2006: 50–58).
5. I make no assumptions in this book about the status of "Q." See further Chapter 8.

theologically the "odd man out." Jesus's relation to the supernatural remains unclear throughout Mark. In contrast, although Matthew and Luke offer somewhat different miracle stories, these stories emphasize each of their Jesuses' supernatural powers and his ability to use them. In each of the synoptic gospels, Jesus's miracles do not cause others to believe in him but instead result from their beliefs. John however has its own distinct miracle stories, and these "signs" (2:11, 18, 3:2, etc.) lead the witnesses to believe in Jesus's close relationship to God.

The gospels all conclude with passion and resurrection stories. Each Jesus is betrayed by a disciple named Judas and condemned by a Roman named Pilate. In Gethsemane, the Jesuses of both Mark and Matthew are unwilling to die, and each one cries out at the moment of his death: "My God, my God, why hast thou forsaken me?" (Mt. 27:46, Mk 15:34). The death of Mark's Jesus is no voluntary sacrifice ("remove this cup from me; yet not what I will, but what thou wilt," 14:36, see also 14:34). Although the gospel of Matthew follows Mark's Gethsemane scene closely, Matthew has Jesus "yield up his spirit" at the moment of death (27:50), instead of simply "breathing his last" as in Mark 15:37. In strong contrast to Matthew and Mark, both Luke and John present Jesuses who are calm and assured as death looms, both in the garden (except for Lk. 22:43–44, which is missing in the oldest manuscripts) and on the cross. The gospel of Luke's Jesus promises to be with the faithful thief "today in paradise" (23:43, compare also 23:34) and John's Jesus sedately arranges for the care of his mother (19:26–27). The final words of Luke's Jesus are "Father, into thy hands I commit my spirit!" (23:46), and John's Jesus says serenely, "It is finished" (19:30). These two Jesuses know all along where they are going. However, the passionless passion of John's Jesus stands in sharp contrast to the crucifixion stories in each of the synoptic gospels.

Despite the efforts of Christians to read meaning into Mark's empty tomb story or to paste on alternative endings, Mark's gospel ends on a note of paradox and fear. According to Mk 16:8, the women at the tomb "said nothing to any one, for they were afraid." However, if the women said nothing to anyone, then Mark's story of the empty tomb and the young man's words to them were never told to any others. Because these matters evidently are being "told" to others in the text of Mark itself, that gospel implies that its story is fictitious.

The shorter and longer endings that were added to the gospel of Mark after 16:8 in various ancient manuscripts do not fully overcome this implication, but they do effectively create at least three different "Marks," for different endings yield different stories. As distinct and contradictory "solutions" to Barthes's hermeneutical "enigma" (1974: 19), these multiple endings produce irreconcilable Marks, alternative textual bodies that describe three different Jesuses. John's gospel also has a problem with ending(s), but there the difficulty is not a failure of denotation, as in Mk 16:8, but rather a super-abundance. According to Jn 21:25, "were every one of [the things Jesus did] to be written ... the world itself could not contain the books that would be written" (see further Chapter 6). Thus John also announces its own deficiencies, but they are quite different deficiencies than those of Mark.

After the crucifixion, the gospel of Matthew narrates an Easter story that is both spectacular and yet abrupt and sketchy, and this quality becomes evident when the end of Matthew is compared to the quite different resurrection stories of Luke and John. Luke and its apparent sequel, the Acts of the Apostles, narrate more extensive encounters between Luke's Jesus and his disciples after the resurrection, as does John (but with different stories). Nevertheless, both Matthew and Luke-Acts reduce the evident fictionality of Mark's ending, and their resurrection appearance stories bring them to definitive and triumphal closure, although again in significantly different ways. Each of these gospels, as well as John, underlines its Jesus's supernatural power and make it clear that he has not only risen from the grave but has met with his disciples and given them authority to create a universal church.

Reality Effect

There are many additional differences between the four Jesuses of the biblical gospels, including narrative disparities that cannot be resolved into matters of minor detail, gaps in one gospel that do not appear in others, or variations in sequence. These narrative differences cannot be reduced to variations of personal, historical, or theological perspective on some single reality – that is, multiple copies of a single model – without seriously mutilating one or more of the gospels. Lurking beneath the numerous differences between these four Jesuses, and producing many of them, are deeper and even more important differences.

My goal in this book is not to produce an exhaustive survey of the differences or similarities between the various Jesuses of the New Testament, for such a survey would be endless. It would require something like a parallel edition of the gospels, which are already plentiful and could be used in this way – although anyone seeking to do so should beware "the vertigo of the simulacrum" (Deleuze 1990: 262). Even so, each gospel's Jesus is the product of the circumstances of reading, the reader's knowledge and interests, and the semiotic codes that are put into play in relation to the actual signifiers of the text,[6] and the possible combinations of these factors would be beyond counting. I address some of these differences in the next four chapters of this book, but others are equally deserving of attention.

Each gospel creates a referential illusion or reality effect. The effect of the real arises when codes of denotation dominate the reading of a text. "Denotation 'translates' reality," says Barthes (1988: 174) – that is, realism is the fictional illusion of reality, and "the real is never anything but a meaning" (1986: 140). In other words, there is no reality without virtuality, as I argued in Chapter 1. According to Barthes, "the 'real' is never anything but an unformulated signified, sheltered behind the apparent omnipotence of the referent" (1986: 139, see also 141–148). The reality effect of a particular text may not denote the lived reality experienced by the reader, and this may be quite explicit (for example, in fantastical or marvelous texts), but even in such cases there will be some engagement of the "reality principle" in relation to which the reader's self and her world are constructed.[7] This reality principle is defined by ideology, which both congeals and is embodied in the reality effect of the text. Even the most unrealistic of fictions must have some coherence and plausibility. This is perhaps most strikingly clear in narratives such as Edwin Abbott's novel, *Flatland* (1884), which is set in a two-dimensional universe. Without such plausibility or coherence, the reader could never become deeply involved in stories of fantasy, other cultures or worlds, the far future, or the distant past.

The reality effect of each of the biblical gospels produces a meaningful story (a virtuality) about a seemingly-real person named Jesus. As distinctive patterns of repetition and difference,[8] these various reality effects are "given" to the reader. The reader alone does not produce them, and she cannot impose on the story whatever perspective she wants, any more than she can choose to make the story signify whatever she wants. However, these effects are also not simply "there" in the texts. They are the products of intertextual negotiations between reader and text, or in other words, "reality" is the effect of semiotic codes, which are themselves profoundly

6. Barthes discusses the codes that he has identified in *S/Z* (1974: 3–21, 26–30). I describe these five codes further in Chapter 9.

7. See further Deleuze (1994: 98–100).

8. "[R]epetition is in its essence symbolic; symbols or simulacra are the letter of repetition itself. Difference is included in repetition by way of disguise and by the order of the symbol" (Deleuze 1994: 17).

ideological, and through which the reader deciphers the text.[9] Therefore although the four gospels' respective reality effects are profoundly subjective phenomena and vary from one reader to another, distinctions between them are not simply made up and cannot be wished away. Each gospel produces a different reality effect, and therefore a different Jesus. The differences between the four Jesuses are quite "real," despite the massive involvement of the subjectivity of the reader.

As reality effects, these four Jesuses are what Gilles Deleuze (among others) calls simulacra. According to Deleuze, "The simulacrum is not a degraded copy. It harbors a positive power which denies *the original and the copy, the model and the reproduction.* ... The simulacrum functions in such a way that a certain resemblance is necessarily thrown back onto its basic series and a certain identity projected on the forced movement" (1990: 262, 265, his emphases). Deleuze's "certain resemblance and identity" of the simulacrum form the pattern of repetition and difference that creates the reality effect. It is on the basis of such patterns that I argue in this book that the Jesuses of the four gospels are four different simulacra.

The simulacrum is not a re-presentation or image of some previously present or independently acknowledged reality, a pre-existing object such as an actual event or person, an eternally-true form or relation, or the intention of an author. Nor is it an illusion. On the contrary, the simulacrum is the effect which *produces* reality by simulating it, the afterlife that generates its precursor: "a single instance which does not exist outside its metamorphoses" (Deleuze 1989: 139). For Deleuze, simulation is not of an original, but of an "originary."

> An originary world is not an any-space-whatever (although it may resemble one), because it only appears in the depths of determined milieux; but neither is it a determined milieu, which only derives from the originary world. ... It is, first of all, Empedocles' world, made up of outlines and fragments, heads without necks, eyes without faces, arms without shoulders, gestures without form. (Deleuze 1986: 123–124, see also 1994: 125)

The simulacrum is a parable that has no explanation, a "secret of the kingdom" that opens itself toward meaning but without definitive denotation or connotation.

Although the simulacrum does not copy an antecedent model, that does not mean that it has no relation to reality. "If the simulacrum still has a model, it is another model, a model of the Other, from which there flows an internalized dissemblance" (Deleuze 1990: 258), or as Jacques Derrida

---

9. This is very capably demonstrated in Barthes's book, *S/Z* (1974).

says, "this very simulacrum still bears witness to a possibility which exceeds it" (1995: 30).[10] Commenting on Deleuze, Alain Badiou says, "the world of beings is the theater of the simulacra of Being" (1999: 25). The simulacrum is a virtual object, produced in relation to actual, physical signifiers through a contingent synthesis of "singularities" and "intensities" that forms the signified (Deleuze 1994: 253–254).[11]

As a reality effect, the simulacrum belongs to the realm of ideology. Systems of simulacra form "sites for the actualisation of Ideas," says Deleuze (1994: 278) – that is, sites of virtuality.[12] In Chapter 1, I identified the Bible as one such virtuality, or system of simulacra. To speak more precisely, it is a canonical system of such systems, for the two testaments, and each of the books within them, are also virtualities. To reduce the different Jesus simulacra of the gospels to variant copies of a single historical model or archetypal entity, as many readers (including biblical scholars) do, requires ideological assumptions that are deeply theological, even if sometimes quite unconscious. It fails to take these Jesuses seriously as distinct simulacra.

Deleuze's understanding that the real is reciprocally determined by the virtual and the actual is deeply relevant to the processes of semiosis. Real signs are constituted by reciprocal relations of individuation between divergent series consisting of virtual signifieds and actual signifiers. The simulacrum is also the product of this semiotic structure, a divergent series of signifiers and signifieds. In Deleuze's words, "The simulacrum is the instance which includes a difference within itself, such as (at least) two divergent series on which it plays, all resemblance abolished so that one can no longer point to the existence of an original and a copy" (1994: 69). Deleuze here echoes Gottlob Frege, who describes "an imperfection of language" such that "combinations of symbols can occur that seem to mean something but (at least so far) do not mean anything, e.g. divergent infinite series" (1952: 70, see also 32–33). Frege's examples include "apparent proper names" and metaphors, both of which play important roles in the gospels' simulations of Jesus.

As a result, Deleuze identifies the simulacrum or symbol as the sign "in so far as the sign interiorises the conditions of its own repetition" (1994: 67). I take this to be the linguistic sign or what both Frege and C. S. Peirce call the "symbol." The simulacrum is a virtual signifier, a sign that creates

10. On the relations between Deleuze's and Derrida's understandings of the simulacrum, see the essays in Patton and Protevi (2003).
11. See further Deleuze and Parnet (2007: 148–152).
12. See Deleuze (1994: 277–278) for description of the characteristics of such systems.

its virtual object. To modify a phrase from Barthes, simulation neither represents nor copies, but only signifies (1982: 89). It is Peirce's "interpretant," understood in Deleuze's analyses as a dynamic phenomenon and in terms of its smallest possible components.[13] As such, the simulacrum deconstructs the binary opposition between reality and representation (Deleuze 1990: 265–266). A character, an event, or even the entire world of a narrative is not the re-presentation or depiction of some prior concept or object, but rather it contributes to the creation of a concept.

Perception of the simulacrum as simulacrum deconstructs the semiotic system, for the simulacrum is always "between" or "in the middle" (two of Deleuze's favorite phrases). No text signifies by itself, and so the simulacrum always appears between signifier and signifer, and between signified and signified – that is, intertextually. Meaning is not located "in" any individual text, but rather it flows between texts and readers, and thus between texts and other texts. This "between" always hovers over an abyss. For the simulacrum, there can be no Final Signified, no ground to the abyss of meaning. In contrast to the modernist concept of the copy or representation, which is always grounded in an antecedent model (and therefore logocentric), the simulacrum is accompanied by the vertigo that accompanies the endless flow of semiosis (Deleuze 1990: 262). As Deleuze says:

> Simulacra are those systems in which different relates to different *by means of* difference itself. What is essential is that we find in these systems *no prior identity, no internal resemblance*. ... What is displaced and disguised in the series cannot and must not be identified, but exists and acts as the differenciator of difference. (1994: 299–300, his emphases)

This is Deleuze's "originary," the field of the simulacrum.

The vertigo of the simulacrum extends beyond denotation and its reality effects to connotation and the plural text, or in other words, from the "readerly" to the "writerly" text (Barthes 1974: 4).[14] Barthes argues that "denotation is not the truth of discourse: ... [denotation is] a particular, specialized substance used by the other [connotative] codes to smooth their articulation" (1974: 128). Denotation must always be negotiated and controlled – it is the singular, paranoid truth of "the real" – but connotation is meaning running wild, schizophrenic, the force behind unlimited semiosis (Eco 1976: 15). For connotation, there is no proper or firm

---

13. On the interpretant, see further Aichele (1997: 63–65). Deleuze (1986) includes an extensive and valuable discussion of Peirce.
14. The readerly and the writerly are discussed further in Chapter 4.

connection between meaning and language. Denotation secures the plurality of the gospels' Jesus simulacra, but connotation opens up a semiotic abyss *within* each Jesus.

The denotation of a sentence or even an entire story may be incomplete or indeterminate.[15] As Frege says, "languages have the fault of containing expressions which fail to designate an object ... because the truth of some sentence is a prerequisite" (1952: 69). These faulty expressions are like variables in a mathematical function which may be "saturated" by yet other functions which themselves contain variables that require saturation by names or yet other functions (Frege 1952: 38–41). Such language opens up a potentially bottomless abyss of semiotic possibilities, and many fantastic, metafictional, or other stories that question reality emphasize this feature, although it is present in all language (see further Chapter 4).

Indeterminate or incomplete denotation can be very unsettling, especially in a text which is thought to be the "Word of God." The reader seeks to close this semiotic opening by completing the incomplete denotations and foreclosing the indeterminate connotations, thereby breaking the flow of semiosis. This offers another way to think what intertextuality does, as I noted in Chapter 1.[16] When these semiotic openings are closed through the reader's understanding and beliefs, what Barthes calls the reality effect appears, and the sentence or story becomes meaningful. The reader must work harder to make sense of some texts (the sort that Barthes calls writerly) than of others – that is, to direct and contain their wild connotations, to saturate their unsaturated functions – and the influence of ideology on reading becomes more evident as a result. Nevertheless, even the least difficult (or in Barthes's terms, most readerly) text means nothing at all unless unlimited semiosis is controlled through some intertextual mechanism to transform the originary into a "determined milieu."

The proper name plays a significant part in this transformation. Frege compares a sentence to a mathematical function which is meaningless until its "empty place" (variable) has been saturated with "a proper name, or ... an expression that replaces a proper name" – that is, words denoting a specific object (1952: 31). In Barthes's words, "As soon as a Name exists (even a pronoun) to flow toward and fasten onto, the semes become

15. Barthes notes that the semiotic properties of sentences apply equally well to stories (1974: 76–77). A story may be as small as a single sentence, or it may consist of many sentences strung together in a sequence. However, all of the sentences in the longest narrative can be analyzed as a single great sentence.
16. See also Deleuze (1990: 29) and Aichele (2001: 200–208).

predicates, inductors of truth, and the Name becomes a subject" (Barthes 1974: 191). The predicates establish character, plot, and meaning, and they may appear, change, or disappear at any moment. Deleuze makes a similar point: "the virtual is never subject to the global character which affects real objects. It is ... a fragment, a shred or a remainder. It lacks its own identity" (1994: 100–101). In language reminiscent of Frege, Deleuze describes the real as the "solution" to the "problem" posed by the virtual, and he compares this to the integration of a differential equation (1994: 209). This mathematical analogy suggests an asymptotic limitation of semiosis, an approach to meaning through an infinite series of approximations. As a result, "The proper name does not designate a subject, but something which happens, at least between two terms which are not subjects, but agents, elements" (Deleuze and Parnet 2007: 51). Therefore even the name does not denote a person, but rather it is the means by which signifying elements are joined together and the narrative function is saturated. The name is thus a shifter of sorts, perhaps not as defined in the classical semiotic tradition, but also not far removed from that.[17]

Narratives draw heavily upon proper names because proper names connect phrases, allowing different connotations to be attributed to the same denoted object. The distribution of proper names in the story allows a fictional illusion of realism to be established. However, depending on the predicates and the ways in which they are linked together, various possible "solutions" to the virtual "problem" may be found. Each of the gospels' Jesus simulacra is nothing more than what Deleuze calls a "partial object": "an isolation or suspension which freezes the real in order to extract a pose, an aspect or a part" (1994: 100). In each gospel, the name of Jesus becomes a metatextual hook on which the story hangs various predicates at different narrative points. The result is like a picture puzzle that can be assembled in different ways. As a simulacrum, each of these Jesuses is a virtual being inhabiting a distinct world, an ideological solution to a different problem, the reality effect produced by a series of signifiers. The stories in which these simulacra appear are not multiple variations on the same story, or even similar stories. Indeed, "The same and the similar no longer have an essence except as *simulated*, that is as expressing the functioning of the simulacrum. There is no longer any possible selection" (Deleuze 1990: 262).

The schizophrenic flow of semiosis is more evident in relatively writerly texts such as the gospels of Mark or John than it is in more readerly texts such as Matthew or Luke. Mark's Jesus, compared to Matthew's or Luke's

---

17. See further Ducrot and Todorov (1979: 252), with reference to Jakobson.

Jesuses, is a disturbing fellow, one who boggles his followers' (and readers') minds, for he continually splits open and comes apart: Christ, son of God, son of man, son of Mary, carpenter, possessed by Beelzebul. John's Jesus also boggles the mind, but in a very different way. As God incarnate, the witnessed and fleshy Word (1:14), he is incomprehensible, like the square root of minus one. Nevertheless, what may be more evident in relation to Mark or John is true also, but in more subtle ways, for Matthew and Luke. As Barthes demonstrates in *S/Z*, even the most readerly text becomes writerly when read very closely. Each gospel's Jesus then becomes a different and distinct partial object, on the verge of coming apart, but in different ways.

As scholars know, even to speak of (for example) "the gospel of John" as though it is a single thing is already to avoid some very serious problems. There is no one gospel of John, except as a virtuality. Instead there are many different manuscripts, printed editions, and translations of John, which for convenience we usually lump together as "the gospel of John." In many cases the differences are slight and the reality effect for any given reader will be the same. However, in some cases, the semiotic potentials of the differences between these texts are considerable. As a result, there are many different simulacra that might be described as "John's (or Mark or Matthew or Luke's) Jesus," and I will note a few of the differences between such simulacra in the following chapters. However, to examine all of the differences would be a truly gigantic (and once again endless) task, and to simplify my discussions in this book I refer to English texts of the gospels that appear in the Revised Standard Version (1971), with occasional additional reference to the Greek texts in the printed editions of Nestle and Aland (1979) or Rahlfs (1979), unless otherwise noted.

Canon and "the Gospel"

Each of the Jesuses of the New Testament is a different simulacrum. This includes not only the four Jesuses of the gospels, but also the Jesuses of Paul's letters, Revelation, and the other New Testament writings. In this book, I say little about these other Jesus simulacra, with the partial exception of Paul's Jesus. This is partly because my point is better made by focusing on the gospels' Jesuses, and partly because there is just not very much to be said about these other Jesus simulacra as such. Each of these other Jesuses, including Paul's, tends to be already absorbed into "Jesus Christ" or "the Lord Jesus" – that is, a different and quite distinct simulacrum. Indeed, the name "Jesus" only rarely appears in these writings apart from the terms "Christ" or "Lord," predicates which become in effect additions to the proper name, and which are like any other predicates by no means interchangeable. Hebrews and Revelation are partial exceptions.

There are numerous different Jesus Christ or Lord Jesus simulacra in the New Testament writings – for example, the Christ of Paul is quite different from that of Revelation or of Jude. These simulacra are certainly worthy of further study, but they will not be considered here. (However, see further Chapter 10 of this book.) In other words, there are probably important differences between these other New Testament Jesus simulacra as well, but they are no longer Jesus simulacra, strictly speaking, and as either Jesus Christ or Lord Jesus simulacra they are more readily assimilated into the Jesus Christ simulacrum of the Bible as a virtual whole, which I discuss below.

In contrast, in the gospels the terms "Christ" or "Lord" are rarely linked directly to the name "Jesus," and one of the differences between the gospels is defined by the different relations between their Jesus simulacra and either the Christ or the Lord. Some absorption of Jesus into Jesus Christ or Lord Jesus does appear in each of the gospels, particularly Luke and John (see Chapter 9), but at least some tension is also apparent between Jesus and Christ or Lord in each one of them.

However, I do regard the Jesus simulacrum of the book of Acts (1:1–9, 7:55, 9:3–6, 10–17, and 16:7) as a narrative continuation of the Jesus simulacrum in the gospel of Luke.[18] I make no assumption about the author(s) of either Luke or Acts, but I regard the Jesus of Luke-Acts in much the same way that I regard James T. Kirk of the "Star Trek" TV series and movies, as in the second example at the beginning of this chapter. If this is not correct, then the Jesuses of Luke and Acts should also be treated as different simulacra. The question of what makes two stories or their simulacra "the same" or different becomes especially significant in such a case. In the Acts of the Apostles, "Jesus" also appears many times in the speeches of various other characters or as a reference to the Jesus, presumably, of Luke. The Paul simulacrum of Acts even quotes a saying attributed to "the Lord Jesus," "It is more blessed to give than to receive" (20:35), that does not appear in any of the gospels.

The differences between the multiple Jesus simulacra of the gospels are pasted over or ignored in Christian ideology, which rejects the possibility of multiple Jesuses. The deep and pervasive logocentrism of Christian

18. See further Chapters 5 and 9, and Green (1997: 6–10). In private conversation, Raj Nadella notes that although both Luke and Acts make it clear that Jesus is "the Lord," the Jesus simulacrum of Acts 9 behaves more like a divine being than does the Jesus of Luke.

theology,[19] which plays an important role in the Christian concept of the Bible and hence in the virtuality of the Bible, continually reinforces this practice. For Christian faith, the Bible is understood to transmit a single message with a single meaning, the Word of God. Therefore the four gospels also must refer to a single truth. In order to maintain these four different stories side by side in the Bible, their four distinct simulacra named Jesus must be absorbed without remainder into a single simulacrum. The name of Jesus must be transformed into a hypertextual link, allowing the various texts to be woven into a single story. This is a very different thing than the semiotic functioning of the proper name in a narrative, that was discussed earlier in this chapter. In this case, the name is extended from one virtuality or world to one or more others, and distinctions between the reality effects of the different narratives are blurred or eliminated.

As a mechanism that controls the meaning of the scriptures, the canon of the Bible performs what Roman Jakobson calls the metalingual function, which is to identify the proper codes for understanding a text (1987: 69). Every simulacrum is always profoundly intertextual, and as a very powerful intertext, a "strong misreading" as it were, the Bible absorbs the disparities between different stories of different Jesuses, and thus between the four gospels. As the one, authoritative Word of God, the canon negates the diverse reality effects of the multiple gospels, in effect translating and unifying the message of the various texts into the singular theological concept of "the Gospel," which is the canonical simulation of Jesus as Christ, Son of God, and Lord. Not surprisingly, the Jesus simulacra of the four gospels stand in various relations to the Jesus Christ simulacrum of the Gospel.

For the Gospel there is only one "real" Jesus: namely, the Lord Jesus Christ, the divine sacrifice who takes away the sins of those who believe in him. This Jesus Christ is the Christian God incarnate in a human body, a unique being whose unjust death and supernatural resurrection guarantees to those who believe in him a heavenly afterlife. The theological entity, Jesus Christ, does not appear in any actual New Testament text, even though the phrase "Jesus Christ" does. Differences between actual gospel texts and their Jesuses pale to insignificance in the Gospel, and the single canonical simulacrum absorbs the various Jesus simulacra of the separate and distinct texts. Jesus Christ is the only Jesus of the one Gospel and the only real Jesus for Christian belief.

Other factors are no doubt also at work in the production of the Gospel of Jesus Christ: in Christian creeds, catechisms, prayers, homilies, and

19. See further Aichele (2001: 15–104).

theological treatises, the ideology of the Gospel plays a very important part. It is no coincidence that the Christian canon of the Bible and the Nicene Creed are both products of the fourth century, the same period in which Christianity was transformed from a diverse array of marginal groups into a united, imperial church. To claim that Jesus is Lord or Christ in a pre-canonical, and therefore pre-Constantinian and pre-imperial, context, as Paul and other New Testament writers do, may have been a radical or even revolutionary thing to do. However, by the time that the New Testament texts are canonized, Christianity is well on its way to becoming an imperial religion and any subversive political implications of this claim either disappear or shift quite significantly.

Nevertheless, the Bible plays a particularly crucial role in the establishment of the Gospel. The gospels' canonical status in the Bible both augments their value and encourages the reader to read them as "the same," weaving together the different stories or treating them as mutually illuminating versions of a single story, which features a single set of characters. Thus Matthew is often called "the Gospel *According to* (Saint) Matthew," and so forth, for the gospels are understood to be four versions of one story. Each gospel then complements and supplements the others, and as a result, the writerly becomes more readerly (see further Part Three of this book). The four simulacra named Jesus are transformed into "versions" of just one simulacrum and understood to be multiple copies of a single model, who is Jesus Christ. The canonical intertext authorizes such reading practices, and the Gospel's simulacrum, Jesus Christ, can then be projected through the canon not only upon the various gospels but also the rest of the Bible, as the theological object of readers' beliefs and desires, the referent of the Bible as a whole. In this way the New Testament gives all of its constituent texts another sense, producing its own reality effect and referring the four gospels to a single, "dynamically equivalent," theological truth – namely, the Gospel.

The canon also excludes other texts – and especially in this case, other gospels with yet other Jesuses – from the authoritative collection. The Gospel is defined not only positively by what the canon includes, but negatively by what it excludes. The inclusion of any text in the canon guarantees that it speaks for God, and since Christians believe in only one God, there can be no multiplicity of message between the texts. The canonical sequence is also important: the fact that Matthew, Mark, Luke, and John appear side by side (although in some manuscripts the sequence of them varies), and the location of the gospels at the beginning of the New Testament encourages the reader to think that these books belong together and to read each of them in light of the other three, as well as the other New Testament writings, perhaps especially the letters of Paul.

The tendency to read the various gospels together appeared well before the New Testament canon was established. The gospels of Matthew, Mark, Luke, and John, or parts of them, were bound together in papyrus codexes (P45 and especially P75) or harmonized (by Tatian) as early as the second century. The codex was already making it possible to arrange the four gospels (and eventually the other biblical writings) as though they were the chapters of a single book. The codex is not the same thing as the canon, but the single codex of the Bible signifies to many readers the fundamental unity of the included texts and thus the non-existence of significant differences between the gospels, including and especially differences between the various Jesuses. Nevertheless, it is the canonizing of the New Testament that gives an authoritative context to the four biblical gospels which the codex alone could not provide.

The coincidence of terminology between Gospel (as theological concept, which I capitalize throughout this book) and gospel (as written text, for which I use the lower case in this book) is confusing, but it is unavoidably there in the discourse of Christianity. The ideological effect of this coincidence not only obscures the distinction between abstract concept and concrete texts, but it also encourages the thought that the four gospels themselves are nothing more than varieties or aspects of the one Gospel, just as the two Testaments are united in the one Word of God, a single Christian Bible. The Gospel is not any of the gospels, nor is it all of them; it is something else, no longer simply a story, like and unlike other stories, as the gospels are. Instead it is a revelation from God, a message of ultimate salvation. The Gospel and its simulacrum, Jesus Christ, are both product and producer of Christian theology, and of Christian readers' desires.

Therefore the pre-canonical collections consisting of only the four gospels that were mentioned above would not have been sufficient to establish the Gospel of Jesus Christ. Once gospel harmonies such as that of Tatian (as well as single gospel canons such as that of Marcion) were rejected, something more was required in order to secure the identity of the gospels' meaning – that is, the virtuality of the single Gospel – and that "something more" appears in other New Testament texts[20] and especially the letters of

---

20. The Old Testament, the Christian name for and appropriation of the Jewish scriptures, also helps to identify the Gospel, but a collection consisting only of the Old Testament and the four gospels would not have been sufficient for that purpose.

Paul. The influence of Paul's writings on the simulation of Christ can hardly be over-emphasized. Paul is far more likely than any of the gospels to conjoin "Jesus" with "Christ" or "the Lord." In addition, Paul's frequent use of the word "gospel" (*euaggelion*) deeply influences understanding of the meaning of that word, and therefore of the texts that are called "gospels." *Euaggelion* appears more often in the undisputed letters of Paul than in the entire remainder of the Bible, both New Testament and Greek Old Testament.

However, Paul does not use this word to designate the kind of story that appears in the gospel texts. He is either uninterested in or unaware of the words and deeds of Jesus, and although the death and resurrection of Jesus are of great interest to him, their chief value is not as narrative events, but as a basis for eschatological and soteriological reflection (and finally as grounds for his own apostolic authority). In Paul's writings, the simulacrum that is Jesus Christ has so absorbed Jesus that Jesus can hardly be considered a virtual object in them.

For Paul, the word "gospel" designates a central element in his own thought, the content of the message that he preaches. Paul defines *euaggelion* as "the power of God for salvation to every one who has faith" (Rom. 1:16). "The gospel" thus acquires a supernatural status in Paul's letters, where it is associated with mystery and power: "For I would have you know, brethren, that the gospel which was preached by me is not man's gospel. For I did not receive it from man, nor was I taught it, but it came through a revelation of *Jesus Christ*" (Gal. 1:11–12, emphasis added). It is in this sense that Paul already preaches the Gospel of Jesus Christ.

In any case, Paul's letters are indispensable to the Gospel of Jesus Christ as a canonical effect. Nevertheless, the only New Testament text where the phrase, "gospel of Jesus Christ," itself appears is Mk 1:1. However, the remainder of Mark's gospel raises serious questions about the relation between Jesus and "Christ, the Son of God," and I have argued elsewhere that in 1:1 and elsewhere in Mark, the word "gospel" connotes the text of Mark itself and therefore does not connote the Gospel (2006: 85–104). Given the highly ambiguous treatment of the word "Christ" elsewhere in Mark (8:29–30, 12:35–37, 13:21–22, 14:61–62), and Mark's very different use of *euaggelion* than in Paul's writings, its appearance in Mark's first verse does not unambiguously indicate the Gospel. Instead, when placed in intertextual juxtaposition with Paul's letters, the gospel of Mark parodies Pauline thought; it does not elaborate or defend it.

The Control of Biblical Meaning

The Christian canon of the New Testament collects the four gospels, places them in a sequence, and follows them almost immediately with a collection of Paul's letters. In effect, the canon quotes each gospel word for word and thereby translates and transforms that text into an organ of a larger entity, recontextualizing the entire text. The canon obscures the actual, physical texts themselves with something else, a signified or at least a signifying potential (a virtuality) that far surpasses any of them. The result of canonizing is not a physical rewriting that transforms or replaces the materiality of the signifier, but it changes the signifier anyway, because it changes the signification. The canon makes possible the Gospel.

However, without Christian belief in the singularity of Christ already established as "right belief," four different gospels would not have been admitted into the Christian canon. This suggests that the Gospel also makes possible the canon. Belief that there is only one Jesus Christ (and thus refusal to think of the gospels as simulations of multiple Jesuses) is essential to orthodox Christian thought. Indeed, the triumph of what Bart Ehrman calls "proto-orthodox" Christianity (1993) following the conversion of the Roman emperor, Constantine, is probably one powerful reason for the canonization of the Bible. Proto-orthodoxy was that variety of early Christianity, over against many others, that would most welcome the canon of scriptures that was then established.[21] Those who favored "different gospels" and "other Jesuses," the ones that Paul attacks in this chapter's second and third epigraphs and elsewhere in his writings, had been or would eventually be eliminated from the Christian movement, in part at least due to the canonical control of meaning.

The ideological influence of the Gospel continues into the present. Even though the Christian Bible no longer functions for many readers as a canon of scripture, the virtual Bible is still a force in today's world. The biblical canon, contained in a single codex, creates the illusion of a self-contained whole, a single, seamless text that conveys the clear, already well-known message of the Gospel of Jesus Christ which lies at the core of the virtual Bible. However, the Christian canon is and has always been at best only a partial success. The codex allows the reader to skip back and forth between the different biblical books. This supports the intertextual effect of the canon and encourages the harmonizing of the gospels' stories. Yet by the same stroke, it brings to light instabilities within the collection, conflicts

---

21. For example, the Marcionites chose a very different "canon," and the Valentinians yet another.

between the gospels (and other biblical texts) that would be mere inconsistencies in a non-canonical collection. Any careful reader is aware of the conflicts, but only to the extent that the canon has failed to control the texts.

That there is a powerful relationship between the theological concept of Jesus Christ and the scholarly concept of the historical Jesus has long been noted. For the last two hundred years or more, scholarly biblical criticism has attempted to resolve the differences between the four Jesuses of the gospels through hypotheses describing trajectories of traditions arising from or about one historical person, Jesus. These trajectories appear in the form of first oral and then written texts produced by a wide variety of early "Jesus communities" and reflecting the differing beliefs of those communities. Lurking behind many of these investigations has been the scholars' belief that it is possible in some degree to recover from these various stories some truths about this one man. It may even be that the problems presented by multiple gospels in the canon is the single most important issue in modern biblical studies.

These biblical scholars accept the canonical reality effect and assume (without question, for the most part) that the gospels serve as four more or less reliable accounts of a single historical truth. They are thought to be four more or less compatible points of view on a single phenomenon, not entirely unlike stories of a single series of events in different newspapers, which differ because they reflect different sources of information, sources which are of varying reliability, or differing perspectives, biases, and writing styles of the reporters and editors who produce them. (This returns us to the second example that I began this chapter with, the multiple stories about E.F.) Even among those who are highly skeptical of the gospels' value as historical sources, it is widely supposed that the stories all denote a single person, albeit falsely, and those who deny that Jesus existed at all also implicitly apply that denial to each of the gospels equally. Although it is widely accepted that distortion of the Jesus stories results from the history of the traditions and differences between emerging theologies, each of the four biblical gospels is thought to denote a single historical reality to some degree, and the differences between them are explained as differences of emphasis or of accuracy.

The resulting reconstructions of this historical person, Jesus, are additional simulacra. The "historical Jesus" functions in a way comparable to the narrative harmonizations of the gospels that began at least as early as Tatian in the second century. Tatian's *Diatesseron* was eventually condemned by the early church, but his efforts and their popularity suggest a deep discomfort with the multiple Jesuses of the New Testament, and especially the gospels. Such harmonizations are still very popular among Christians today, probably for similar reasons, but now they often take the form of novels or movies about Jesus that piece together the diverse New Testament texts as though they narrated a single, coherent story. These too are reconstructions of the "historical Jesus," although usually of a less scholarly and more sentimental or pious sort. The net effect in any case is a super-gospel that owes much to the canonical Gospel of Jesus Christ.

In these ways, both Christian faith and modern biblical scholarship reject the thought of four distinct Jesus simulacra. To think otherwise would destroy both a fundamental tenet of the faith and an indispensable presupposition of much of the scholarship. In either case, the one Christ simulacrum is constructed canonically, out of the four distinct Jesus simulacra of the gospels, supplemented by other biblical sources in both the Old and New Testament writings, and especially Paul's letters. The canon legitimizes certain understandings of the texts and delegitimizes others, controlling the way that the Bible is read and thereby encouraging the theological concept of the singular being, Jesus Christ. The Bible is read as the coherent Word of God, smoothing over differences of narrative and implication between the various gospel texts and resolving them into a greater truth. Such a reading turns four different gospels into the one Gospel, and it turns four different simulacra who share the name of Jesus into the one simulacrum who is the Lord Jesus Christ, the divine Savior and Son of God. As a result (again, in either case), the reader can comfortably ignore the otherwise disturbing implications of four different Jesuses among the gospels.

Belief in the unity of the canon as the Word of God makes the multiplicity of the gospels tolerable for Christian faith, and the inclusion of four gospels in the New Testament even plays a major role in Christian rejection of the multiplicity of Jesus simulacra. The inclusion of multiple gospels in the New Testament does not encourage diversity, as some have claimed recently, but instead it *subjects* diversity to a greater unity (Gamble 1985: 24–35, 75). The reader will only "see" the different Jesus simulacra and the theological difficulties that they present if she frees the gospels' respective texts from the canon, and from each other.

Part II

Four Jesuses

Chapter 3

MATTHEW'S GOSPEL ACCORDING TO PASOLINI

By close-ups of the things around us, by focusing on hidden details of familiar objects, by exploring commonplace milieus under the ingenious guidance of the camera, the film, on the one hand, extends our comprehension of the necessities which rule our lives; on the other hand, it manages to assure us of an immense and unexpected field of action. ... Evidently a different nature opens itself to the camera than opens to the naked eye. (Benjamin 1968: 236)

[F]rom the outset, Christianity and revolution, the Christian faith and revolutionary faith, were the two poles which attracted the art of the masses. (Deleuze 1989: 165)

Readers who have little prior experience with reading the Bible or with Christian thought may encounter the Bible's books as they would encounter other books – that is, relatively free from canonical control. However, there are few such readers in the Western world, at least, for even if you (assuming that you have grown up in the West) have never read any part of the Bible and are not a Christian, you have still probably lived your entire life in a culture steeped for hundreds of years in biblical traditions. In addition, for readers such as myself, who are somewhat familiar with the Bible, simply to read the gospel of Matthew or any other biblical text as though it were a separate book, apart from the canon, is not really a viable option. The canonical intertext will have its way, and the larger biblical message of the "Word of God" will influence the reading through what Roland Barthes calls codes of reference (or culture) and of symbols (1974: 19–20), and perhaps other intertextual codes as well. The reader has little conscious control over the influence of these codes, whether or not she is a faithful Christian. This canonical influence will perhaps be more prominent in regard to more familiar biblical texts, such as the gospels, than it is for others.

Nevertheless, as I noted in Chapter 1, the semiotic machine that is the Bible is now breaking down. Both the meaning and authority of the biblical texts are in jeopardy, and increasingly each of these texts sinks or floats in contemporary secular culture, just as non-canonical texts do. One measure of the mordant status of the biblical canon is the freedom with which popular mass media translate and recycle formerly-canonical texts, freeing them from traditional theological readings.[1] Texts that include language, themes, and images from the Bible appear in countless other books, as well as movies, television shows, comic books, and other works of popular culture. Each of these new texts offers a rewriting of one or more formerly-biblical texts that in turn implies a different reading – that is, a reading of that text at least somewhat apart from any canonical context. In relation to the gospels, in such a reading what I call "the Gospel" (see Chapter 2) has little or no part. Sometimes these rewritings may be shocking or disturbing. This production of non-canonical biblical texts can be painful and violent and sometimes even dangerous.

When Scripture Is Not Scripture

Pier Paolo Pasolini's controversial film, *The Gospel According to St Matthew* (1964), is one such rewriting of a biblical text. Unlike most other "Jesus movies," which draw upon implicit canonical understandings of the Bible's narrative material (often in the form of sentimental piety) in order to freely rearrange the texts, Pasolini does not play fast and loose with the text of Matthew's gospel.[2] Instead, he lifts the entire story of Matthew out of the Bible, and while this might seem quite respectful of the gospel text itself, it is not at all respectful of the canon. Pasolini's film is written text, spoken words, and moving image all at once, and therefore it is not "scripture." Pasolini has created a non-scriptural gospel of Matthew. By freeing Matthew's text from "the scriptures," the movie liberates the gospel of Matthew from canonical control and thus from the Gospel. Whenever it mentions "the scriptures," as Matthew does so often, the movie necessarily refers to a different medium, and a different virtuality. The intertextual nexus formed by the canon has disappeared, at least in relation to this story.

I noted in Chapter 2 that the biblical canon in effect quotes each gospel word for word and places them in an intertextual context that controls their meanings and absorbs their multiplicity, turning them into versions of the one Gospel of the one Jesus Christ. Pasolini's *Matthew* de-canonizes

---

1. See further Aichele (2001, especially 218–231), as well as the essays in Aichele and Walsh (2002). See also Chapters 5 and 7 in this book.
2. For a detailed survey of 18 Jesus movies, see Staley and Walsh (2007). For another approach to the relation between Pasolini's movie and the gospel of Matthew, see Walsh (2003: 95–120).

the biblical gospel of Matthew by also quoting it (nearly) whole, but as though it were isolated from the rest of the Bible. The title of the English version of the movie unfortunately, and against Pasolini's own wishes,[3] includes the word "Saint," which does not appear in the Italian title, *Il Vangelo secondo Matteo*. Matthew (the purported author) can only be a saint according to the Christian church, and this change in the title suggests an attempt to reclaim Matthew (the story) for the canon. The selective capitalizing of certain nouns, such as "Kingdom" and "Heaven," in the subtitled English version of the film also tends to stress a dogmatic dimension that the film's spoken dialogue, or the written Greek text of the gospel of Matthew, leaves open.

Despite this, Pasolini's film "translates" Matthew's gospel, moving it from its long-time "location" in the biblical canon to another site, that of popular culture. In this case, the two locations take the forms of two distinct but related media. The film is an instance of what Roman Jakobson calls intersemiotic translation – that is, a "*transmutation*" or "interpretation of verbal signs by means of signs of nonverbal sign systems" (1987: 429, his emphasis). The nonverbal sign system is here constituted by the medium of cinema, but since modern cinema is not a purely nonverbal medium, Pasolini's movie is not a purely intersemiotic translation. I would prefer to call it an intermedial translation (see Aichele 2001: 61–63). Pasolini describes the film's relation to the written gospel as an "analogy" (Barański 1985: 80).[4]

The film also translates the written Italian words[5] of the already-translated gospel of Matthew into the spoken Italian words of the movie's actors, in a nearly word for word recital of dialogue from Matthew's story. For those (including myself) who do not know Italian, the English subtitles or dubbing then further translates – interlingually, in Jakobson's terminology – the spoken Italian words of the actors into written or spoken English words. I refer in the following to the English subtitled videotape version of *Il Vangelo secondo Matteo*, as well as the English dubbed DVD version (both Pasolini 1964).

Like any noteworthy translation, Pasolini's movie involves a thoughtful and close reading of its source text. It also offers a curious instance of what Walter Benjamin calls "literal translation" (1968: 69–82).[6] Benjamin's ideal

3. Friedrich (1982: 125, n. 15).
4. See also Deleuze (1989: 26–27).
5. *Il Vangelo di Gesù Cristo*, third edition. Assisi: Edizioni Pro Civitate Christiana, 1963.
6. See also Barthes (1977: 64–65).

of literal translation is the interlinear translation of the scriptures, in which the "source" and "target" texts are actually written beside one another, word by word (1968: 82). In Pasolini's *Matthew*, this interlinearity between media is most fully realized in the written English subtitles that appear on screen at the same time as the Italian words are spoken, but something like it is also manifest in the dubbed English words that come out of the mouths of actors who are evidently speaking another language. Indeed, when the subtitles are absent, as they are occasionally, or in the disparity between the dubbed words and the movements of the actors' mouths,[7] the viewer who knows no Italian is presented with what Benjamin calls "pure language," which is "a language completely devoid of any kind of meaning function, … pure signifier, … paradoxical in the extreme" (de Man 1986: 96–97). These two texts barely touch one another, as Benjamin says, like "a tangent touches a circle … at the infinitely small point of the sense" (1968: 80), and they make manifest the intersemiotic tensions between the respective languages and media.

Although it is in the tension between the subtitles or dubbing and the speaking images that literal translation is most evident in this movie, it is also true in a more complex way that the entire film translates the written gospel "literally" (Testa 1994: 184). Benjamin argues that the desire for meaning is an obstacle to translation, and that "[literal] translation must in large measure refrain from wanting to communicate something, from rendering the sense" (1968: 78). Instead of transferring meaning, and indeed quite like Benjamin's related concept of mechanical reproduction of the work of art, literal translation "reactivates the object reproduced" (1968: 221). Pasolini's movie is such a mechanical reproduction – indeed, a mechanical reproduction of a mechanical reproduction. In this movie, the verbal signs consist of cinematic recordings of oral recitations (in Italian or English) of the printed text of a translation of Matthew's gospel, which is itself a mechanical reproduction of handwritten Greek texts.[8] For those who access this movie on videotape or digital disk, as I do, or by means of a TV channel, the video presentation has also "translated" and mechanically reproduced the film into yet another medium. Thus this movie reflects a very complex intermingling of translations and mechanical reproduction.

---

7. The voice of Enrique Irazoqui, the Spanish actor who plays Jesus, was dubbed even in the Italian version of the film (Barański 1985: 100–101).

8. On printing as a technology of reproduction, see Benjamin (1968: 219, as well as 83–109), and Eisenstein (1979). See also Deleuze (1989: 253–255) and Chapter 1 of this book.

The virtuality of a movie is different than the virtuality of a book. The written text of a book is passive and the reader treats it however she will: she can pick it up and put it down, skim or skip over certain parts, jump back and forth, or reread difficult passages. This has consequences for her experience and understanding of its contents. In contrast, in the movie theater, the moving pictures and resonating sounds dominate the viewer for the moment, and she must either let them have their way, or leave the theater. Cinema is the realm of denotation, and connotations have less power in that medium than they do in literature. As Benjamin says:

> the distracting element of [a movie] is also primarily tactile, being based on changes of place and focus which periodically assail the spectator. ... No sooner has his eye grasped a scene than it has already changed. It cannot be arrested. ... The spectator's process of association in view of these images is indeed interrupted by their constant, sudden change. (1968: 238)

This is what Gilles Deleuze calls the "movement-image," which refers both to the practical techniques required by the cinematic medium and to the phenomenology of the viewer's experience (1986, especially 56–70). Indeed, as Deleuze says:

> The movement-image does not reproduce a world, but constitutes an autonomous world, made up of breaks and disproportion, deprived of all its centres, addressing itself as such to a viewer who is in himself no longer centre of his own perception. (1989: 35)

Although the viewer of a movie on videotape or DVD may be able to rewind it or skip around much as the reader of a printed book can, even so the viewer's experience of the video text will be profoundly different than the reader's experience of the written text, and closer to the theatrical experience of the cinema, because of the movement-image.[9]

Like mechanical reproduction, literal translation re-creates the source text and transforms it into an "original" (Benjamin 1968: 71). The translation enables the viewer or reader to see the text in ways that she hadn't been able to before it was translated. This reveals the text but also critiques it. Among other things, Pasolini's movie produces a different Jesus simulacrum, a transformed reality effect which "reactivates" the written gospel of Matthew's Jesus simulacrum and transforms it into a precursor, illuminating Matthew's Jesus in interesting and provocative ways. Any translation does as much for the simulacra of its source text, although some reactivations will be more "illuminating" than others.

9. See also Deleuze's comments on fascism and cinema, and his analysis of Artaud (1989: 159–162).

Pasolini's camera "speaks" its own highly articulate language (Greene 1990: 121), featuring a mix of intense frontal close-ups (faces of Jesus, the disciples, and others) with striking *cinéma-vérité* long shots (the baptism, Jesus and the disciples walking through the countryside, the two trials, Jesus's post-resurrection appearance), and he draws on familiar European artistic traditions for many of the film's images. However, Pasolini also resists those artistic traditions, as Naomi Greene demonstrates (1990: 74–75), and this gives the film a quasi-documentary quality that the written gospel does not share. Deleuze notes that:

> [Pasolini's] camera does not simply give us the vision of the character and of his world; it imposes another vision in which the first is transformed and reflected. ... [W]e are caught in a correlation between a perception-image and a camera-consciousness which transforms it. (1986: 74).[10]

According to Deleuze, "What characterizes Pasolini's cinema is a poetic consciousness, which is ... mystical or 'sacred'" (1986: 75).

There is gain and loss in any translation, both for the signifier and for the signified. Like any reading, a translation is an ideological act, an act of *eisegesis*.[11] In an intersemiotic translation such as Pasolini's *Matthew*, betrayal of the source text also arises from inescapable differences in the signifying potential of the respective media. Pasolini uses a sequence of translated words (mostly Jesus's words) from Matthew's gospel as a matrix in which to distribute narrative elements of the story. These elements are simulated in the movie through nonverbal sign systems for which the translation must be quite non-literal. The film necessarily gives flesh and blood to characters and scenes that the reader imagines for herself when she reads the written text,[12] and because of this, in translation from writing to cinema, Benjamin's reactivation of the simulacrum is also a constraining or focusing of its semiosis.

Pasolini's *Matthew* is dominated by what Deleuze calls the "affection-image," seen in the numerous close-ups of the faces of Jesus, his mother, and his disciples and opponents.

> [A] film ... always has one type of image which is dominant: one can speak of an active, perceptive, or affective montage ... [T]hree kinds of spatially determined shots can be made to correspond to these three kinds of varieties:

10. See also Deleuze (1989: 27, 168–170) and Barański (1985: 99–100, 104, n. 34).
11. There is no such thing as exegesis, but only various forms of eisegesis. What biblical scholars often call "exegesis" is eisegesis that pretends (as an ideological move) to be objective.
12. See Benjamin (1968: 246–247, n. 11); Testa (1994: 195); Deleuze (1986: 74).

the long shot would be primarily a perception-image; the medium shot an action-image; the close-up an affection-image (Deleuze 1986: 70).[13]

Deleuze later notes that "as its substance [the cinematic close-up] has the compound affect of desire and of astonishment – which gives it life – and the turning aside of faces in the open, in the flesh" (1986: 101). In this regard, Pasolini's movie stands in striking contrast to Matthew's gospel, in which thinking or feeling elements that appear in the affection-image are minimal, even in the birth and post-resurrection scenes (in contrast to Luke at both of these points). However, what Deleuze calls perception-images also play very important parts in Pasolini's movie, and at these points it is more closely aligned with the written text of Matthew.

Only the biblical text appears in the film in the words of Pasolini's Jesus or other characters, or in rare but significant voice-overs or voice-offs. These words have been scarcely altered from the written text, although sometimes what is indirect quotation in the Bible becomes direct quotation in the movie. Voice over narration reproduces some of Matthew's quotations from the Old Testament, such as Jeremiah's words about Rachel weeping during the slaughter of the innocents scene (Mt. 2:17–18, quoting Jer. 31:15). Very few words in *The Gospel According to St Matthew* are not either citations from the Jewish scriptures or the spoken words of characters, and the latter are nearly always taken directly from the written text of Matthew's gospel. Two exceptions are noted here. First, in the film, Jesus speaks aloud the names of the twelve disciples, but the written text simply lists the names in diegesis (Mt. 10:2–4). Second, in the film, when Judas returns the betrayal money to the chief priests, the priests utter the words, "the Field of Blood," which appear as part of a diegetic comment in the text (27:8). Generally, however, comments such as these from the written text are absent from the movie.

Uncovering Matthew

Unlike most Jesus movies,[14] *The Gospel According to St Matthew* depicts a gospel story freed from its canonical captivity, and it thereby releases a

13. Unfortunately, Deleuze does not discuss Pasolini's *Matthew* explicitly in his books on cinema, except for a passing reference in a note (1989: 315, n. 38). However, his comment on Dreyer's film, *Passion of Joan of Arc*, stands in striking tension with Pasolini's *Matthew*: "it is itself Passion … and enters into a virtual conjunction with that of Christ" (1986: 108).

14. Two other notable exceptions are Terry Jones's film *Monty Python's Life of Brian* (1974) and Denys Arcand's *Jesus of Montreal* (1989), although whether either of these films strictly qualifies as a Jesus movie could be disputed.

revolutionary gospel, a materialistic Matthew, from within the biblical security of Christian ideology. In so doing, it creates a Jesus simulacrum who stands in a very peculiar relation to the gospel of Matthew's Jesus simulacrum, a distorted reflection that nevertheless uncovers its double. As Benjamin says, "no translation would be possible if in its ultimate essence it strove for likeness to the original. For in its afterlife ... *the original undergoes a change*" (1968: 73, emphasis added). That is, the translation changes the original – not its signifiers, but the signifieds.

Pasolini's *Matthew* generally follows the sequence of the spoken and cited words in Matthew's gospel. Several reviewers have noted Pasolini's strong interest in the poetry of Matthew's text, and the movie's close adherence to the gospel text heightens the viewer's awareness of the text's writerly incoherencies. This mimetic interlinearity results in strange, dreamlike scenes, such as the encounters early on between Pasolini's Joseph and Mary simulacra, in which no word is spoken. In addition, the disciples are for the most part silent. These silences highlight the articulation of diegesis and mimesis in Matthew's "laconic" story (Testa 1994: 182, see also 197). Indeed, many elements for which the film has been criticized – for example, the isolation and "distance" of Jesus from his followers, or the silence and anonymity of the crowds – also characterize the written gospel. Viewers want movie directors to produce readerly, "novelistic" Jesus films that require no particular effort to view, such as Franco Zeffirelli's *Jesus of Nazareth* (1977) or Mel Gibson's *The Passion of the Christ* (2004), much as readers want a Bible that is easy to read and speaks the Gospel clearly and with a harmonious "voice." Pasolini does not oblige such viewers.

Adele Reinhartz argues that "the movie draws a sharp distinction between Jesus and his followers on the one hand, and the Jewish authorities on the other. This distinction is emphasized through the visual presentation. One striking aspect of this presentation is headgear" (2001). It is true that the odd-looking hats worn by Jesus's opponents make it easy to identify them, but such hats were worn by wealthy medieval Christians, not Jews, according to Jeffrey Staley and Richard Walsh (2007: 45, 194, n. 10). The movie is anti-Semitic because it focuses heavily on the "hypocrite" sayings of Matthew 23, as Reinhartz says, but this is because it follows closely a single source text, in which an entire chapter is devoted to these harsh words. Other "hypocrite" sayings of Jesus appear elsewhere in the gospel of Matthew (at 6:2, 16, 7:5, 15:7, 22:18, and 24:51), and several of these (Mt. 6:16, 15:7, and 24:51) are not among the sayings of Pasolini's Jesus.

The movie's fault in this regard is perhaps that is is too good a translation, although even then, the movie's larger story suggests that the "scribes and Pharisees" that its Jesus simulacrum denounces are stand-ins for the powerful and oppressors, not for the Jews as such. Reinhartz also notes that "Pasolini's stated goal was to compare the conflict between Jesus and the Jewish authorities in first century Palestine to religious conflict in twentieth century Italy." In other words, the opponents of Pasolini's Jesus are not so much the specifically Jewish Pharisees and scribes of the written gospel as they are the bureaucrats, owners, and bosses of every age and culture, and particularly of modern capitalism.[15] In this way the movie, like the gospel, depicts these words of Jesus in a manner consistent with prophetic attacks on sinful behavior that are common in the Jewish scriptures.[16]

Speaking of his never-completed film, *Saint Paul*, Pasolini said that he sought a series of "transpositions, founded upon analogy" to replace the "conformism" of the Jews "with a contemporary conformism: which will thus be that typical conformism of current bourgeois civility."[17] In this light it may be significant that the movie also includes the infamous words of self-accusation in Mt. 27:25 ("His blood be on us and on our children!"), but in the film the words are spoken anonymously and off-screen by a single voice, not a voice over, but also not "all the people" as in the gospel of Matthew. Might this voice be speaking for the (civilly bourgeois) viewer?

Another revealing distortion of the gospel of Matthew appears in the "stupendous, interminable"[18] Sermon on the Mount, which occurs in the film out of the sequence of the written text. The sequence of sayings within the sermon has also been rearranged, but the sayings themselves follow Matthew's text closely. In the written text, the sermon takes the form of a lengthy series of loosely related sayings of Jesus that run throughout the entirety of Matthew 5, 6, and 7.[19] Although Matthew explicitly describes this material as "sayings" or "words" (*logous*, 7:24, 26, 28), and never as a sermon, the text presents the sayings as though they were joined in a single long speech – indeed, the longest uninterrupted speech of any of the synoptic gospels' Jesus simulacra.

These sayings are also often interpreted as a continuous speech or sermon, even though many scholars suspect that this continuity is more the result of editorial activity on the part of the gospel of Matthew's author

---

15. See Barański (1985: 94) and Greene (1990: 76).
16. See Carroll (1997: 104–105).
17. Sketch for *San Paolo*, translated by and courtesy of Elizabeth Castelli.
18. Pasolini's words, quoted in Testa (1994: 184).
19. Compare Lk 6:20–49.

than of any historical accuracy. Pasolini's film translation of the sermon effectively highlights this uncertainty about the sayings' context, presenting most of the sermon through a lengthy and uninterrupted series of head shots of Jesus speaking, but varying the background sky: night, day, storm clouds, lightning, and wind. Only Jesus's head and the sky behind it are visible throughout the sermon, and it is the changes in the sky and the lighting that draw the viewer's attention. The resulting sequence of images may be either a single, extraordinarily long speech event, lasting several days, or it may be a variable string of more or less distinct sayings that were repeated on different but otherwise unknown occasions. No audience is evident in the movie, unlike the written gospel, where the audience is the crowds and the disciples (5:1, 7:28). The effect is disconcerting: Pasolini defamiliarizes Matthew's Sermon on the Mount and highlights its intrinsic discontinuities without substantially changing the sermon itself.

There is little sentimental piety in *The Gospel According to St Matthew*, unlike the Hollywood tradition of Jesus movies, and despite Pasolini's tendency to romanticize the peasants. The crowds that rush to see the risen Jesus at the movie's end belong more to Marxist neo-realism than they do to Christian iconography. There are few special effects in the film, with the notable exception of the walking on the sea episode. This is an ideological move, an attempt to create a sense of realism using pseudo-documentary filming techniques. However, Pasolini's approach also creates a sense of mystery, since special effects often tend to de-mystify the uncanny or fantastic.[20] Miracles happen suddenly and without any clear explanation, in the seam of the montage. The otherwise earthly-looking angel also appears and disappears abruptly, and the apocalyptic overtones of the resurrection scene are decidedly muted (contrast Mt. 28:2–3). Although the birth story in the movie follows the written gospel closely, it also makes clear by implication that the gospel of Matthew's Christmas story is decidedly less supernatural than Luke's story. The angel appears in Joseph's dreams and the wise men bring gifts (as well as information for Herod), and these events emphasize the baby's importance, but this is not a story of the incarnation of God.

A sudden receding of the camera suggests that something has happened at Jesus's baptism while a voice-off speaks, "this is my beloved Son" (Mt. 3:17). However, once again, whose voice is speaking? The viewer is left in

20. In this respect, Pasolini's film is curiously similar to Daniel Myrick and Eduardo Sánchez's *The Blair Witch Project* (1999), and especially to Wim Wender's *Wings of Desire* (1987).

uncertainty. Neither the written gospel nor the movie answers that question, but by removing the gospel from the canon, the movie retrieves the deep ambiguity of this scene – and even more so, since unlike the written text of Matthew, the film offers no opened skies, no dove, and especially no descending "Spirit of God" (3:16) to clarify things. In addition, Pasolini's movie omits the gospel of Matthew's transfiguration scene, with its voice from the cloud, echoing the voice at the baptism, and its shining Jesus in conversation with Moses and Elijah. In the written gospel, the transfiguration scene reinforces not only the message of the baptism but also the miraculous aspect of Jesus's birth. Without its reinforcements, the birth and baptism stories in the movie raise important questions about the identity of Pasolini's Jesus, but they leave the answer unsettled.

What appear to be summary statements of repeated actions in the written text of Matthew's gospel either must be depicted as specific events in the film, as when Jesus cures a tower filled with demoniacs, or else they cannot be depicted at all. Statements such as the following do not describe a single event:

> And he went about all Galilee, teaching in their synagogues and preaching the gospel of the kingdom and healing every disease and every infirmity among the people. So his fame spread throughout all Syria, and they brought him all the sick, those afflicted with various diseases and pains, demoniacs, epileptics, and paralytics, and he healed them. And great crowds followed him from Galilee and the Decapolis and Jerusalem and Judea and from beyond the Jordan. (Mt. 4:23–25)

Even through the mere juxtaposition of visual images with spoken words – especially the words of Jesus – the movie rewrites the gospel. Pasolini's Jesus picks up a child as he says, "my yoke is easy and my burden is light" (Mt. 11:30), but no children appear in the written context. He weeps after the execution of John the Baptist, but the gospel of Matthew's Jesus "withdrew from there in a boat to a lonely place apart" (14:13), and no weeping is mentioned. This is the "free indirect discourse" for which Pasolini is justly famous (Deleuze 1989: 143–144). These cinematic conjunctions are not coincidental, and they indicate significant differences between Matthew's and Pasolini's Jesus simulacra.

In addition, sudden shifts of scene and other gaps in the flow of narration that are usually ignored by readers of the canonical text are more disruptive and evident in the movie. Some transitions are translated into significant juxtapositions, such as the image of John the Baptist in prison as a voice-over recites the words of Isa. 9:2 quoted in Mt. 4:15–16:

> The land of Zebulun and the land of Naphtali, toward the sea, across the
> Jordan, Galilee of the Gentiles – the people who sat in darkness have seen a
> great light, and for those who sat in the region and shadow of death light has
> dawned.

This passage, which in the movie becomes a commentary on John's situation,
appears in the written gospel immediately after Jesus hears that John has
been arrested. However, in the written gospel's context, the quote serves as
a prophecy that was being fulfilled by Jesus, not John. At these points, the
film (like any translation) does not merely quote the text, but it also
transforms it. Other transitions in the written narrative, such as "when he
heard that John had been arrested" (4:12) or "as he entered Capernaum"
(8:5), disappear entirely in the film.

When the written narrative transitions have been silenced by the film,
or when the film makes evident an absence of transitions in the written
text, the film's viewer becomes aware of the incoherence of the gospel of
Matthew's story, narrative failures of the written text that the ideological
functioning of the canon covers up or supplements in various ways.[21] As
Bart Testa argues, even the film's alterations to the written text "bring the
evangelist's narrative segmentation to the fore" (1994: 193).

Deviations

Pasolini has not shown every detail that appears in the gospel of Matthew's
28 chapters, nor could he in a movie that lasts only 136 minutes. The
movie's omissions or other deviations from the written gospel lead to serious
consequences for the differences and similarities between the two Jesus
simulacra. The selection of possible meanings to be excluded or included
is always ideological, and when it comes to Jesus movies, it is always and
especially a matter of controversy. Yet these disparities also draw attention
to the written text, apart from or in tension with the Gospel.

Several exceptions to the film's "interlinearity" with the written text
produce significant alterations of the narrative sequence.[22] In the movie,
when Jesus and his disciples withdraw after the death of John the Baptist,
an anonymous voice-over speaks words that include Isa. 14:31 ("Wail, O
gate; cry, O city; melt in fear, O Philistia, all of you! For smoke comes out of
the north, and there is no straggler in his ranks"), a text that does not seem
especially relevant to the story and moreover, that is not cited in the gospel

---

21. See Greene (1990: 73). Testa details the stylistic correspondences between Pasolini's
     film and Matthew's gospel (1994: 187–197); see also Barański (1985: 86–87).
22. See Testa (1994: 206, nn. 28, 29).

of Matthew. Perhaps more important, at Mt. 13:14–15 – that is, well before his crucifixion – Jesus utters the words of Isa. 6:9–10 in modified form:

> You shall indeed hear but never understand, and you shall indeed see but never perceive. For this people's heart has grown dull, and their ears are heavy of hearing, and their eyes they have closed, lest they should perceive with their eyes, and hear with their ears, and understand with their heart, and turn for me to heal them.

In the film, these words are spoken at the moment of Jesus's death by an anonymous narrator – yet another voice-over – during a momentarily black screen[23] just before the crucified Jesus reappears to utter what are also the last words of the gospel of Matthew's Jesus, "My God, my God, why hast thou forsaken me?" (27:46). This rearrangement of sayings is a significant alteration of the story. Is there a connection between these and other voice-overs in the movie? Who speaks these voice-overs from Isaiah? God? the prophet? Pasolini?

A different type of departure from the written text appears in the movie's nonverbal soundtrack. As the voice-overs and voice-offs make plain, the written text cannot speak itself, and the actor's voices – not just that they have resonant voices, but the specific qualities of those voices, like the images of their bodies – give the movie a physical (or "tactile," as Benjamin says, 1968: 238) dimension that writing alone can never have. The long silences in Pasolini's movie are accentuated by and themselves serve to emphasize the occasional background noises, such as the neighing of a horse, the cries of demoniacs, the screams of crucified men, or the laughter of children.

There is also a musical soundtrack, which I find largely distracting although it is often praised, which generally "spiritualizes" the story and often contextualizes the visual images in ways that encourage traditional or pious emotional responses. However, there are several noteworthy exceptions. The folk singer Odetta's mournful rendition of the blues classic, "Motherless Child," as the baby Jesus and his parents flee to Egypt, and again when Jesus appears to be baptized by John, seems especially appropriate to Pasolini's very human, earthy Jesus, even though he is neither motherless

---

23. On the use of a black screen as an "irrational cut," see Deleuze (1989: 192–193): "the series of anterior images has no end, while the series of subsequent images likewise has no beginning, the two series converging towards the white or black screen as their common limit." Deleuze is speaking here of the films of Philippe Garrel. On disjunctions between speech and the visual image, see Deleuze (1989: 242–247 and 315, n. 38).

nor "a long way from home." Another blues song, "My Oh My,"[24] when Jesus is sentenced by the council and delivered to Pilate and which then continues during Judas's repentance, also suits the film well. In addition, the rich African harmonies and rhythms of the *Missa Luba* (which often sound at particularly intense moments in the film) defamiliarize the traditional Latin texts of the Mass and turn them into a cry for liberation.

Unlike most of the other musical selections in the soundtrack, these musical intertexts contribute to the film's suggestion that the relation between Jesus and the institutions of imperial Christianity, which would include the biblical canon, is at best highly problematical.[25] The juxtaposition of quite different musical forms in the soundtrack also produces a curious dissonance. Perhaps it expresses Pasolini's fascination with the relation between what he called the "prehistoric" and the world of history. Deleuze describes Pasolini's concept of prehistory as "the abstract poetic element, the 'essence' co-present with our history, the archaean base which reveals an interminable history beneath our own" (1989: 234). However, this dissonance also has something to do with Pasolini's cinematic translation of the gospel of Matthew. Once again the differing media strain against each other in ways that raise questions about each text and that encourage the viewer to return once again to the source text, as any literal translation will, to find it supplemented and liberated from its traditional context (Benjamin 1968: 74, 80).

There is no point in asking whether Pasolini's film depicts "the historical Jesus," that dream of Western modernism. It is more interesting to ask instead whether Pasolini's Jesus is a Marxist Jesus, and perhaps also a gay Jesus, as we might expect. Curiously, the role of the aged Mary, Jesus's mother, who witnesses his crucifixion "from afar" (Mt. 27:56, assuming that "Mary the mother of James and Joseph" is Jesus's mother), is played by Pasolini's own mother, Susanna. In addition, the mother of Jesus has a much more significant part in this movie than she does in the written text of Matthew, perhaps reflecting Pasolini's Catholic background. However, we must be cautious about assuming that an author or director will simply project her own interests and desires upon her principal character. In his own life, the "Catholic Marxist" Pasolini was perhaps as often in conflict with Marxists as he was with Catholics. Nevertheless, Pia Friedrich argues that "The autobiographical component in the figure of Christ, radically 'diverse' in that he is socially heretical, inflexible, and vehement, is evident"

24. I have been unable to find any identification of the singer.
25. See Greene (1990: 76).

(1982: 21).[26] The film gives us a reading of the gospel of Matthew that allows possibilities such as these to be entertained, and perhaps even affirmed, but without simultaneously ruling out other options, and even contrary possibilities.

Litmus Test

Richard Walsh claims that familiarity with the written text of Matthew helps the viewer to better understand *The Gospel According to St Matthew* (2003: 97). As Walsh notes, Matthew draws heavily on the Jewish scriptures for precursor texts and to claim authoritative status for itself, but Pasolini's movie instead draws heavily on Matthew's gospel as its precursor (2003: 96, 98). In addition, although Walsh comments that "'secondo' [in *Il Vangelo secondo Matteo*] can mean 'following, subsequent, secondary' as well as 'according to'" (2003: 115, n. 6), the film makes no pretense to be "scripture."

It seems unlikely that the viewer would understand Pasolini's film at all if she didn't at least know of Matthew's gospel. I want to push this point even further, but in a somewhat different direction: what sort of understanding would a reader have of Matthew, or indeed any of the biblical gospels, if she did not already know the canonical "story of Jesus" – that is, the Gospel? The reader's ideological understanding of "how the story goes" depends in this case on a *theological* pre-understanding, in which the Christian canon may play a very large role, even if that reader is not a Christian (and more so if she is). Such understanding affects and overshadows even the most serious and critical scholarly analyses of the texts, both biblical and cinematic. Perhaps, to invert Walsh's comment, a careful viewing of Pasolini's film would "liberate" the written gospel from canonical control (and the Gospel) and thereby help the reader to better understand Matthew's text by "defamiliarizing" it. After all, Pasolini's film shows the viewer things about the gospel of Matthew that the reader might not see otherwise. This is often the case when biblical texts are read "outside" of the canon, in different intertextual contexts where different semiotic flows are opened up.

In this way Pasolini's movie becomes a litmus test of the viewer's preconceptions of Matthew's story. In particular, the contrasts between Pasolini's Jesus and Matthew's Jesus illuminate distinctive features of the two simulacra. Even though different readers will inevitably see different Jesuses in the gospel of Matthew, for reasons noted in Chapter 2, any careful reader will see important differences between Matthew's and Pasolini's

26. See also Barański (1985: 106, n. 41); Greene (1990: 219–220); Testa (1994: 181).

Jesuses. One one hand, there are few miracles in the movie, and fewer parables. The film skips the genealogy of Jesus (Mt. 1:1–17) and with it his status as a "son of Abraham" (compare 3:9) and of David, among other material.[27] The apocalyptic discourse of Chapter 24 is missing, and although the movie's Jesus is undoubtedly a prophet, he has little interest in the end of the world. Like any revolutionary, he would rather change it.

Matthew's two parables Chapters, 13 and 25, are also both missing from the movie, except for the transposition noted above of 13:14–15 (quoting the book of Isaiah) from midway through the gospel's story to near the end of the movie.[28] However, this also highlights the importance of parables in the written text, for the Isaiah quote, as rewritten in Matthew, explains Jesus's use of parables (13:13). The modified words emphasize the stupidity of the crowds ("because seeing they do not see, and hearing they do not hear, nor do they understand"), but the saying does not fit so well into Pasolini's depiction of the relation between Jesus and the crowds (see further below). The quote fits better at the movie's end, as a challenge to the viewer.

On the other hand, numerous visual details do not appear in the written gospel but stand out in the movie. Among these are the lengthy and disturbingly graphic slaughter of the innocents, the child Jesus held in Joseph's arms, the physical appearance of the angel (apparently always the same one, and looking like a young girl – thus probably not Gabriel, as in Luke), James and John running along the beach drying a fishing net, and Salome playing with her jacks just before she dances. In other cases, details may deviate from those mentioned in the written text(s): the newborn Jesus is sheltered in a cave, not a house (as in Mt. 2:11), Jesus embraces the disciple John in Gethsemane (hinting perhaps at the gospel of John's "beloved disciple"), and Jesus's mother reacts very emotionally and at some length to his crucifixion (again perhaps hinting at John's gospel, or perhaps just Mary traditions in general).

We see and hear the movie's Jesus simulacrum, whereas the gospel of Matthew can only write the words of its Jesus and other simulacra. The nearly continuous presence of the disciples throughout the story is evident in the movie, for they are often on screen (particularly Judas, including another scene from the gospel of John).[29] However, Matthew's gospel must

27. Some of this material is listed in Barański: (1985: 82–84, 104, nn. 29–30).
28. In an email to me, Richard Walsh notes that "While [Pasolini] filmed Matthew 13, 24–25, he decided not to include them [in the movie]. Matthew 23 thus replaces the apocalyptic discourse as Jesus's response to the elite" (21 May 2010).
29. See further Barański (1985: 85, 104, n. 23); Staley and Walsh (2007: 45); Walsh (2003: 103–104).

periodically remind the reader that disciple simulacra are accompanying its Jesus, and it is not always clear to whom Jesus is speaking. The written text of Matthew tells the reader nothing about what Jesus, Mary, or Judas looks like, and any film's concrete depictions of the bodies of characters in a written story will always be at variance with the reader's own inevitable imaginings, no matter how much detail the story includes.[30] Several film critics even complained about the appearance of the actor (Enrique Irazoqui) who plays Pasolini's Jesus, apparently because they thought he didn't look like Jesus should. While this may seem silly, Pasolini also chose to shoot the film in southern Italy rather than Israel because he felt it looked more like first-century Palestine (Barański 1985: 77).

It might be interesting and not entirely frivolous to ask people what each of the various Jesus simulacra of the New Testament writings looks like. For example, does Matthew's Jesus look like John's Jesus, or like Paul's Jesus? I would not expect people to agree in their descriptions of how they imagine each Jesus, but would they tend to agree about the differences between the "appearances" of the various simulacra? Would anyone sincerely claim that they all look the same? However, if they don't all look the same, then how could they possibly be the same? In such judgments ideology is hard at work, and surely the presence or absence of influence from the Gospel would be a factor in any answers to these questions.

Pasolini's Jesus is at once less rugged than John the Baptist and less serene than the angel. He does not fit the stereotype of a laborer (Staley and Walsh 2007: 45), although most of his disciples do. One effect of seeing these bodies is that the viewer becomes quickly aware of their feelings and emotions (Deleuze's "affection-image"). The movie's Jesus simulacrum is pleased by the children, upset by his disciples, angered by his opponents, anxious in Gethsemane. He is lively and fully human, for despite his abnormal birth and the voice from heaven at his baptism, there is nothing evidently divine about him. In this he is unlike Matthew's Jesus simulacrum, who must always be somewhat of a blank page, and who like any literary character, must be constructed by the reader who fills in countless narrative gaps and "spots of indeterminacy."[31] In the gospel of Matthew as in much ancient literature, the personalities of characters are much less developed

---

30. For example, in *The Lord of the Rings* Tolkien goes into great detail describing the appearance of Frodo the hobbit and Aragorn the man, among many others. In his movie of those books, Peter Jackson follows Tolkien's descriptions closely, but Elijah Wood and Viggo Mortensen in makeup as those characters still varied considerably from this reader's imaginings.
31. See further Aichele (2005: 45–60). The phrase is from Roman Ingarden.

than they are in modern literature. The feelings of Matthew's Jesus must usually be inferred by the reader, and there will be more opportunities for contrary inferences than in a movie.

Perhaps the most common emotional state of Pasolini's Jesus simulacrum is a kind of stern (even pensive) determination, which also appears in Pasolini's depiction of John the Baptist. The movie emphasizes the strong bond between Jesus and John the Baptist, and the impact of John's arrest and execution on Jesus's activities is considerable. Although a powerful figure in his own right (and physically more striking than Jesus), Pasolini's John simulacrum is clearly the forerunner, who willingly gives way before his greater successor. The bond between John and Jesus is also a theme in Matthew (3:13–15, 4:12, 14:10–12; see also 11:2–15, 21:25–27, 32), but the film makes this theme even more prominent. Like Pasolini's John, Pasolini's Jesus is a fiery prophet, who is not at all averse to violence. Perhaps his violence is even that which Matthew's Jesus describes in 11:12, "From the days of John the Baptist until now the kingdom of heaven has suffered violence, and men of violence take it by force" (compare Lk. 16:16). Pasolini's Jesus is executed primarily because he threatens the status quo, and not in order to fulfill the scriptures, as in the written gospel (Barański 1985: 92).

The gospel of Matthew contrasts the crowds as those who do not understand ("This is why I speak to them in parables," 13:13) on one hand, and the disciples who "know the secrets of the kingdom of heaven" (13:11; see also 13:10, 16–17, 51, and 16:16–17) on the other. As was noted above, one consequence of the movie's transposition of Matthew 13:14–15 to the crucifixion scene is that this contrast does not appear in it. For Pasolini's Jesus, in contrast to Matthew's Jesus, there is no insider/outsider binarism, no significant division between informed disciples (or viewers) and "dull" crowds. The miracles of Pasolini's Jesus simulacrum may be mysterious, but his words are not. In other words, for this movie there is no division between an elite group of "the elect" (24:24, 31) – the wise and faithful ones, the sheep as opposed to the goats (25:32–34) – and everyone else.

This is particularly evident in the movie's scenes of the "hypocrites" sayings (from Matthew 23), where the disciples become part of the larger crowd, but it also is indirectly evident in Pasolini's Sermon on the Mount, where neither disciples nor crowd are on screen – and as a result, again there is no division. As I also noted above, the movie skips the parables of Matthew 13, which divide insider disciples from outsider crowds, as well as the apocalyptic discourse and further parables of Matthew 24–25, which the gospel of Matthew's Jesus simulacrum addresses to the disciples and thus also to the reader, but apparently not to the crowds.

The apparent lack of division or opposition in the movie between disciples and crowds also appears in other ways. The council trial of Pasolini's Jesus is filmed from Peter's point of view at the back of a crowd, and Pilate's decision is filmed from the disciple John's point of view, again in the midst of a crowd and unlike the gospel of Matthew. The effect in each case is that the viewer hears the words but can only barely see the action, like those who were "actually" present. Neither Peter nor John, nor the viewer, knows any more about what happens on those occasions than the crowd does. "Objective and subjective images lose their distinction, but also their identification, in favour of a new circuit where they are wholly replaced, or contaminate each other, or are decomposed and recomposed" (Deleuze 1989: 144). Finally, Pasolini's resurrected Jesus simulacrum is greeted by and speaks to a sizeable crowd that includes the disciples, in contrast to Matthew's Jesus simulacrum, who speaks only to "the eleven" (28:16–20). Zygmunt Barański argues that the emphasis that Pasolini gives to the crowds and disciples reduces the gospel of Matthew's focus on Jesus (1985: 91), but this emphasis also diminishes the elite status of the disciples. These changes contribute strongly to Pasolini's simulation of a political Jesus, as opposed to the supernatural Christ of the Gospel. Pasolini's Jesus belongs to the people.

The other side of this contrast between written text and film is noted by Walsh: "What Pasolini omits in his reproduction of Matthew, and which is, thereby, highlighted by reading Matthew with his film, is Matthew's use of Jesus to create a new institution" – that is, the church (2003: 113, compare Mt. 10:1, 27, 16:18–19, 18:17–18, 28:19–20). Walsh argues that the gospel of Matthew is already deeply involved in creating an institutional myth, and the clear distinction between authorized insiders and ignorant outsiders plays an important part in the construction of an institutional hierarchy. What I here call the Gospel would be one important component of this myth. In contrast, in Pasolini's movie, despite its dedication to Pope John XXIII and its friendly reception in the Catholic Church (Walsh 2003: 112),[32] there is no significant distinction, and thus no hierarchy. The movie does include the saying of Jesus to the disciple Simon in Mt. 16:18–19:

> you are Peter, and on this rock I will build my church, and the powers of death shall not prevail against it. I will give you the keys of the kingdom of

32. According to Liukkonen (2001), *Il Vangelo secondo Matteo* was partly financed by the Catholic Church.

heaven, and whatever you bind on earth shall be bound in heaven, and
whatever you loose on earth shall be loosed in heaven.

However, Barański notes that Pasolini wanted to delete this
ecclesiologically-important passage from the film but finally deferred to
pressure from friends in the Italian Catholic Church (1985: 90).

For the written gospel of Matthew, the trade-off for a Jesus in solidarity
with the people, as in the movie, is a Jesus who institutes the church, as
well as a story that will serve as a valuable bridge between the two biblical
testaments. However, this is already to situate Matthew once again within
the virtual Bible and its Gospel. Unlike Pasolini's Jesus, the written
Matthew's Jesus simulacrum lives in a tension between the old and the
new. He draws upon the traditional scriptures, but in order to "fulfill" and
thus transform them into something else. He is both the new Moses and
the social radical at once, and thus he is something more: "I tell you,
something greater than the temple is here" (12:6). And yet he is also less,
precisely because he is so divided, and it may even be this which tears him
from the people, just as new wine tears old skins (9:17).

Pasolini's movie highlights this tension by way of contrast. Considered
apart from its canonical context and the Gospel, it becomes evident that
the gospel of Matthew both creates and wrestles with this division within
its Jesus simulacrum. Perhaps it is even this (and not the Romans or the
Jewish leaders or "all the people" or God or Satan) that leads finally not
only to Jesus's death but also to his resurrection. That is, perhaps it is finally
Matthew's readers who utter the fateful words, "His blood be on us and on
our children!" (27:25).

No translation is ever a complete or exact reproduction of its source
text. However, any film also shows its viewer *more* than any corresponding
written text could. Pasolini's Jesus simulacrum is not the second Moses of
the written gospel, the giver of a new divine law. Neither is he a Cynic
philosopher, as many contemporary New Testament scholars would argue,
nor an apocalypticist, as others claim. Pasolini's Jesus preaches neither pie-
in-the-sky escapism nor withdrawal into wisdom, but rather down-to-
earth revolution. He is not interested in contemplating the world, or in
fleeing it, but instead he wants to change it – he understands Karl Marx's
eleventh thesis on Feuerbach – and it is only in that sense that this movie's
Jesus might be called Christ. He shows a distinct preference for the poor,
and he is more concerned with social oppression than he is with individual
sin (Greene 1990: 77).

Given Pasolini's own Marxist beliefs, the movie's emphasis on the
political, human side of Jesus is not surprising. This Jesus simulacrum is

arguably less supernatural, and more political, than the written gospel's Jesus (Staley and Walsh 2007: 44, 46). If Matthew's Jesus simulacrum had been more like this movie's Jesus, how different would the Bible be! However, could such a version of Matthew's gospel ever have made it into the biblical canon? Alternatively, if the written gospel of Matthew had been read as Pasolini reads it, would it have been accepted into the canon? Under such circumstances, would the Gospel have been able to absorb it? However, it is also possible that the gospels of Luke and John, with considerable help from the letters of Paul,[33] have managed to neutralize, through their canonical proximity to Matthew, the human, political activity and teaching of Matthew's Jesus. (This point is developed further in Chapter 9.) In other words, it is possible that the gospel of Matthew's Jesus is *already* more like Pasolini's Jesus than readers today can otherwise know. What might this imply about the Gospel's responsibility for class oppression, and more generally its power to contextualize texts in ways that allow only more "spiritual" – that is, less political – readings?

Pasolini did not begin the de-canonization of the gospel of Matthew. That process began long ago, at least as far back as the beginnings of print culture during the Renaissance and Reformation, and it has been growing and accelerating ever since.[34] Matthew's gospel had already escaped the Christian canon when it attracted this film maker's attention, and if it had not already done so, it might well not have attracted his attention. What Pasolini's film does is to help its viewers to see a new Matthew, a text that continues to live outside of the semiotic control formerly provided by the Christian Bible – that is, a gospel that is not the Gospel. Could anyone say that she "believes" Pasolini's *Matthew* in the way that someone might say that they "believe" the Bible? Or rather, "Has he [Pasolini] not, like Nietzsche, torn belief away from every faith in order to give it back to rigorous thought?" (Deleuze 1989: 170).

---

33. At the time of his death, Pasolini was preparing to film a movie titled *Saint Paul*, which apparently would have been quite different from his *Matthew*. See Friedrich (1982: 44–45) and Testa (1994: 198). I am especially grateful to Elizabeth Castelli for sharing with me her notes on Pasolini and his work on this film.
34. See further Chapter 1, and Aichele (2001, especially 38–60).

Chapter 4

CHILD AND KINGDOM: ON SOME UNSETTLING LANGUAGE IN THE GOSPEL OF MARK

[T]he Bible constructs its readers as children and explicitly calls them the "children of Israel" or the "children of God." In that important sense, the Bible quite literally presents itself as a book for children. The question then is whether it is a book of instruction, or of entertainment, or a book which itself deconstructs that opposition. Is it a book of paternalistic conformity ... or is it a subversive spur to the risks of creative play? (Pyper 2005: 151–152)

Text of bliss: the text that imposes a state of loss, the text that discomforts ..., unsettles the reader's historical, cultural, psychological assumptions ... brings to a crisis his relation with language. (Barthes 1975: 14)

Pasolini's movie, discussed in the previous chapter, is primarily a translation of the gospel of Matthew from one medium to another. Some of the more daringly literal interlingual translations of individual biblical texts also, and in similar ways, counter the influence of the canon on the semiotic codes through which those texts are read. These include Stephen Mitchell's translation of the book of Job (1979) or Richmond Lattimore's translations of the gospels (1979). Such translations, precisely by virtue of their "literality," are less eager to render the text in a readerly manner and more likely to allow its writerly otherness and incoherence – that is, its resistance to canonical control – to be manifest. By attending to the signifier, literal translation reproduces the source text's uncertainties of meaning, instead of the interpretations that would resolve them. The closer one gets to a truly word by word translation, as Benjamin suggests, the more troublesome the translated text becomes, and very literal translations, such as Hölderlin's translations of Sophocles, are sometimes quite writerly (Benjamin 1968: 81–82).

In addition, there are other ways in which biblical texts can be de-canonized, and I explore some of them in this and the following chapters. One way deliberately refuses to dismiss or explain away textual phenomena that otherwise appear to be minor anomalies or irregularities in the texts, and instead it regards these awkwardnesses as fissures that may be pried open to reveal or expose the text in different, non-canonical ways – to negate the ideological effects of the virtual Bible and the Gospel – much as literal translations do, with less interest in meaning and more attention to physical aspects of the text. This is the approach that I take in the present chapter, as well as in Chapters 6 and 8 of this book.

The First Entrance

According to Roland Barthes, some texts are "texts of pleasure" (1975: 14). These texts are readerly: they open themselves to the reader, seemingly withholding nothing (at least, not for long), and they satisfy her desire for meaning. They are easy and enjoyable to read. In contrast, other texts are "texts of bliss," which produce in the reader intense excitement (*jouissance*), frustration, or irritation. These are writerly texts: their gaps and excesses force readers to become writers, provoking desires for but simultaneously withholding some satisfaction that they may never give (1974: 4–5). Barthes says that "The writerly text is *ourselves writing*, before the infinite play of the world ... is traversed ... by some singular system ... which reduces the plurality of entrances" (his emphases). That "singular system," which may take many forms, transforms and constrains the writerly text of bliss by explaining it. The canon of the Bible is one such system.

In this chapter, some language in the gospel of Mark, one of the more writerly texts in the Bible, has subversively "spurred me to the risks of creative play," as Hugh Pyper says (invoking Prov. 8:30), in the first epigraph of this chapter. In order to read that gospel outside of its traditional canonical enclosure, I explore some of the "plurality of entrances" offered by the "infinite play" of Mark's text, but with the hope that I do not thereby reduce its writerly plurality too much, replacing one controlling context with another. My creative play in this case is prompted by my own excitement and irritation at the use by Mark's Jesus simulacrum of the Greek words *teknon* and *paidion*, translated as "child/children" or sometimes "son," in five passages in the gospel of Mark, in contexts where they connote what are or might well be adult human beings.

These passages, which I will call "lexias" following Barthes,[1] are:

1. "[I]t will suffice that the lexia be the best possible space in which we can observe meanings" (Barthes 1974: 13). However, I will not use these lexias in exactly the same manner that Barthes does in *S/Z*.

1. And when Jesus saw their faith, he said to the paralytic, "My son [*teknon*], your sins are forgiven" (2:5).

2. And he said to her [the Syrophoenician woman], "Let the children [*tekna*] first be fed, for it is not right to take the children's [*teknōn*] bread and throw it to the dogs." But she answered him, "Yes, Lord; yet even the dogs under the table eat the children's [*paidiōn*] crumbs" (7:27–28).

3. And he took a child [*paidion*], and put him in the midst of them; and taking him in his arms, he said to them, "Whoever receives one such child [*paidiōn*] in my name receives me; and whoever receives me, receives not me but him who sent me" (9:36–37).

4. And they were bringing children [*paidia*] to him, that he might touch them; and the disciples rebuked them. But when Jesus saw it he was indignant, and said to them, "Let the children [*paidia*] come to me, do not hinder them; for to such belongs the kingdom of God. Truly, I say to you, whoever does not receive the kingdom of God like a child [*hōs paidion*] shall not enter it" (10:13–15).

5. But Jesus said to them [the disciples] again, "Children [*tekna*], how hard it is to enter the kingdom of God!" (10:24).

Two distinct Greek words, *paidion* and *teknon*, are used in these five lexias.[2] *Paidion* is the diminutive of *pais* and may connote innocence or dependency upon others, while *teknon* relates to *tiktō* and connotes birth or parentage. Both words appear frequently in each of the gospels to denote children but also sometimes to connote, as in these passages, adult human beings. Both the paralytic in lexia #1 and the disciples in lexia #5 are adults, or at least the reader has no reason to think otherwise. The words are being used metaphorically in these two lexias. In addition, although the immediate referent of the words of Mark's Jesus to the woman in lexia #2 is her daughter (*thugatrion, thugatros*, 7:25, 26, 29), who is evidently a child, metaphoric overtones of both Jesus's words and the woman's reply suggest a much wider connotation. Lexias #3 and 4 form one of the gospel of Mark's well-known doublets. In each case, *paidion* in Jesus's words plays upon a narrative context in which children are present, but that context does not restrict understanding of *paidion* in either lexia to denote children only, especially if these two sayings are understood to belong somehow with the other three.

---

2. There are no major variations in the oldest manuscripts on *teknon* and *paidion* in these lexias.

Jesus's use of *teknon* in lexia #2 may connote the Jewish people, as "the children of Israel," and the woman's use of *paidion* may suggest that she is talking about her daughter, a specific child, despite the aphoristic quality of her words. However, the direct interplay between the two words in this single brief dialogue indicates some degree of semiotic interchangeability between them and their signifying potentials. The unnamed woman's change of wording becomes part of her clever transformation of Jesus's aphorism, which then leads him to acknowledge what she has done for her daughter: "For this saying you may go your way; the demon has left your daughter" (Mk 7:29; contrast Mt. 15:28). It might even be argued in relation to the narrative development of the gospel of Mark's larger story that this interchange leads Jesus to use *paidion* later on in lexias #3 and 4. But if that is the case, then why does he shift back again to *teknon* in lexia #5, just a few verses after lexia #4? Would such a shift imply that *tekna* such as the disciples are not yet ready to receive the kingdom of God, but *paidia* are? Or are the shifts back and forth between these words not especially significant in the unfolding of the gospel of Mark, as the dialogue in lexia #2 indicates?

I find myself "unsettled" (as Barthes says) by these texts in Mark. But what makes them writerly? There is nothing particularly paradoxical, incoherent, or incomplete about the language itself. All humans are the children of someone or other, no matter our ages, and we may be so described. Nevertheless, in contemporary North American mainstream culture – my culture – when an adult addresses or describes another adult as "child" or "son/daughter," even if the usage is clearly affectionate, the language may well be understood as disrespectful, patronizing, and demeaning, and often it is an exercise of intimidation and display of superior power. If I call you "child" or "son/daughter" (or "boy/girl"), it is because I *can* call you that: in other words, because I am your superior (elder, teacher, employer, etc.).

Children are larval human beings, on the way to something else, and except for the privileged, childhood is a time of ignorance, misery, weakness, and fear – and prior to the development of modern medicine, of high mortality rates. In this sense, adults *are* superior to children. Perhaps sensibilities were otherwise in the ancient Hellenistic world, but I know of no reason to think that "child" was a term of respect in that culture. Indeed, Francis Moloney says that "In antiquity the child was 'the last of all'" (2002: 188, n. 77), and Alan Cadwallader notes that children were "the most vulnerable and least textualized members of ancient society" (2008: 161). Jesus's attitude toward children is sometimes described as exceptional, but these five lexias in the gospel of Mark are better described as confusing, or perhaps simply confrontational. Each of these five lexias is situated in a context of conflict or amazement (see also Mk 2:6–7, 12, 9:34–35, 10:26), to which Jesus's child-language may contribute.

However, other readers of these five passages are apparently not unsettled by the child-language of Mark's Jesus, although some are troubled by the ambiguity of the phrase, "receive the kingdom of God like a child," and the context of lexia #4. Instead, Jesus's words in these lexias are described as affectionate (Taylor 1953: 195, 431; Johnson 1960: 56), or if they are taken in more symbolic ways, as referring to Jews (Johnson 1960: 137; Fowler 1991: 117) or to less significant or more humble or more receptive people (Taylor 1953: 405–406; Johnson 1960: 163, 172, 175; Moloney 2002: 188–189, 196–198) or even to Jesus himself (Fowler 1991: 189). Sometimes readers pay no attention at all to these words, or they are more bothered by Jesus's use of dog-language in lexia #2, in apparent reference to the Gentiles, and thus strongly implying that the woman and her daughter are less than human. However, Jesus's child-language, which may also imply sub-humanity, apparently neither irritates nor excites these scholars.

If the reader understands Jesus to be the Lord and Savior, the Messiah and Son of God, or even the incarnate Word of God, as the Gospel and Christian faith would have it, then perhaps this child-language on the part of the gospel of Mark's Jesus simulacrum is appropriate and even good. In that case, he is indeed superior to every other human being, a higher, super-human entity, perhaps even an angel or god, and he is entitled to address or refer to humans as children, in the same way that humans address or refer to children or even beloved pets with this sort of language. If Mark's Jesus simulacrum were clearly Lord and Savior, Messiah, Son of God, or Word of God, then his child-language in relation to adults would not be unsettling.

However, the gospel of Mark's Jesus simulacrum is not clearly any of these. Apart from Mk 1:1 (and then only in some manuscripts), he is described as "son of God" only by human opponents or demons, and he is never described as savior. The Syrophoenician woman calls him "Lord" (7:28), but it is very unlikely that she regards him as divine. The alleged "messianic secret" only makes sense if the reader has already read Matthew, Luke, or John, and thus already expects that a gospel will present Jesus as some sort of messiah. Mark's Jesus is either an inept keeper of secrets, or else there is no secret, but merely profound obscurity: "Neither will I tell you by what authority I do these things" (11:33). This saying appears also in Mt. 21:27 and Lk. 20:8, but the reader of either of those gospels knows what is the authority behind its Jesus simulacrum – that is, he is the messiah or Son of God. This is not the case in Mark.

Mark's Jesus simulacrum does appear to have magical powers, and he attracts supernatural beings, both angels and demons, but it is never clear exactly what sort of being he is.[3] He may be a superior being, one who might properly address adult humans as "children," or he may be just as human as you and I are, in which case his child-language is either a "spur to the risks of creative play," or else merely arrogant and offensive. His words and actions in this case require the reader's intervention in a way that similar words and actions of the other gospels' Jesus simulacra do not. As a result, if the reader does not understand Mark's Jesus to be a deity or super-human being, then this child-language on his part opens one or more different "entrances," to use Barthes's term, into the text of Mark: it becomes unsettling and writerly. These entrances lead to a reading of Mark's gospel and its Jesus simulacrum that lies beyond canonical control and is quite contrary to the Gospel.

The Jesus simulacra of the stories of Matthew, Luke, and John are clearly superior to any other human being. Each of these gospels explicitly states in its own way and from the very beginning of its story than its Jesus is super-human, or even divine. This superiority is reiterated throughout each of these stories. Despite this, however, all of these gospels tend to tone down the child-language of their Jesus simulacra in lexias that are similar to Mark's five lexias. Luke 5:20 has "man [*anthrōpe*]" instead of *teknon* in lexia #1, making it clear in that gospel that the paralytic is an adult but also removing the potential insult (compare Jn 5:9–10). Matthew 15:26–27 uses *teknon* only once and *paidion* not at all, in contrast to lexia #2, and so the interchangeability of these words does not appear in Matthew's dialogue. Neither Luke nor John has a comparable lexia. The ambiguities of lexias #3 and 4 are clarified in otherwise similar lexias in the other gospels. Luke 9:48 has "this child" (apparently denoting a specific child) instead of "one such child" as in lexia #3, although Luke 18:15–17 follows lexia #4 closely. Matthew 19:13–15 does not have the phrase, "like a child," that appears in lexia #4, and in Mt. 18:3–4, Jesus says, "Truly, I say to you, unless you turn and become like children, you will never enter the kingdom of heaven. Whoever humbles himself like this child, he is the greatest in the kingdom of heaven," strongly associating the child with humility. John 3:3–8 suggests that a spiritual (re)birth is involved. There is no lexia in Matthew, Luke, or John that is comparable to lexia #5.

3. The fantastic qualities of Mark's Jesus simulacrum are discussed further in Aichele (2006).

Nevertheless, there is no lack of child-language applied to adults by the respective Jesus simulacra of the gospels of Matthew, Luke, and John. *Teknon* appears in Mt. 9:2 (connoting the paralytic), 15:26 (see above), and 21:28 (for the son of the vineyard owner), and in Lk. 15:31 (for the non-prodigal son) and 16:25 (connoting a rich man). *Teknion*, the diminutive of *teknon*, appears only in Jn 13:33 (connoting the disciples). *Pais* appears at Mt. 21:15 (connoting the crowds) and Lk 12:45 (where it is translated as "manservant"), and in Acts 4:27 and 30, *pais* (translated as "servant") describes Jesus. *Paidion* appears in Mt. 11:16 (compared to "this generation") and 18:4 (compared to "whoever"), in Lk. 7:32 (compared to "the men of this generation"), and in Jn 21:5 (connoting the disciples). These instances of *teknon* and *paidion* also suggest, although indirectly, a degree of interchangeability of these terms. Jesus simulacra also use *nēpios*, "infant," for their followers in Mt. 11:25 and Lk. 10:21, and in the quote from LXX Ps. 8:3 in Mt. 21:16 (assuming that Mt. 21:15 connotes adults). None of this language seems inappropriate, for again, each of these gospels makes it clear in various ways and at numerous points that its Jesus simulacrum is indeed superior to other people. As the unique son of God, each of these Jesuses quite properly treats others as children of God, and by no means his equals.

Child-language that connotes adults is rare in the Jewish scriptures, and only a few precursors to this practice in the gospels may be found there. In order to trace the exact words, I refer to the Septuagint, the Greek translation of those scriptures. These words describe the Israelites as children of God in Isa. 30:1, "'Woe to the rebellious children [*tekna*],' says the Lord, 'who carry out a plan, but not mine,'" and 63:8, "For he [God] said, Surely they are my people, sons [*tekna*] who will not deal falsely," and also Hos. 11:1, "When Israel was a child [*nēpios*], I [God] loved him, and out of Egypt I called my son [*tekna*]." Similarly, Zech. 9:13 prophesies, "I will brandish your sons [*tekna*], O Zion, over your sons [*tekna*], O Greece." Although *paidion* is common in the Septuagint, it apparently is not used to connote adults.

In striking contrast to the Jewish scriptures, the Pauline writings of the New Testament frequently use *teknon* to connote adults. In the undisputed writings, Paul uses *teknon* to connote Christians as children of God in Rom. 8:16, 17, 21, 9:8; Gal. 4:28; and Phil. 2:15. In the disputed writings, this usage appears at Eph. 5:1. Paul also uses *teknon* to connote Christians as his own children in 1 Cor. 4:14, 17; 2 Cor. 6:3, 12:14; Gal. 4:19; 1 Thess. 2:7, 11; and Phlm. 10. In the disputed writings, this usage appears at 1 Tim. 1:2, 18; 2 Tim. 1:2, 2:1; and Tit. 1:4. However, *paidion* appears only in 1 Cor.

14:20, where the connotation is negative ("Brethren, do not be children [*paidia*] in your thinking; be babes [*nēpiazete*] in evil, but in thinking be mature"). Paul also uses *nēpios*, but the connotations also tend to be negative, as in the often-quoted 1 Cor. 13:11 ("When I was a child, I spoke like a child, I thought like a child, I reasoned like a child; when I became a man, I gave up childish ways"). Similar language appears in Rom. 2:20 and Eph. 6:4. *Pais* and *teknion* do not appear in the Pauline writings.

If we read the gospel of Mark within its New Testament canonical context, then Mark's simulation of Jesus is absorbed into the canonical Christ simulacrum, which the writings of Paul play a major role in establishing (see Chapter 9). The Christ simulacrum of the Gospel is undoubtedly a super-human being, and perhaps a god, but in any case he is of a distinctly higher order than the rest of humanity. As a result, in the context of the Gospel, Mark becomes more readerly, a text of pleasure, and once again there is no problem with its Jesus simulacrum speaking to adults as though they were children.

However, that Mark's story and its Jesus simulacrum do not fit comfortably within the virtuality of the New Testament and its Gospel of Jesus Christ is indicated by Jesus's child-language in these five lexias (among other things). Perhaps Pauline usage of *teknon* may serve as precursor to the uses of *teknon* in Matthew, Luke, or John, but the gospel of Mark's ambiguous use of *paidion* in lexias #3 and 4, and the semiotic interchangeability of *paidion* and *teknon* in lexia #2 (which does not appear directly in any other gospel), count strongly against a Pauline precursor. Furthermore, if Pauline thought is not reflected in other Markan language, as I have argued elsewhere (Aichele 2006: 85–104), then we might read these five Markan passages in some other way as well.

The Second Entrance

Other sayings and deeds of the gospel of Mark's Jesus simulacrum also suggest an alternative understanding of these five lexias. Two other sayings use neither *teknon* nor *paidion* but have very similar connotations. First, in Mk 9:42, just a few verses after lexia #3, Jesus refers to "little ones [*mikrōn*] who believe in me," perhaps referring to the child of that lexia, but the more immediate context of these words is his mention of those who "do a mighty work in my name" or who "give you a cup of water to drink because you bear the name of Christ" (9:39, 41).[4] The combination of sayings in Mk

4. Matthew 18:6 and Lk. 17:2 also have *mikrōn* but change the context (and thus the connotation) significantly.

9:35–42 reinforces the thought that the "one such child" of lexia #3 is not just a child. In addition, the shifting and uncertainty of "your name/my name/the name of Christ" that appears in 9:38–39 and 41, as well as in lexia #3, appears whenever Jesus mentions the word "name" in Mark. Just as no Jesus ever explicitly says in any synoptic gospel that he is the son of man, so none of them ever says what "my name" is. In itself, that omission may not be so odd, but added to each Jesus's repeated use of the phrase "my name," it raises a question: What name does he have in mind?[5]

Second, in Mark 5, the hemorrhaging woman is placed in tandem with Jairus's twelve-year-old daughter, and Jesus even specifically addresses this unnamed adult woman as "daughter" (*thugatēr*, 5:34, see also 5:23, 35; compare Mt. 9:20–26; Lk. 8:42–55). Like the Syrophoenician woman of lexia #2, whose own words[6] have worked the miracle of exorcizing her "little daughter" (Mk 7:25, 29), the bleeding woman performs a "mighty work" when she improperly touches Jesus's garment, and he tells her that "*your* faith has made you well" (5:34, emphasis added).

Elsewhere I have argued that what Tzvetan Todorov calls the "oneiric logic" (1973: 173) of postmodern fantasy shapes the narrative of the gospel of Mark and its Jesus simulacrum (see Aichele 2006: 31–58, 131–166). Mark's Jesus simulacrum corresponds to what Gilles Deleuze calls an oneiric phantasm, for it is composed of "images which correspond to desire or … dream images." Oneiric phantasms are "apt to merge together, to condense and dissipate, and are too swift and too tenuous to offer themselves to sight." In contrast, Matthew, Luke, and John describe Jesus simulacra that correspond to what Deleuze calls theological phantasms, "which intersect spontaneously in the sky, forming immense images out of the clouds – high mountains and figures of giants" (1990: 275).[7] In these other gospels, Jesus's words become the statements of a superior being. One consequence of this difference of the simulacra is that Jesus's child-language in Mark signifies differently than it does in Matthew, Luke, or John, even if the words are the same. Jesus's child-language in Mark is a product of the oneiric logic of fantasy, and thus it is spoken not only by a different simulacrum, but by a different kind of simulacrum.

5. See further Chapter 2, and Aichele (2001: 200–208).
6. Lattimore's translation of Mk 7:29 makes this more explicit: "Because of this saying [of the woman], go; the demon has left your daughter" (1979). In contrast, the comparable passage in Mt. 15:28 makes it clear that Matthew's Jesus has granted the woman's request.
7. Matthew's Jesus simulacrum is a mix of the oneiric and the theological; see further Chapter 9.

Another major feature of the gospel of Mark's oneiric narrative logic is the "secret of the kingdom of God" (4:11), which even though it has been "given" to the disciples, neither the disciples nor the reader ever "gets." Again, both Mt. 13:11 and Lk. 8:10 describe the kingdom as "secrets," but in each of them, the disciples understand the parables. In contrast, in Mark the secret message was sent but not received, and the mystery remains. The kingdom of God is central to the message of many of Jesus's sayings, and it is explicitly connected to the child in Mark's lexias #4 and 5. Richmond Lattimore's translation of lexia #4, here closer to the Greek (*toioutōn estin hē basileia tou theou*) than the Revised Standard Version, even says "of such is the Kingdom of God" (1979: 27). Furthermore, if "receives me" and "receives … him who sent me" in lexia #3 correspond somehow to "receive the kingdom of God" in lexia #4, then the kingdom is strongly implicit in that lexia as well. In these two lexias, either the kingdom of God or Jesus and the one who sent Jesus are to be received, and this reception is compared to the reception of children (*paidia*).

In addition, if the "children" whom Jesus mentions twice in lexia #2 are indeed the children of God – that is, the recipients of God's covenant with Israel – then the kingdom of God is implicit in that lexia also. Furthermore, although like lexia #2, lexia #1 does not mention the kingdom as such, both of these passages are set in contexts of a miraculous restoration of health, a "mighty work" or earthly moment in which something that is unwhole amazingly becomes whole. The healing of the hemorrhaging woman in Mark 5 is another such moment. These are moments or events of a fantastic kingdom growing secretly, as in Jesus's parable of Mk 4:26–29. Finally, the saying about "little ones who believe in me" is the very text that connects Jesus's comment about a man seen doing "a mighty work in my name" to his discussion about entering the kingdom in Mk 9:43–47, which I discuss further below.

In other words, the adult "children" of the five sayings in the gospel of Mark that were noted above all stand in some sort of conjunction with the kingdom of God. In Matthew, Luke, and John, this connection also appears, but it is less pronounced, in part at least because the child-language of their Jesus simulacra is less unsettling, for the reasons noted above. Nevertheless, apart from sayings in these other gospels that are similar to the five Markan passages (also noted above), and where the child-language is often toned down, child-language describing adults appears in conjunction with the kingdom of God (or Heaven) only in one text. In Lk. 16:25, "son [*teknon*]" is evidently used in a patronizing or even belittling way when Abraham speaks to Lazarus. This conjunction does not appear at all in the Acts of the Apostles, unless one counts 4:27, which identifies the "servant [*pais*]" Jesus as the "anointed one" or king. Nor does it appear in the Pauline writings.

In this phrase, "the kingdom of God," as spoken by Mark's Jesus, there is another bit of language that "discomforts" my sensibilities, unsettling historical, cultural, and psychological assumptions, as Barthes says. Again, in the other gospels, each of their Jesus simulacra is clearly a king of sorts – that is, the messiah or Christ (albeit in different ways). As such each of them is entitled to talk about his kingdom. However, the messianic qualities of Mark's Jesus are far from clear, and therefore when he speaks these words, questions arise – questions that Mark does not answer. In other words, this phrase, "the kingdom of God," offers a second set of "entrances" into the text of the gospel of Mark, as well as further tensions with its New Testament canonical context and the Gospel.

Kings and kingdoms were common in the ancient world, and perhaps in such a world to claim the God of Israel or his messiah as your king was even a subversive and liberatory act. However, to think of God or Christ today as the absolute ruler of a kingdom, a Lord (whether in heaven or on earth) who demands unquestioning obedience from docile subjects, is at best a foreign and unpleasant metaphor and at worst simply a dead one, a meaningless string of words that are reiterated for custom's sake. Both "the kingdom of God" and "the will of God" need to be seriously reconsidered from a postmodern and indeed posthuman perspective, and perhaps the "entrances" offered by these phrases into Mark's gospel are points at which such a rethinking becomes possible.

These entrances open into Mark's text but they open within it as well, for the kingdom of God is itself described in the gospel of Mark as something to be entered. Popular fantasy literature contains many stories of an alternative, extra-ordinary reality, a "secondary world" (or in this case, kingdom) in tension with but accessible from the everyday "primary world" (Tolkien 1966: 49, 60), and perceivable or accessible only to those who know the way or who live in some sort of marginal state (such as oppression, disease, psychosis, drug abuse – or childhood). Sometimes events occur in that secondary world which have great repercussions for both the extra-ordinary and the ordinary worlds. Yet all around these marginalized people, others (usually the great majority) live ordinary lives in the primary world, often entirely unaware of the alternative reality. Sometimes even the people who know or believe in the secondary world have great difficulty entering or re-entering it, and they suffer or sacrifice greatly in the attempt. However, once they have experienced that secondary world, they cannot live for long away from it. They would unhesitatingly cut off an arm or pluck out an eye to get back.

However, in the most subtle fantasies of all – such as the writings of Franz Kafka, Italo Calvino, or Gabriel García Márquez – there are not two distinct worlds at all, one ordinary and the other extra-ordinary, but merely one world which is somehow both ordinary and extra-ordinary. It is an uncanny narrative world, in Sigmund Freud's sense of "uncanny," at once familiar and strange (1955).[8] In such a world, "entry" is not a matter of passing back and forth, but rather living in the one world in two contrary ways at once, without diminishing either of them. The gospel of Mark's writerly text of bliss belongs among these fantasies.

My discomfort with both the words of Mark's Jesus that refer to adults as children and his words about the mysterious kingdom of God alerts me to the connection suggested in that gospel between them. The gospel of Mark's Jesus does not present the kingdom of God as some other-worldly place, a distinct and spiritual secondary world to which we might escape from this one. Nor is it simply a this-worldly realm, a different and exotic country to which we might travel. Instead, Jesus's words suggest that the kingdom of God is (a) secret. It is this world, but seen "through the looking-glass," as it were, and the child-language of Mark's Jesus connotes those people who perceive this world as such a mysterious place, and who live in it accordingly.

In the gospel of Mark, the kingdom of God is "at hand" (1:15, compare Mt. 4:17), and some people are "not far from the kingdom" (12:34). It is coming or even "has come with power," and "some standing here ... will not taste death before they see" its arrival (Mk 9:1, compare Mt. 16:28; Lk. 9:27). Yet the kingdom is also a seed that grows mysteriously by itself in the earth, "he knows not how" and "of itself" (Mk 4:26–27), a tiny thing that becomes huge (4:30–32, compare Mt. 13:31–32; Lk. 13:18–19). If the kingdom of God is utopian, it is not because it is "not here" or "not yet," but rather because it is something to be "entered," and entering it is not easy (Mk 10:23, compare Mt. 19:23; Lk. 18:24). You may even have to mutilate yourself in order to get in (Mk 9:43–47, compare Mt. 5:29–30, 18:8–9). However, the kingdom is "life" (*zōē*), as opposed to the unquenchable fires of Gehenna.

Even though it is called "the kingdom *of God*," God is conspicuously absent from Jesus's descriptions of the kingdom in the gospel of Mark, as he is also from "kingdom" statements made by the Jesus simulacra of Matthew and Luke. (John's Jesus has very little to say about the kingdom of

8. Freud's use of "uncanny" is quite similar to Todorov's more general concept of the fantastic.

God [see 3:3, 5].) According to Mark's Jesus simulacrum, God is "not God
of the dead, but of the living [*zōntōn*]" (12:27, compare Mt. 22:32; Lk.
20:38), and perhaps this use of *zaō* in Jesus's dialogue with the Sadducees
in Mk 12:18–27 also allows us to connect the kingdom of God with the
"resurrection," yet another concept that remains mysterious in Mark, but
much less so in Matthew, Luke, or John, thanks to their Easter episodes. In
Mark 9:10, the three disciples "question … what the rising from the dead
meant" (this does not appear in the other gospels), and Mark ends at 16:8
without a resurrection appearance of Jesus.

In any case, despite his association with "the living" in 12:27, God's
relation to the kingdom of God remains a mystery in the gospel of Mark.
Mark's Jesus simulacrum talks about "the gospel of God" (1:14), and he
urges people to have faith in and side with God (7:8–9, 8:33, 10:9, 11:22,
12:29–30), but these statements say relatively little about God, and more
about people. He says that "No one is good but God alone" (10:18), and
that "all things are possible with God" (10:27, see also 11:25, 12:24), but
it is unclear how seriously either of these extreme statements should be
taken. In addition, God is conspicuously absent as a character from the
larger narrative of the gospel of Mark, and here there is sharp contrast
between Mark and both Matthew and Luke. Unlike the angelic delegates
and explicitly identified Holy Spirit in those latter gospels, there is no
evident God simulacrum in Mark's story.

God's relation to Jesus is also a mystery throughout Mark, and the
vineyard parable in 12:1–9 does not clarify it (compare Mt. 21:33–41; Lk.
20:9–16): even if the vineyard owner is assumed to be God, it is not clear
that Jesus is his heir, the one, beloved son. A spirit descends on Jesus at the
moment of his baptism (Mk 1:10), but it is not described as God's spirit (as
it is in Mt. 3:16 and Lk. 3:22), and the voice from the sky or cloud that calls
Jesus "my beloved son" in 1:11 and 9:7 is not identified as coming from
God. The required inferences may be obvious, but only to the reader who is
already familiar with the canon and the Gospel. The similar voices from
the sky or cloud are also not further identified in Matthew (3:17, 17:5) and
in Luke (3:22, 9:35), but again this absence is not felt so sorely in either of
those gospels, where the reader already knows whose son Jesus is. Indeed,
Matthew, Luke, and John each make clear in various ways and with various
connotations that each of their respective Jesuses is the son of God, although
only John's Jesus says as much (10:36, 11:4). In contrast, there is no miraculous
virgin birth or incarnation story in Mark to make Jesus's divine paternity or
origin explicit; instead he is called, perhaps insultingly, the "son of Mary"
(6:3; see further Chapter 5).

Because it is never clear who the father of Mark's Jesus simulacrum is, it is perhaps not surprising that he receives no response when he prays to "Abba, Father" in Gethsemane (14:36, see also 13:32). As a result, the non-response of the "Father" in comparable scenes in Matthew and Luke (but see 22:43) signifies differently. The Jesuses of Mt. 26:64 and Lk. 22:70 can afford to be coy at the council trial, for it is clear elsewhere in each of these gospels that its Jesus truly is the son of God. In contrast, the apparent bluntness of the response of Mark's Jesus to the high priest's question (14:61–62) is on closer inspection deeply paradoxical.[9] Otherwise Jesus never identifies himself as God's son in Mark, and he is described by other humans as the son of God in only two other places: in 1:1 (but only in some manuscripts), perhaps mockingly by the implied author, and again perhaps mockingly by an enemy, the Roman centurion, in 15:39.

The demons, who are much more clearly evident in the gospel of Mark than God is, associate Jesus with God (1:24, 3:11, 5:7), but they too are enemies and should not be trusted in any case. Even Jesus's phrase "him who sent me" in lexia #3 is murky: perhaps Beelzebul has sent him, as the scribes say (3:22), or perhaps he is the resurrected form of John the Baptist, as Herod thinks (6:16). Although similar language appears in Mt. 12:24, 14:2, and Lk. 11:15 (but contrast Lk. 9:9), once again the larger stories of these gospels leave little doubt. Finally, as Mark's Jesus dies, he cries out that God has abandoned him (15:34). The darkness during the crucifixion and the tearing of the Temple curtain merely add to the mysteries (15:33, 38). Again Matthew and Luke have similar stories (except that Luke has very different last words), but the resurrection appearances of their respective Jesuses change the meaning of these scenes.

Mark's Jesus simulacrum says that the kingdom is "life [*zōē*]," and one meaning of *zōē*, according to Liddell and Scott's lexicon (1996), is "way of life." This is Liddell and Scott's third definition, following "substance, property" and "life, existence" (as opposed to death).[10] This understanding of *zōē* further supports the connection between the kingdom of God and Jesus's child-language in the gospel of Mark. Jesus tells a rich man who wishes "to inherit eternal life [*zōēn aiōnion*]" to keep the commandments and then also to "sell what you have, and give to the poor, and you will have treasure in heaven; and come, follow me" (Mk 10:17–21). In the first part of this chapter, I noted that Jesus's disturbing child-language in Mark's

9. See further Aichele (2006: 136–141).
10. Bauer (1957) reverses the order of the first two definitions and follows them with various forms of "supernatural life," listing the passages noted here.

gospel is also conjoined with talk about or an act of faith: to "believe in me," to act "in my name" or "bear the name of Christ," to perform "mighty works" or utter powerful words, to receive a child or like a child. To sell or give away everything in order to "follow me" is another such act of faith, a giving or losing of one's "life" or soul (*psuchē*, Mk 8:35, 10:45, 12:30) which amounts to entering the earthly way of life that Mark's Jesus calls *zōē*, or the secret kingdom of God.

Read with this understanding of *zōē*, this saying supports the idea suggested above that in the gospel of Mark, "eternal life" and perhaps also "resurrection" and even "heaven" are not about some other, secondary world that is distinct from this primary world, but instead they have a great deal to do with how one lives in this world.[11] According to the gospel of Mark's Jesus simulacrum, entering the kingdom requires giving up all that you own and even losing your soul. It involves a significant change in your way of life. Perhaps this is why the disciples react with amazement (only in Mk 10:24, but see also 10:26 and Mt. 19:25) to Jesus's remark about the difficulty of entering the kingdom that concludes the encounter with the rich man, and this then leads to lexia #5.

Nowhere in the gospel of Mark is this more forcefully stated than Jesus's advice in 9:43–48, shortly after lexia #3, to cut out body parts that might otherwise "cause you to sin" and thereby keep you from entering the kingdom, or "life." Entering the kingdom – that is, taking on this different way of life – may require not only giving away wealth, but also radical change of body as well as of mind (*metanoia*, "repentance," as in 1:15). Perhaps this is what "be salted with fire" means in Mk 9:49. Even the paralytic and the demon-possessed girl of lexias #1 and 2 must change, and it may cost them as much to lose the incapacity of a leg or even a demon as it does to lose your eye or hand. Those who have always been whole may never understand that. An amusing scene in the movie, *Monty Python's Life of Brian* (Jones 1979), makes this serious point. A former leper complains that Jesus has deprived him of his livelihood as a beggar, without his permission.[12] Might the paralytic in Mark 2 also be objecting to this transformation of his way of life all the while that he is brought into the house and even as Jesus heals him?

---

11. See Cadwallader (2008: 162–164) for a Marxist treatment of this idea.
12. For a similar story with a different spin, see Langguth (1968: 144). As one who has been crippled since birth, I do not belittle the real desires of handicapped people to be made whole. However, our handicaps become part of who we are, and we may become as attached to them as we are to our more positive qualities.

The Third Entrance

In lexia #5, Mark's Jesus simulacrum refers to the disciples as "children [*tekna*]." Just a few verses later, in Mk 10:29–30, Jesus says to the disciples, "there is no one who has left house or brothers or sisters or mother or father or children or lands, for my sake and for the gospel, who will not receive a hundredfold now in this time, houses and brothers and sisters and mothers and children and lands, with persecutions, and in the age to come [*ho aiōn ho erchomai*] eternal life [*zōēn aiōnion*]." *Teknon* is used twice in this saying, and the children are described once as abandoned and once as received, in a pattern that appears elsewhere in the gospel of Mark (4:24, see also 4:3–8, 26–29, 8:35, and 10:21). In addition, as in Mk 10:17, the word *zōē* is once again coupled with the word *aiōn*, which appears twice in 10:30, for the "age to come" with its own distinctive (*aiōnion*) way of life that is the kingdom of God, which is also "now in this time."

This assemblage of Jesus's sayings in the gospel of Mark suggests that those who have left everything, giving up even their "lives" (or souls, *psuchēn*) "for my sake and for the gospel" are the "little ones," the children who enter the mysterious kingdom and receive *zōē*, "life."[13] Perhaps it is this, even more than the thought that rich people will have a hard time entering the kingdom, that astonishes the disciples in Mk 10:24 and 26. These adult "children" who have left everything are the posthuman beings[14] whom only Mark's Jesus simulacrum calls the sons of men. As I noted in Chapter 2, in Mark 3:28 Jesus tells the crowd around him that "all sins will be forgiven the *sons of men*, and whatever blasphemies they utter" (emphasis added), and a bit later he refers to this crowd as his "brother, and sister, and mother" (3:35), in language that is echoed in 10:29–30. The multiplicity of these male and female sons of men infects the entire son of man story that Jesus tells throughout Mark's gospel, including the passion predictions and apocalyptic sayings.[15] In Mark, Jesus is but one among many sons of men. This significantly distinguishes Mark's Jesus simulacrum from the other Jesuses, just as it distinguishes Mark's son of man story from son of man stories in Matthew, Luke, and John. In each of the other gospels and in Acts, there is only one son of man, who is probably or even certainly (Jn 8:28, 9:35–37) Jesus himself.

In other words, the unsettling adult children in the words of the gospel of Mark's Jesus are sons of men, and not children of God as Paul says (see

13. Compare Cadwallader (2008: 176).
14. See further Hayles (1999) and Carlson (2008).
15. See further Aichele (2001: 151–172).

above) and as Matthew, Luke, and John each imply. Here Mark stands in very strong contrast to Paul's "gospel" and with it to the Gospel or canonical message of the Christian Bible. Indeed, the phrase "son of man" does not appear at all in the Pauline writings, except for "sons of men," connoting human beings, in Eph. 3:5. For Mark's Jesus simulacrum, the sons of men are the "many" men and women who have been "ransomed" by the son of man (who is also plural) when he "gives his life [*psuchē*]" for them (10:45). However, although many, the sons of men are the "elect" (see 13:20, 22, 27), for not everyone is a son of man. In other words, in Mark's story, this giving of life is not the one-time sacrifice of a unique son of man who dies on a cross to save souls (*psuchēn*) that it is in the Gospel.

Instead, according to Mark's Jesus, if you wish to enter the kingdom then you must give or lose your own *psuchē* and not try to save it (see 8:35). In contrast, *zōē* is not something to be given or saved but rather a way of life or state to be entered. The plural sons of men give their lives in words and deeds, including those of Jesus but also many others (such as the Syrophoenician woman or the man who casts out demons "in my name"), and these mighty works open the way of life (*zōē*).[16] This opens yet a third set of "entrances" into the gospel of Mark's text, which like the first two sets appear only from an extra-canonical perspective, for they require reading Mk 3:28 as a "son of man" saying, something most biblical scholars and other readers are reluctant to do, for apparently theological reasons. The undeniable plurality of the sons of men in this saying runs strongly counter to the Christian Gospel, and since this is the only saying of any of the gospels' Jesus simulacra that contains this plurality, the simplest theological "solution" has been simply to deny that it is a son of man saying. Many recent translations of the New Testament erase the problem altogether by translating "sons of men" in Mk 3:28 as "people" (NRSV) or with other gender inclusive language, but retaining the singular phrase "son of man" in the words of the gospels' Jesus simulacra, encouraging a reading for which that phrase connotes Jesus exclusively.

After all, if Mk 3:28 is read as a son of man saying, then the gospel of Mark's sons of men may include Jesus among their number, but they are not innocent, unique saviors – indeed, they are sinners and blasphemers (3:28), and their relationship to Abba/Father/God is polyvalent and conflicted. One one hand, they will come in the Father's glory and power, with angels, and to gather the elect (8:38, 13:26–27, 14:62) – that is, other sons of men. On the other hand, only the Father knows "when the time will

16. See further Aichele (2006: 203–221).

come" (13:32–33), and until then the sons of men will be betrayed, tortured, and killed (8:31, 9:12, 31, 10:33–34, 14:21). These sons of men "do the will of God" (3:35), but if Mark's Jesus simulacrum is a son of man, then to judge from his fate (when his time comes?), the "will of God" in Mark's story appears to be that they should die, misunderstood by their friends, alone, and reviled by their enemies (14:36, 15:29–34; see also 8:34).

Nevertheless, these elect Markan sons of men are "children of humankind"[17] whose "creative play" (to quote Pyper again) uncovers the extra-ordinariness of the ordinary, and the familiarity of the strange. They enter the kingdom (Mk 10:29–30) as its posthuman heirs, as in Dan. 7:13–14:

> behold, with the clouds of heaven there came one like a son of man, and he came to the Ancient of Days and was presented before him. And to him was given dominion and glory and kingdom.[18]

Language in the noncanonical gospel of Thomas suggests a similar idea. In saying 37, the disciples ask Thomas's Jesus simulacrum when he will be revealed to them. He replies, "When you disrobe without being ashamed and take up your garments and place them under your feet like little children and tread on them, then [will you see] the Son of the Living One, and you will not be afraid."[19] In saying 22, Jesus says: "These infants being suckled are like those who enter the Kingdom" and then "When you make the two one, and when you make the inside like the outside and the outside like the inside, and the above like the below, and when you make the male and the female one and the same, so that the male not be male nor the female female; and when you fashion eyes in place of an eye, and a hand in place of a hand, and a foot in place of a foot, and a likeness in place of a likeness; then will you enter [the Kingdom]." In Thomas's saying 106, Jesus says, "When you make the two one, you will become the sons of man, and when you say, 'Mountain, move away,' it will move away." Finally, in saying 28, Jesus says, "My soul became afflicted for the sons of men, because they are blind in their hearts and do not have sight; for empty they came into the world, and empty too they seek to leave the world. But for the moment they are intoxicated. When they shake off their wine, then they will repent."

17. As in Marvin Meyer's inclusive-language translation of saying 106 in the gospel of Thomas (Kloppenborg *et al.* 1990: 152).
18. See further Aichele (2008).
19. Unless noted otherwise, quotations from the gospel of Thomas are taken from Thomas O. Lambdin's translation (Cameron 1982: 25–37).

I do not want to over-emphasize the similarities between the Jesus simulacra of the gospels of Thomas and Mark or their sayings, but the discomfort produced by the text of bliss that is Thomas here invites creative play with the text of bliss that is Mark. Thomas's Jesus says that "when you make the two one" – like an infant being suckled – you enter the kingdom (saying 22), but you also become sons of men, with miraculous powers (saying 106). This scenario is enacted in the "mighty works" of Jesus and several other characters in Mark's narrative. According to Thomas 28, the sons of men are currently blind and drunk (sinners and blasphemers?), but when they sober up they will repent, and then perhaps they will see, like naked, shameless children, and not be afraid (saying 37). By saying these things more or less explicitly, Thomas's Jesus simulacrum allows the reader to consider the possibility that Mark's Jesus simulacrum might say something similar, although less explicitly, in his child and kingdom sayings.

In the gospel of Mark, the kingdom of God is a secret, and it is secret. It may be in plain sight, like a deer or a unicorn standing beside the road, but you never see it because you don't know how to look, or where, or when. You are blind or drunk, as Thomas's Jesus says. Or as Deleuze says, "all the powers have an interest in hiding images from us, not necessarily in hiding the same thing from us, but in hiding something in the image" (1989: 20). Moloney and others rightly emphasize the characteristic of receptivity in children as crucial to the metaphor of "child" in the unsettling language of Mark's Jesus. Deleuze also says that "in the adult world, the child is affected by a certain motor helplessness, but one which makes him all the more capable of seeing and hearing" (1989: 3). This is particularly evident in lexias #3 and 4 – that is, in relation to *paidion*.

However, child-like receptivity is often understood to be naive innocence, simple passivity, even weakness or gullibility, or in other words, Pyper's "paternalistic conformity," which would accept whatever it is given without question, perhaps like the suckling baby of Thomas 22. This suggests an already-established kingdom that is given to the child as *fait accompli*, but it is not how the sayings of Jesus in the gospel of Mark bring together the child, the kingdom, and the son of man – at least, not if the reader seeks to understand Mark apart from the Gospel of Jesus Christ, or rather in much the same way that she would read the gospel of Thomas or other extra-canonical texts. For such a reading, the widely-noted ambiguity of lexia #4 becomes important, perhaps even decisive: "whoever does not receive the kingdom of God like a child [*hōs paidion*] shall not enter it" (Mk 10:15). Should *hōs paidion* in this saying be read as meaning that you must receive the kingdom of God "in the way that a child would," or should it be read instead as saying that you must receive the kingdom "as you would receive a child," much like lexia #3 – although in that saying, too, reception is qualified by the shifting uncertainties of "in my name"? For an adult it is fairly easy to receive a child, but much greater effort is required to become a child (as opposed to being merely childish, which is rather easy).

As humans we are all larval beings and hence child-like, perpetually incomplete and on the way to something else.[20] It is this as much as anything else that constitutes our posthumanity. And perhaps it is this more than any other characteristic which illuminates Jesus's child-language applied to adults. However, if we are already in some sense perpetual children, then why have we not already "entered the kingdom"? Or have we perhaps already entered the kingdom but somehow just don't know it – that is, are we already in an uncanny world, like the ones described earlier in this chapter? Nevertheless, as adults we are only "like" children, and the metaphoric "like [*hōs*]" that is explicit in Mk 10:15 marks a division and tension between what is and what is not. Only if you are not a child can you be like a child. There is nothing simple or naive or innocent about it.

Indeed, apart from sentimental romanticizing or major brain damage, how could an adult ever become a child (not merely *teknon* but *paidion*)? To paraphrase the disciples in Mk 10:26, who then can enter the kingdom of God? Perhaps this is also Nicodemus's question in Jn 3:4 ("How can a man be born when he is old? Can he enter a second time into his mother's womb and be born?"). The reply of John's Jesus simulacrum to Nicodemus ("unless one is born of water and the Spirit [*pneumatos*], he cannot enter the kingdom of God," 3:5–6) is both more absolute than the words of Mark's Jesus in 10:27 but also suggests a spiritual transformation, and his elaboration two verses later ("The wind [*pneuma*] blows where it wills, and you hear the sound of it, but you do not know whence it comes or whither it goes," Jn 3:8) hints at uncertainty and perhaps even violence.

In any case, in the gospel of Mark, there is no nostalgia involved in becoming a child, and it is not a return to the womb. Mark's Jesus simulacrum answers the disciples' question by saying, "With men it is impossible, but not with God; for all things are possible with God" (10:27). Once again God is invoked, but presumably this is the same God that eventually abandons Mark's Jesus on the cross: that too is possible. This answer may offer some hope, but it also describes the extreme improbability of success, and it leaves the secret of the kingdom unrevealed.

20. See further Deleuze (1994: 78–79) and Carlson (2008: 26–29).

Furthermore, Jesus's words about self-mutilation in Mk 9:43–49 describe an entry into the kingdom of God or *zōē* that may be far more demanding and unpleasant than spiritual transformation. Perhaps for the gospel of Mark's Jesus, becoming a child describes another form of such unsettling self-mutilation. To become a child requires becoming something that the adult reader is not: something alien, posthuman, even monstrous. She must become what Mark's Jesus calls "the son of man." Only then can she find that way of life for which the world is a fantastically uncanny place, at once extra-ordinary and ordinary, and thereby enter the secret kingdom of God.

This is a matter of activity, not passivity. The child receives the kingdom in order to enter it, but it is the risky "creative play" in this act of reception that *makes the kingdom happen*. The many male and female sons of men "leave everything" (10:28, see also 8:35), and they do not merely receive *zōē*, but they take it. In lexias #3 and 4, the Greek word translated as "receive" is *dechomai*, but in Mk 10:30, the word so translated is *lambanō*. Mark 9:36 likewise begins, "And he took [*labōn*] a child." Liddell and Scott's lexicon allows *dechomai* to have more active meanings than "receive," such as "understand," "welcome," or "entertain," and *lambanō* can also mean "understand" (1996). These readings seem more appropriate to the argument presented here. Unlike the disciples in Mark, Jesus understands children, and the sons of men understand the kingdom.

Reading the gospel of Mark outside of the canon opens up unsettling entrances into Mark's text, and if the reader passes through those portals – perhaps if she even enters or understands the kingdom of God – she encounters the possibility that entering or understanding that kingdom requires that she become a child *without ceasing to remain an adult* (and thus not a child). Perhaps the strange "young man" or men who appear in Gethsemane and again at the tomb in Mk 14:51 and 16:5 (and who appear only in Mark) are examples of such posthuman monsters, adults who have made themselves children in order to enter the kingdom, and perhaps it is because of the young man's disturbing aspect, and not the emptiness of the tomb, that the women flee in speechless fear at the end of that gospel (16:8). The young man is the child, and he is also the resurrection.

Chapter 5

Dark Conceptions: The Two Fathers of Luke's Jesus

The Incarnation is nothing else than the practical, material manifestation of the human nature of God. (Feuerbach 1957: 50)

[F]ictional transfiguration [requires a ...] narrative in which the characters and the action, irrespective of meaning or theme, are prefigured to a noticeable extent by figures and events popularly associated with the life of Jesus as it is known from the Gospels. (Ziolkowski 1972: 6)

What did Joseph and Mary say to each other before having the child?
– Jean-Luc Godard. (quoted in Deleuze 1989: 298)

The metaphysical frameworks supplied by ancient Greek philosophy helped Christian thinkers of the first several centuries CE to navigate the conceptual difficulties involved in the idea of divine incarnation. This idea remains a central feature of the Gospel of Jesus Christ. However, these ancient philosophical frameworks no longer provide viable intellectual options. Neoplatonism is no more plausible today than is the idea of a flat earth. We can understand that people once believed that the Earth was flat, and perhaps even why they did so, but we cannot make ourselves believe this. Similarly, living in a highly secularized, scientifically sophisticated world, we find it difficult to believe in traditional concepts such as the god-man, because the concepts themselves no longer cohere with reality as we understand it. We no longer think of "natures" or "persons" in the ways that these terms functioned in classical christological discourse.[1] These concepts assume an ideology that is no longer acceptable and perhaps even incomprehensible.

---

1. From the Chalcedonian confession: "Our Lord Jesus Christ is ... the same perfect in Godhood and the same perfect in manhood, truly God and truly man, the same of a rational soul and body; consubstantial with the Father in Godhood, and the same consubstantial with us in manhood, ... two natures without confusion, without change, without division, without separation" (Kelly 1960: 339–340).

The ancient ideologies provided philosophical concepts in terms of which early Christians read and understood the Bible. Because those ideologies no longer control our reading, modern readers who want to believe in biblical texts as the Word of God must find alternative concepts in order to make sense of them. However, like the non-flat planet Earth, these alternative concepts may jeopardize the Gospel and entail understandings of the texts that exceed the control of the canon of the scriptures. In this chapter, concepts derived from an intertextual juxtaposition between Luke's gospel and a modern novel open up a way to read Luke in a non-biblical context. As in the previous two chapters, this effectively de-canonizes that gospel and releases its Jesus simulacrum from the virtuality that is the Jesus Christ of the Gospel.

The God-Man

Christians believe that the messiah or Christ is Jesus of Nazareth, a man who lived two thousand years ago in Roman Palestine and who rose from the dead to sit forever at the right hand of God, as the savior and judge of humanity. They also believe that this remarkable being conjoins two distinct and even contradictory natures, divine and human, in one person. In other words, Jesus Christ is a mysterious and unique union of the supernatural and the natural, the god-man, a human being who is also somehow God. This god-man concept is among other things a Christian compromise between the Jewish idea of a human messiah and the gnostic idea of a divine redeemer. The concept was developed in order to resolve theological differences between various early Christian groups concerning the identity of Jesus and his status as "the Son of God." However, although this concept solves some problems, it creates others.

Although the Christian doctrine of the two natures of Christ did not emerge until well after the gospel of Luke was written, the biblical narrative in which this mysterious union of the divine and the human is most explicitly stated is Luke's Christmas story. According to this story, the Spirit of God (or perhaps the angel Gabriel, acting on God's behalf) impregnates Mary, the future mother of Jesus. Gabriel tells Luke's Mary simulacrum, "The Holy Spirit will come upon you, and the power of the Most High will overshadow you; therefore the child to be born will be called holy, the Son of God" (1:35). The Greek phrase translated as "the Holy Spirit" in this verse is *pneuma hagion*, "holy spirit," and the capitalizing of "Holy Spirit" and addition of the definite article in the Revised Standard Version translation makes explicit a theological dimension that is only a possibility in the Greek text.[2] However, in Luke's story of Jesus's baptism, it is indeed *the* holy spirit (*to pneuma to hagion*) that descends as a dove (3:22; contrast Mt. 3:16; Mk 1:10), just as a voice from the sky calls Jesus "my beloved son." "Son of God" is not a metaphor when applied to Luke's Jesus simulacrum.

Luke 1:35 does not specifically quote the Old Testament book of Ruth, but the intertextual resonance between the "shadow" of "power" over the "handmaid" Mary (Lk. 1:35, 38) and Ruth 3:9, in which the man Boaz "spreads his skirt" over his "maidservant" Ruth, is striking.[3] The words in Ruth are Ruth's invitation to Boaz to have consensual sex with her, but in Luke they are Gabriel's announcement (not an invitation) to Mary. In each case it is a scene of imminent intercourse. According to Luke, God will mate with Mary, and Jesus will be the result (1:31).

The birth stories of the gospels of Luke and Matthew are often woven together so thoroughly in Christmas celebrations that many readers are unaware that there are differences between them. However, as I noted in Chapter 2, there are many significant differences between the Christmas stories of Luke and Matthew, and they should not be considered as two versions of a single story. Matthew's entire account of Mary's impregnation is merely "before they came together she was found to be with child of the Holy Spirit [*pneumatos hagiou*]" (1:18), and although these words allow a christological view involving divine incarnation, they do not strongly encourage it. In addition, in Mt. 1:20, the unnamed angel says to Joseph, "that which is conceived in her is of the Holy Spirit [*ek pneumatos estin hagiou*]." The Greek text again omits the definite article. However, apart from these few words, Matthew says nothing to indicate that its Joseph simulacrum is not the genetic father of Jesus. Furthermore, apart from the quotation of Isa. 7:14 in Mt. 1:23, in the Septuagint translation which mentions a virgin, Mary is not described as a virgin in Matthew's birth story, in contrast to Lk. 1:27 (twice) and 34. Since Joseph would probably not be the first father in history to get cold feet when his girlfriend told him she was pregnant, Matthew's story is much less clear than Luke is about how Mary got pregnant, or about the metaphysical or biological nature of the resulting child. Similarly, the gospel of John says nothing to indicate that its Joseph simulacrum is not the biological father of its Jesus, or that Jesus's mother was a virgin. There is no mention of either Joseph or of Mary's virginity in Mark.

2. See also Brown (1993: 125).
3. Brown discounts any connection between these passages (1993: 290), but Schaberg disagrees (1987: 117). Schaberg maintains that Luke's story conceals a human act of rape, a conclusion that Brown rejects (1993: 635–637).

As a result, only the gospel of Luke's birth story emphasizes that the Jesus simulacrum that results from this supernatural conception is both physically and metaphysically a son of God. However, he is not some cobbled-together monster, like a mermaid or a sphinx, or even Dr Frankenstein's creature. It is not the case that his top half is human and his bottom half is divine (or vice versa). Nor is he analogous to a cyborg, the biomechanical mingling of human being and machine from science fiction stories that appears more and more in the reality of our everyday lives.

Instead, Luke's Christmas story strongly implies that the union of God and human being in Jesus is analogous to that of the two genetic strands contributed by the father and the mother, and combined and manifested in the body of any normally-conceived child. That one of those strands is supernatural in this story makes little difference to the analogy. Luke's Jesus simulacrum is a hybrid, not unlike a mule, of which every cell is half horse and half donkey.[4] Given the place of the god-man within Luke-Acts's presentation of Jesus as the Lord "in Jerusalem and in all Judea and Samaria and to the end of the earth" (Acts 1:8), as well as within later post-Constantinian theology, he is a hybrid who will rule an empire. As half-God he is the king, not merely in Israel but everywhere. This has immense consequences for the gospel of Luke's Jesus, for even when his narrated words or deeds are identical to those of Matthew's or Mark's Jesus simulacra, they signify differently, for they are the words or deeds of a man who is also god. Similarly, when Luke's demons identify Jesus as the "Son of God," and when the voice from the sky or cloud that speaks at his baptism and transfiguration calls Jesus "my Son" (Lk. 3:22, 9:35), there can be little doubt whose voice it is or how these titles are to be understood.[5]

However, this genetic analogy is complicated by widespread modern belief that God is a spiritual, transcendent being, who does not have a physical body. Despite the resonance with the book of Ruth, it is not generally imagined that God actually copulates with Mary, and commentators often assume that the gospel of Luke's Mary simulacrum remains a virgin despite the conception. Raymond Brown says that "There is never a suggestion in Matthew or in Luke that the Holy Spirit is the male element in a union with Mary," and Jane Schaberg agrees.[6] According to

---

4. Compare Moore (1994: 59). However, Moore is discussing the gospel of John.
5. Elsewhere in Luke, however, "son of God" language is used of others in what appear to be metaphorical ways (6:35–36, 11:2, 13, 12:30–32).
6. Brown (1993: 124, see also 290, 314, 523); Schaberg (1987: 76, 117). See also Bultmann (1971: 62–63, n. 4).

the Christian ideology, the Holy Spirit produces no sperm, chromosomes, or DNA to contribute to the child that results. Luke's language describing a divine power that overshadows Jesus's mother is understood to refer to a non-physical being, a spirit without a body.

Here modern readers begin to have difficulty with traditional christological concepts. We understand the reproductive process fairly well today – we can inseminate artificially, increase or terminate fertility, and even clone living beings – but we do not understand how a spiritual (non-physical) being could fertilize a woman's ovum. We understand reproduction as a function of physical bodies that draws upon genetic codes. For this understanding, in order for God to have physical intercourse with Mary, God (as the Holy Spirit) would have to be already incarnate, as in ancient polytheistic tales of embodied gods coupling with human beings (and as in Gen. 6:1–4), and that would be unacceptable to Christian belief.

Indeed, the gospel of Luke does not specifically state that Mary has been impregnated by a non-physical being,[7] for the Greek word for "spirit," *pneuma*, can also mean "breath" or "wind" – in other words, an airy physical body. Nevertheless, Luke's claim that the spirit of God will "overshadow" Mary and impregnate her is often understood as though it were a more detailed version of the gospel of John's story of the incarnation of the divine Word (1:1–14). The disturbingly "pagan" physical overtones of Luke's Christmas story are ameliorated and absorbed in Johannine logocentrism. (The christological affinities between Luke and John are pursued further in Chapter 9.)

This canonically intertextual reading of Luke's Christmas story extends beyond Matthew and John. The creation stories of Genesis 1–3 provide another nexus for understanding the virginal conception of Jesus. Brown maintains that the virginal conception stories of Matthew and Luke are in effect creation stories.

> [T]he Spirit that comes upon Mary is closer to the Spirit of God that hovered over the waters before creation in Gen. 1:2. The earth was void and without form when that Spirit appeared; just so Mary's womb was a void until through the Spirit God filled it with a child who was His Son. (1993: 314)

> [The virginal conception] was an extraordinary action of God's creative power, as unique as the original creation itself (and that is why all natural science objections to it are irrelevant, e.g., that not having a human father, Jesus' genetic structure would be abnormal). (1993: 531)

7. See Feuerbach (1957: 70–73 and 293–297).

However, if this fetal creation is *ex nihilo*, as Brown's references to Genesis 1 imply, then Jesus is no more Mary's natural son than he is Joseph's. Mary provides nothing more than a surrogate womb ("a void") in which the divinely created embryo gestates. An extreme form of this view may be suggested in the Valentinian Gospel of Philip 17: "Some say Mary was impregnated by the Holy Spirit. They err. They do not know what they say. When did a woman become pregnant by a woman? Mary is the virgin whom no power corrupted" (Cartlidge and Dungan 1980: 65). This passage apparently reflects the view that the Holy Spirit is female, and it also hints that Jesus is not at all human. In order to counter that heretical possibility, the creation analogy must be modified with help from Genesis 2 to describe Jesus as a second Adam, created when the divine breath/spirit blows over the molded dust of Mary's genetic material (an "earth … without form"). Luke's Jesus is then the son of Mary in the same way that Adam is the son of "mother earth," and Jesus is the second Adam.[8] Luke's genealogy even traces Jesus back to "Adam, the son of God" (3:38).

Both the christological tradition and the Christian canon of the scriptures encourage readers to weave together the gospels of Luke, John, and Matthew, so that each gospel complements and supplements the others, and in order to comprehend the god-man. Interpretation of Luke's Christmas story intertextually with the Genesis creation stories is also encouraged by the canon and by Christian theology. It is likely that the Christian canon was adopted (insofar as one can say that it was ever adopted) in the fourth century CE, at about the same time that the god-man concept became part of the church's confession, and this is probably not a coincidence. Canon and christology reinforce one another, and both play important roles in the imperial successes of "orthodox" Christianity and the Gospel of Jesus Christ.

The Rat-Man

Nevertheless, the ideological failure of traditional theological and philosophical categories in the modern world has been accompanied by the intertextual failure of the canon, as I noted in Chapter 1. The Bible's authority as the Word of God is fading away. The two creation stories of Genesis 1 and 2–3 do not neatly complement one another, and they also do not suffice to explain to the modern reader how Mary could get pregnant without intercourse. Anyone who pays careful attention to the Christmas

---

8. See Romans 4–5 and 1 Corinthians 15, as well as Schaberg (1987: 122); Dunn (1980: 254–255); and Boyarin (1994: 269, n. 44).

stories becomes aware of irreconcilable differences between the gospels of Matthew and Luke, and for all their possible compatibility, Luke and John do not tell the same incarnation story. Luke lacks any hint of John's idea of the pre-existence of the divine being who becomes incarnate, and John does not describe specifically how the Word becomes flesh. This further challenges the reader's understanding of the biblical texts.

Although the narrative worlds (the reality effects) of the four gospels are not the same, each of them is consistent for the most part with the ordinary, everyday world of the reader's experience, what J. R. R. Tolkien calls the "primary world" (see Chapter 4). Most of the characters in the biblical gospels are realistic characters, who talk and act much like people do in the everyday primary world, and the same is true for most of the events and the settings of those events. These reality effects are not identical to reality, but they reflect readers' beliefs about reality. They are constructed illusions, virtualities, the products of ideology. The exercise and degree of realism varies from one gospel to another, but their narrative worlds are not by and large fantastical "secondary worlds" inhabited by goblins, dragons, or unicorns, or by extra-terrestrial aliens, and even though direct appearances of God or other supernatural beings interrupt their realism, they are precisely that: interruptions from a marvelous other-world.

Luke's narrative realism leads the reader to expect that the events that occur in its story, no matter how unusual, can be explained in terms of her understanding of the primary world. The contemporary difficulty in comprehending the god-man appears in the problem of reconciling the realistic qualities that dominate most of Luke's gospel with supernatural elements of its Christmas story. In contrast, ancient readers of the gospel of Luke lived in a primary world considerably different from ours, a world in which gods, demons, and other supernatural beings played important everyday roles, including mating with human beings. The ideology reflected in their beliefs about the world made credible the traditional christological formulas. Such readers might have little difficulty in fitting Luke's Christmas story with its account of human-divine intercourse into a realistic narrative context, for such was their "reality."

For modern readers, working with quite a different ideology, the "fit" of such other-worldly interruptions presents a serious problem. To such readers, the Christmas events, and especially the miraculous conception of Jesus, appear to be contrary to their beliefs about reality. Additional marvelous interruptions of reality appear in several other stories in the gospel of Luke, most notably the transfiguration of Jesus (Lk. 9:28–36) and his resurrection from the dead (Luke 24), and these are similarly problematic. Jesus's healing miracles may also present difficulties, and the references to demons, but at least some of these stories might be given natural explanations, although whether they should be so explained is another question.

The attempts that were described above to clarify the virginal conception story within traditional canonical structures are at best only as strong as the biblical canon. At the same time, the modern disintegration of the canon allows texts such as the gospel of Luke to drift away from their biblical context into new and fluid juxtapositions with extra-biblical texts, giving rise to intertextual tensions that allow readers to understand them in ways other than they had previously. New intertextual configurations produce new understandings, readings of the biblical stories that often stand outside of or even contrary to the ideologies of believing communities, even as they also illuminate the extra-canonical texts in strange and suggestive ways.

One way to understand such stories is to regard them as fairy tales or fantasies. In such stories the need for rational or scientific explanation of bizarre events is suspended, and the withholding of explanation becomes itself an important feature of the story.[9] One such alternative understanding of the Christmas story, and the consequent belief that Jesus is the son of God, appears when the gospel of Luke is brought into play with China Miéville's urban fantasy novel, *King Rat* (1998). The narrative world of Miéville's story is what Gilles Deleuze calls "originary": "the originary world only appears when the invisible lines which divide up the real, which dislocate modes of behaviour and objects, are supercharged, filled out and extended" (1986: 124). The story achieves at points a dream-like quality, not unlike stories by Mervyn Peake or Franz Kafka. A similar oneiric quality appears at various points in Luke's gospel, and Mary's encounter with Gabriel would certainly be one instance. Nevertheless, despite these fabulous overtones, the narrative world of *King Rat* and most of the characters living in that world are realistic, much as they are in Luke.

In Miéville's novel, the traditional tale of the Pied Piper of Hamelin is retold from the rats' standpoint. According to Miéville's story, the Piper is not simply the Ratcatcher who saves the townsfolk of Hamelin from a plague of rats, and who then takes the town's children away with him when the citizens renege on their agreement to pay him. Instead of the traditional story, or in addition to it, the Pied Piper of *King Rat* is a supernaturally evil being who is able to lure and catch whatever living creatures he wants with

---

9. See further Aichele (2006: 15–58).

seductive flute music. Hearing his music, the creatures enter a trance state in which they dance themselves to death. "Pete" the Piper is "the Lord of the Dance" (Miéville 1998: 188); he is the Devil.

Standing opposed to the Ratcatcher is the King of the Rats, along with his allies, Anansi and Loplop, the respective rulers of the spiders and the birds. Mention is also made of the leaders of various other species – including "Mr Bub, the Lord of the Flies" (Miéville 1998: 134, alluding to 2 Kgs 1:2–3) – but these characters do not appear in the story. Miéville describes these bizarre characters as "animal archetypes" (Morgan 2001), but they are neither noetic structures nor Platonic forms. Nor are they transcendent, disembodied spirits. Instead, they are finite deities transplanted from various fairy tales and nursery rhymes into the modern, secular, urban world.

Like his supernatural colleagues, the rat king is not just another one of his species. He is formed more like a man than a rat, but he is also not a human being, and he displays distinctly rat-like characteristics and abilities. Timothy Beal observes that the vampire Orlok, in F. W. Murnau's film, *Nosferatu*, appears primarily as "a human rodent with rat teeth, pointed ears, and ever-growing fingernails dangling from arms that he holds in front of himself like paws" (2002: 143). This is a fitting description of King Rat (compare Miéville 1998: 29–30). Like the rat king, vampires are supernatural parasites, and both rats and vampires are strongly associated with plague.

King Rat possesses strength and powers beyond those of any natural rat or human. He is the rat God. He is also a physical being – that is, King Rat and his supernatural allies have not temporarily "assumed" semi-anthropomorphic bodies, to be discarded later, as in ancient stories about divine incarnations and avatars. They are not materializations of beings that are "really" non-physical. Instead, they are completely and permanently embodied. Although he is very old ("I was here when London was born," Miéville 1998: 125), King Rat is also evidently mortal. He too was subject to the Piper's musical enchantment on that fateful day in Hamelin,[10] but he was able to free himself at the last moment, just in time to watch hundreds of his rat subjects dance themselves to death under the influence of the enchanting flute music. Because he survived without saving them, the rats regard their king as a failure and a traitor, and they have turned

10. Miéville (1998: 127–131). The Pied Piper story may have some basis in medieval plague outbreaks in Europe. The town of Hameln in Germany claims to be the site of the event, which allegedly occurred on June 26, 1284. For information on this story, see Kuhn (2009). See also Barthes (1985: 211).

away from him. The rat kingdom has failed, not because of a foreign conqueror, but because the rats have rejected their God.

This failure on his part consumes King Rat. He has lived for hundreds of years in the knowledge that he was unable to save the Hamelin rats from the Piper. It seems that there is nothing that he can do about the situation, for the Piper's power to overwhelm even the king's rat sensibilities is absolute. Finally, the rat king realizes that the Piper can play only one tune at a time, and since each species requires its own, distinct tune of enchantment, this means that he can overcome only one species at a time. King Rat forcibly rapes a human woman, and the resulting child possesses both human nature and rat nature. This child is a straightforward, albeit miraculous, hybrid of two genetic strands: a rat-man, both fully man and fully rat. He will be able to defeat the Piper, for if the Piper plays a rat-seducing tune, then the rat-man's human nature will be impervious to it, and if the Piper plays a human-seducing tune, his rat nature will be unaffected (Miéville 1998: 134, 146). In contrast to the imperial god-man of Constantinian Christianity, Miéville's rat-man comes close to the post-colonial concept of "hybridity."[11]

The rat-man is named Saul Garamond. The biblical connotations of Saul's first name play no explicit part in Miéville's story, but the story would be a different one if the rat messiah did not share the name of the first "anointed one" of Israel. Saul appears to be human, and he grows up believing that he is a human being like any other. Saul's (unnamed) mother dies giving birth to him, and he is raised in a kind but somewhat distant manner by her husband (also unnamed), whom Saul believes to be his father. This man knows that Saul is a child of rape, but he does not know about Saul's rat heritage. Only after his human father also dies – murdered by King Rat – does Saul discover who his true father is.

His human father's murder triggers Saul's first meeting with King Rat. When the rat king comes to recruit Saul for the fight with the Piper, he has to reveal the truth. The revelation of his true identity and his true father is profoundly disturbing to Saul. He despises this monstrous being who raped his mother and destroyed the happiness and eventually the life of his human father, but at this point his own rat-powers begin to emerge. From then on, Saul's rat nature is continually at war with his human nature. This conflict between his two natures cripples him, but it also frees him from the Piper's

---

11. See Bhabha (1994). Hybrid mixtures of human beings with other living things, including beetles, frogs, cacti, lobsters, eagles, and mosquitos, appear in several of Miéville's more recent novels, *Perdido Street Station*, *The Scar*, and *Iron Council* (2000, 2002, 2004).

control: "I'm not rat plus man, get it? I'm bigger than either one *and I'm bigger than the two*. I'm a new thing" (Miéville 1998: 301, his emphasis). The rats venerate Saul and regard him as their true king, the son of God, and he shares their disdain for King Rat.

However, King Rat has taken too long to implement his plan, and technology has caught up with him. Miéville's story is set in contemporary London, where electronic recording and production of music have become well known. The Piper knows about Saul, and in his efforts to destroy him, he kills or kidnaps several of Saul's friends, including Natasha Karadjian, a popular musician who creates and performs by recording multiple "tracks" that play simultaneously, using sophisticated digital synthesizers and recording devices. From her, the Piper learns how to record multiple flute tunes to be played at the same time, tunes that when combined will seduce several different species at once (Miéville 1998: 293). In this way he hopes to be able to overcome and destroy the rat-man.

Material Christology

Yvonne Sherwood's summary of the "afterlives" of the book of Jonah in modern poetry applies rather well to *King Rat's* transformation of the gospel of Luke: "The book is still discernible in the shadows, but is radically re-sorted almost beyond recognition" (2000: 173). Like Luke's resurrected Jesus simulacrum (24:16), this metamorphosed story may be hard for readers to recognize at first. Miéville's novel does not translate Luke, but instead it transfigures that gospel. As Theodore Ziolkowski says about "fictional transfigurations" of Jesus:

> In all these cases ... the structure of action establishes the parallel between the original source and the modern counterpart: the meaning can range from a serious reinterpretation to the most blatant parody. (1972: 8)

Ziolkowski also notes that "the parallels are essentially formal, not ideological." Nevertheless, the intertextual tensions between these two texts bring to light ideological factors in the reading of Luke, and especially presuppositions that the reader brings to that text.

Miéville's story serves as a re-mythologizing of Luke's gospel, recycling that gospel outside of the biblical canon, just as Pasolini's movie, *The Gospel According to St Matthew*, effectively removes the gospel of Matthew from the biblical canon, although using very different techniques (see Chapter 3). *King Rat* narrates merely one of many contemporary afterlives of Luke's Christmas story, differing flows of semiosis. Thereby Miéville's novel creates the story of Luke as one of its precursors, in the sense that Jorge Luis Borges says that Franz Kafka's texts create his precursors: "In each of these texts we find Kafka's idiosyncrasies to a greater or lesser degree, but if Kafka had never written a line, we would not perceive this quality; in other words, it would not exist" (1964: 201). There is no reason to think that Miéville is deliberately resituating, rewriting, or referencing Luke, any more than Kafka was necessarily aware of his precursors. There is no mention at all of Christianity or of Christ, except as an expletive (for example, Miéville 1998: 165).[12] Nevertheless, numerous intertextual tensions between *King Rat* and Luke "translate" the troublesome ancient god-man concept into a contemporary secular form.

The gospel of Luke's Jesus is godlike. His power to perform miracles and "mighty works" (19:37) is not unlike that of the "immortals" of Greek and Roman legend (Schaberg 1987: 140). He can even transfer power to his followers (Lk. 9:1, 10:1–17). God seems to awaken the supernatural power of his "beloved Son" at his baptism (3:22), but Jesus's power was apparently given to him at his conception, aligning him with God through "holy spirit" (1:35, see also 2:49). Likewise, Saul's supernatural rat father must awaken him to his rat-powers. Saul also has power to do things beyond the ability of a normal man or rat, and it appears that he too has received this power at conception. Whether he will live for hundreds of years, like his father, is unknown.

Luke's Jesus simulacrum announces the arrival of the "kingdom of God," a realm in which he will play a crucial role as the Son of his divine Father (10:21–22, 22:29–30, see also 1:31–33).[13] This kingdom is "in the midst of you" (17:21), but also still to come (19:11–27). Like God, King Rat rules a kingdom, which consists of the cities of this world (Miéville 1998: 159, 172). His abode in the sewers of London is even described as a "cathedral," complete with a throne (1998: 89). However, although Saul eventually obeys the will of the rat king, it is for reasons of his own and in constant hostility to his supernatural father. Furthermore, this hostility is mutual: King Rat has sired his hybrid son solely as a weapon, to be sacrificed in order to destroy the Piper, and so that he can reclaim his former power over his rat subjects – that is, for his own salvation. He has no desire to pass the kingdom on to his son, or to rule it with him.

---

12. Nevertheless, other Miéville stories and novels indicate that he is familiar with the Bible and Christian thought.
13. Compare Mt. 11:25–27, 19:28. On the relation of Mark's Jesus simulacrum to the kingdom of God, see Chapter 4.

The gospel of Luke's Jesus simulacrum is described as a "friend of tax-collectors and sinners" (7:34), but this is presented as an insult, and whether he has any friends at all, even among his disciples, is unclear. In contrast, although Saul is followed blindly by hordes of rat disciples (Miéville 1998: 162–169), it is his connections to human friends, Natasha Karadjian and Fabian Morris, that become decisive factors in his decision to confront the Piper. Saul is even willing to "lay down his life for his friends" – a phrase that does not appear in Luke, but instead in John 15:13 – and although he does not die, he endures great sufferings for them. In other words, Saul's self-sacrifice has nothing to do with the will of his divine father (contrast Lk. 22:42).

Luke's Jesus simulacrum rejects Satan's temptations (4:1–13), and he announces the defeat of Satan: "I saw Satan fall like lightning from heaven" (10:18). Jesus's conflict with Satan is an ongoing topic in the gospel of Luke (10:19–20, 11:18–20, 13:16, 22:3, 31). The Piper never tries to tempt Saul, but he mesmerizes Saul's friend, Natasha. Thanks to the "dissonance" between his two natures, Saul is able to resist the Piper's multi-track melodies (Miéville 1998: 299–300), and accompanied by armies of rats and spiders fired with "millennial fervor" (1998: 255), he leads a cataclysmic battle against the Piper, culminating in the evil one's descent into hell.

However, the most important intertextual tensions between the gospel of Luke and the novel concern the relationship between Jesus or Saul and their respective parents, both human and divine. When King Rat rapes Saul's mother, it is a physical, sexual act, not unlike ancient polytheistic stories of gods with human or animal bodies who rape human women. The Piper and the rat king, like the other animal deities in *King Rat*, are all splendidly physical, fully embodied, and disturbingly human beings. In this respect, they are reminiscent of other recent superhuman heroes, such as Superman or Buffy the vampire slayer, as well as many of the champions of antiquity. They are not non-material spirits. Indeed, the only hint of "spirit" in *King Rat* appears in the physical breath that the Piper expends while playing his enchanting flute music, and in the title of the music that he and Natasha compile, "Wind City" (Miéville 1998: 150, 208–210), which nearly leads to his triumph over Saul.

Like Saul's mother, Luke's Mary simulacrum has been raped by a god (or his angelic delegate). Mary's impregnation is a physical act. Angels in the Bible are often explicitly physical as well as godlike beings – for example, the "man" (often described as an angel but also implied to be God) with whom Jacob wrestles in Gen. 32:22–32. In Lk. 1:35, the angel Gabriel speaks of a holy spirit (or breath, or wind) that "comes upon" Mary. The phrase, "come upon," in this verse translates a term, *epeleusetai*, that has negative overtones in Lk. 11:22, 21:26, 35, and Acts 8:24, 13:40. If this "spirit" is more physical than Christians usually allow, or indeed if it is Gabriel himself as an embodied being, then the gospel of Luke's birth account resembles the pagan stories of divine rape. Brown denies that such stories have anything to do with the Christmas stories (1993: 523), but Schaberg is not willing to rule out this similarity, although she holds that Jesus's biological father is a human rapist (1987: 121–127, 194).

The gospel of Luke describes Mary's initial reaction to the angel's words as deeply confounded, troubled, or confused (*dietarachthē*, 1:29). Brown notes Mary's reluctance but insists that she consents to the pregnancy at Lk. 1:38 and that conception occurs only after her consent (1993: 306, 406), and Schaberg appears to agree (1987: 131–132). This implies that God has given Mary a choice, and that she could have declined the pregnancy. But what choice does Mary have? In the nine verses between her initial confusion at the angel's greeting and her statement of compliance as "the handmaid of the Lord" (1:38), she speaks only briefly, again stating confusion and perhaps even refusal: "How shall this be, since I have no husband?" (1:34).

The initial concern and reluctance of Luke's Mary when the angel addresses her suggest that her impregnation is not voluntary. The Holy Spirit (or Gabriel) forces itself upon her, overwhelming her. Schaberg observes that Luke's avoidance of "themes of a woman's anger, struggle, and protest, in favor of the themes of protection, trust, and gratitude can be judged to confine the character of Mary in a personal powerlessness that only God can break" (1987: 143). Gabriel does not ask for her permission, for God's offers are unrefusable, as he even says: "with God nothing will be impossible" (1:37). How significant then is Mary's consent? Indeed, it is surprising that the gospel of Luke describes Mary's concerns at all. Perhaps if she were not unwilling, that would be unseemly – as though this scene were not already unseemly enough!

Both Zechariah (John the Baptist's father) and Mary are "greatly troubled" by their respective meetings with Gabriel at the beginning of the gospel of Luke, and both of them are told, "do not be afraid" (*mē phobou*, 1:12–13, 29–30). However, Zechariah and perhaps his wife, Elizabeth, have apparently been praying for a child. Mary, as an unwed virgin, presumably has not. Zechariah is also not as troubled as Mary. Both Zechariah and Elizabeth respond positively to the angel's announcement of the miraculous conception of John (1:11–25), but in their case Zechariah is the child's biological father ("Elizabeth will bear *you* a son," 1:13, emphasis added), not God. In contrast, Mary is presumably not barren and thus differs considerably from Elizabeth as well as from Hannah, the prophet Samuel's mother, in the similar scene in 1 Samuel 1. Therefore, although Mary's language echoes Hannah's, as Elizabeth's does, the meaning of her words is quite different. Schaberg notes the suggestion of ominous power in Lk. 1:35, and she hints at the thought that God might be an oppressor in this scene, in the parallel that she draws to the story of Hagar in Genesis 16 (1987: 107, 112–114, see also 135). Nevertheless, on the whole, Schaberg views God as Mary's defender.[14]

Luke's Mary simulacrum eventually acquiesces to the angel's announcement (1:38), and a bit later she welcomes her extra-marital pregnancy with enthusiasm, in a surreal scene with Elizabeth (1:46–55). Nevertheless, the gospel of Luke also tells the reader later, twice, that "Mary kept all these things, pondering them in her heart" (2:19, 51). Saul's mother also decides to bring her pregnancy to term and to keep the initially unwanted child, despite her husband's concerns (Miéville 1998: 182), but she dies in childbirth, and her husband's knowledge of Saul's conception in an act of rape stands as a painful barrier between him and his son. In Mt. 1:18–21, Joseph's response to the news that his betrothed is pregnant by another father bears some resemblance to Saul's father's reaction to his wife's rape and pregnancy. However, Luke's Joseph simulacrum makes no response at all to Mary's extra-marital pregnancy. Joseph is mentioned five times in Luke's story, but with no suggestion that his paternal relation to Jesus might be affected by the fact that Mary's pregnancy was caused by another.

The Estranged Son

Indeed, in the gospel of Luke there is no indication that the relationship between Jesus and Joseph is troubled by anything like the distance between Saul Garamond and his human father. Schaberg notes a similar problem in relation to Mary (1987: 143). Likewise, there is no tension between Jesus and God in Luke's gospel, in sharp contrast to the bitter relationship between Saul Garamond and King Rat in Miéville's novel. God lays claim to Luke's Jesus simulacrum at his baptism, by way of the Holy Spirit (3:21–22), much as he has previously laid claim to Mary (1:28, 30). God's claim on Jesus is repeated during the transfiguration (9:35), and perhaps once more on the

14. See also Daly (1978: 85).

Mount of Olives (22:43–44[15]), in the latter case through an angel, as with Mary.

King Rat also repeatedly lays claim to Saul, but Saul is constantly tormented by the truth of his own identity. Because Luke's Jesus is not so tormented, Luke's God simulacrum is much more effective than the rat king in obtaining his son's acquiescence. God vindicates and rescues Jesus, raising him first from the dead, and then to heaven (Lk. 24:51; Acts 1:9), and this post-mortem vindication emphasizes the divine side of Jesus's heritage. Saul is also rescued by his supernatural father in the climactic confrontation with the Piper, but this action does nothing to reduce the hostility between them. Saul even describes the rat king as a "Judas" (Miéville 1998: 310).[16]

Luke's references to Jesus's mother and human father contrast in significant ways to the other gospels. The gospel of Mark's Jesus simulacrum is described as the "son of Mary" (6:3), hinting that he was regarded as a bastard whose father was unknown. Similar views are suggested in the gospel of Thomas's saying 105, Jn 8:41, the *Acts of Pilate*, the writings of Celsus, and the Talmud and other rabbinic writings.[17] Some sources suggest that Jesus's father was a Roman soldier whose name (or nickname) was Pantera. This supports Schaberg's argument that the Christmas stories are cover-ups for a human rape that was embarrassing to early Christians. Schaberg denies that Luke's Mary is at fault in her pregnancy (1987: 119). In contrast, in a modern version of the Pantera stories, the movie *Monty Python's Life of Brian* (Jones 1979) portrays the mother of Brian (who is a parody of Jesus) as a Jewish prostitute whose customers were Roman soldiers.[18]

For the gospel of Mark, there is no Joseph simulacrum and there is no Christmas story or other account of Jesus's origin. Those who do the will of God may be the mother, brother, or sister of Mark's Jesus simulacrum, but

15. These verses are missing from the oldest manuscripts of Luke. See further below.
16. These themes are also linked in Miéville's short story, "The Tain": "Aghast, he had decided that he was chosen for something. For this. He granted himself authority to speak for his people. To surrender. Judas-messiah. ... *Perhaps this isn't why they leave me alone at all – what if the chosen one misunderstands what he's been chosen for?*" (2005: 300–301, Miéville's emphases).
17. Brown (1993: 534–542) surveys this material, as does Schaberg (1987: 156–178).
18. On multiple meanings given to "Mary" in early Christianity, see Shoemaker (2001: 555–595), and Gospel of Philip 32 (Cartlidge and Dungan 1980: 67). On the value of *Monty Python's Life of Brian* for biblical studies, see Davies (1998).

no father is mentioned in 3:35. Likewise, those who have suffered "for my sake and for the gospel" will receive "brothers and sisters and mothers," but again no father is mentioned, although "father" is included among those who have been abandoned in Mk 10:29–30.[19] Perhaps these are ways of suggesting that God is the only father of Jesus or of his followers, but Mark's gospel says nothing to encourage that idea (see further Chapter 4). Although Jesus speaks of an apparently divine "Father" in Mark, that Father appears to abandon him in the end (14:36, 15:34; see also 8:38, 11:25, 13:32).

In addition, the relation between the gospel of Mark's Jesus and his mother is troubled. In Mark 6:4, immediately after he is described as the son of Mary, Jesus says, "A prophet is not without honor, except ... among his own kin, and in his own house." Mark's Mary simulacrum may be present at the crucifixion and on Easter, if she is "Mary the mother of James the younger and of Joses" (15:40, 47, 16:1). However, she may also be among "his family" when they try to "seize" Jesus, thinking that he is crazy (3:21), and soon thereafter he rejects both her and his brothers in favor of "whoever does the will of God" (3:31–35). The gospel of Luke divides up these scenes and removes or at least reduces the familial conflict (8:19–21).

The gospel of John, like Luke, describes a Jesus simulacrum with two fathers, but Joseph almost disappears, being mentioned only twice and both times in passing (1:45, 6:42). In addition, John develops the relationship between its Jesus simulacrum and his divine Father much further than the other gospels (for example, 1:1–18, 10:25–30). God is by far the more significant of the two fathers of John's Jesus. Jesus's mother appears at the wedding in Cana (2:1–5, 12), in the question in 6:42, and with the beloved disciple at Jesus's crucifixion (19:25–27), but her name is never mentioned. Brown notes that the exchange between Jesus and his parents in Lk. 2:48–49 is comparable to Jesus's dialogue with his mother in Jn 2:3–4 (1993: 491).[20]

As is well known, the gospel of Matthew tells a Christmas story in which its Joseph simulacrum is the protagonist, and Luke tells a Christmas story in which its Mary simulacrum is the protagonist. Matthew mentions Joseph six times, and Matthew alone among the canonical gospels specifically describes Joseph's concern over Mary's premarital pregnancy and the supernatural events that are required to assuage his misgivings (1:19–25). Luke does not have anything like Matthew's story of the flight into Egypt (2:13–21), in which Joseph is instrumental, and with it the ominous story

19. See also Schaberg (1987: 162–163).
20. See also Brown (1993: 488, n. 29 and 491, n. 42).

of the slaughter of the innocents, with its overtones of divine violence reflected in the quote from Jeremiah. Matthew both maintains the dual paternity of its Jesus simulacrum, like Luke and John, and struggles more openly with the consequences of it than either Luke or John do. Matthew alone associates Mary, through Jesus's genealogy, with Old Testament precursors of dubious virtue: Tamar, Rahab, Ruth, and Bathsheba (1:3, 5, 6). In addition, Matthew's gospel says nothing about Mary's reaction to her pregnancy or about the birth of John the Baptist, both of which serve in Luke to elaborate the birth story. Matthew's Joseph is closer to Saul Garamond's father, in his relationship to his son, than Luke's Joseph is. Luke's Mary is closer to Saul's mother than Matthew's Mary, in her experience of forced impregnation.

Two non-canonical "infancy gospels" also suggest something like the gospel of Matthew's concern regarding the relationship between Jesus and Joseph, but in combination with features from Luke. The Protevangelium of James describes at considerable length Joseph's discomfort with Mary's pregnancy, as well as Mary's fear (9:2–14:2; see further Chapter 9). The Protevangelium also emphasizes the virginity of Mary, both after she has conceived (16:1–3) and again after she has given birth (19:3–20:1), as though there was some nervousness about the miraculous nature or non-natural causation of her impregnation. The apparent harmonization of Matthew's and Luke's Christmas stories in the Protevangelium serves to heighten the similarity between all three of these Christmas stories and *King Rat*.

The Infancy Gospel of Thomas does not narrate a Christmas story, but rather a number of stories about the relationship between Joseph and the young boy Jesus (Chapters 2–7 and 12–16).[21] Hints of anger and tension between Joseph and Jesus appear throughout that gospel (such as "Do you not know that I am yours? Do not vex me," from Jesus to Joseph in 5:3), but also stories of affection. These stories describe the behavior of a child who is truly superior to his human parents and other adults, including a story very similar to Lk. 2:42–49, Jesus's childhood visit to the Temple (Infancy Gospel of Thomas 19). Both of these infancy gospels emphasize supernatural Jesus simulacra with relatively little humanity, and the god-powers of each of these Jesuses become apparent at a very early age, or even at birth. The gospel of Luke shares the infancy gospels' interest in the pre-baptismal life of Jesus, but Luke's Jesus simulacrum displays no clear god-powers prior to his baptism.

---

21. The Infancy Gospel of Thomas and the Protevangelium of James may be found in Cartlidge and Dungan (1980: 92–97 and 107–117), and also Cameron (1982: 109–121 and 124–130).

In Miéville's novel, the alienation between Saul and his father results from the father's bitterness at the rape and death of his wife. It is a thoroughly human distance, unlike the distance between a god and a mortal being.[22] Similarly, the stories featuring Joseph simulacra in the infancy gospels and especially in the gospel of Matthew stand in striking contrast to Luke's silence regarding the impact of Mary's peculiar pregnancy on the relationship between Jesus and Joseph. It is a significant silence, perhaps even an embarrassed silence. That both Matthew and at least the Protevangelium of James note this issue indicates that this is not just a matter of modern sensibilities. Indeed, if Luke is to some degree a rewriting of Matthew's gospel (see further Chapter 8), this raises questions about why Luke would change the Christmas story in these ways. Both the tension between Luke and Miéville's story, and the contrast between Luke and the other gospels, suggest that Luke's narrative negates any thought that, as with Saul and his two fathers, Jesus's knowledge of his true paternity would permanently scar the relationship between Joseph and Jesus as well as the relationship between Jesus and God.

The gospel of Luke, like Matthew, says more about its Joseph simulacrum than either Mark or John, but Luke still says very little about him, and *King Rat*'s depiction of the strained relations between a father and his son highlights this deficiency. Joseph functions in Luke's story as nothing more than a stand-in for God, a father surrogate to forestall any hint of Jesus's illegitimacy (Schaberg 1987: 139). Joseph disappears from Luke's story after 2:50, although his name is mentioned in two further passages in which his paternal relation to Jesus is questioned (3:23, 4:22). In contrast, Luke's Mary simulacrum appears again at 8:19–20 and perhaps in the Easter story, if she is "Mary the mother of James" (24:10). Although Luke's Joseph is evidently present at Jesus's birth (2:6–7, 16), it is only Mary who keeps "all these things, pondering them in her heart" (2:19).

It is often assumed that Joseph was an older man when he married Mary, and that he died soon after Jesus was born, but Luke gives the reader no reason to think that. Indeed, that Mary's husband Joseph has died is not stated anywhere in the Bible. Perhaps God even kills Joseph, just as King Rat murders Saul's father, but Luke is silent about Joseph's fate, and the disappearance of this significant character remains unexplained

22. See Miéville (1998: 24–27). One of Freud's more famous patients was the "Rat Man," Ernst Lanzer, who was "plagued by powerful obsessions involving rats, torture, and punishment. Lanzer's obsessive acts and thoughts were traced to his deep ambivalence about sexuality and about *his father*" (Library of Congress WWW page 2009, emphasis added). See also Docker (2001: 159).

throughout Luke's story. The miraculous story of Jesus's virginal conception and birth in Luke's gospel masks the narrative effacement of Joseph. This disturbance is the narrative correlate of a theological difficulty.

Just as there is no indication in the gospel of Luke of any personal connection between Jesus and Joseph, so there is no hint of any resistance or tension between Jesus and God. Luke's Jesus alone among the canonical gospels' Jesus simulacra is evidently aware from very early in his life that Joseph is not his actual father, and he accepts his supernatural parentage without question (2:42–49). Luke simulates a Jesus who is not only unscarred by his divine paternity, but quite comfortable with it. Perhaps this Jesus is even less human than Christians claim, and more like the Jesus simulacra of the infancy gospels than is generally thought. Jesus's non-relationship with Joseph coheres closely with his complete acquiescence to God's will. He willingly becomes the god-man simulacrum that Saul Garamond refuses to be. In contrast to Saul, Luke's Jesus is completely possessed by the god who is his true Father, and he is unable (or unwilling) to seek his own way. Once again, Lk. 2:49 ("I must be in my [divine] Father's house") is a crucial text, a motto over Luke's entire gospel.[23]

Luke's Jesus simulacrum prays only once on the Mount of Olives (22:39–46), in contrast to the Jesus simulacra of Matthew and Mark, each of whom prays three times in Gethsemane, with the implied consequence that Luke's Jesus accepts his divinely-ordained suffering more willingly than either Matthew's or Mark's Jesus does. Prior to his death, Luke's Jesus is not "troubled" as the Jesuses of Mk 14:33 and Mt. 26:37 are; instead, in Lk. 22:45, it is the disciples who are sorrowful. Luke 22:43–44 describes "an angel from heaven, strengthening [Jesus]" while he prays. Jesus then continues his prayer "in an agony ... more earnestly" while sweating "great drops of blood." Once again, a dream-like quality appears. These verses do not appear in many ancient manuscripts of Luke, and they provide the only indication in Luke's passion narrative of any agonizing on the part of Jesus. Nothing like the angelic support or bloody sweat appears in either Matthew or Mark. Schaberg notes that the juxtaposition of the angel and Jesus's prayer to his "Father" mirrors Luke's conjunction at 1:35 between Gabriel and the holy spirit that overshadows Mary: "Jesus' agony facing death was one that Luke could openly write about; Mary's agony was one that he could not or would not" (1987: 135).

On the cross and again in contrast to the other two synoptic gospels, Luke's Jesus simulacrum is confident and attuned to his divine Father.

23. See Moore (1992: 121–123).

Only in the gospel of Luke does Jesus engage in conversation with one of the robbers with whom he is crucified, telling him that "today you will be with me in Paradise" (23:43), and only Luke's Jesus speaks the dying words: "Father, forgive them; for they know not what they do," and shortly thereafter, "Father, into thy hands I commit my spirit" (23:34, 46). In contrast, the Jesus simulacra of both Mk 15:34 and Mt. 27:46 cry out as their final words, "My God, my God, why hast thou forsaken me?," quoting Ps. 22:1. This phrase aptly describes Saul Garamond's estrangement from the rat king, although in the final showdown, King Rat does not abandon Saul.

The joint effect of these differences and of Luke's failure to address Jesus's relationship to Joseph is to suggest that nothing, not even excruciating death, disturbs this Jesus simulacrum's intimacy with his divine Father. They are in complete harmony, so closely aligned as to be nearly indistinguishable. As Jesus says, "he who rejects me rejects him who sent me" (Lk. 10:16). The relation in this statement is an exclusive one, in contrast to "he who receives me receives him who sent me" in both Mt. 10:40 and Jn 13:20.[24] Nevertheless, the intimacy suggested by Lk. 10:16 is not unlike the relation of John's Jesus simulacrum to God: "I and the Father are one" (10:30). Again there is a reciprocity between the gospels of Luke and John that neither shares with Matthew or Mark. This contributes to the logocentric reading of Luke described above.

Christological Fantasies

Miéville's novel, *King Rat*, describes a secondary world in which the physical and the spiritual are not separable. It is also a polytheistic world. Despite or perhaps because of its many gods, and in contrast to ancient polytheisms, Miéville's story inhabits a profoundly secular world, which is otherwise not at all unlike our primary world.[25] Nevertheless, the idea of multiple, finite, physical gods such as Pete the Piper, King Rat, and the others remains in the realm of the marvelous, and Miéville's rat-man may be no more plausible or even comprehensible to the modern scientifically-oriented reader than the god-man of Christian orthodoxy is. However, along with the canon and traditional, logocentric theologies, monotheism is on the wane in our contemporary world, and a polytheistic theology may be

24. See also Jn 12:45, as well as Mk 9:37 and Lk. 9:48, which are discussed further in Chapter 4.
25. Other recent fictions have also depicted similar blends of polytheism and modern secularity; for example, Gaiman (2003) and Phillips (2007).

appropriate to its fragmented realities and plural discourses.[26] Therefore this story may be less implausible than one might at first think.

The rat-man of Miéville's novel is not a Jesus simulacrum, but he is a secularized Christ, who sacrifices his own interests in order to save others. Saul Garamond is a material messiah, a mortal and permanently embodied god-man in a world that does not comprehend non-physical, transcendent spirit. Like the Christ simulacrum of the Chalcedonian formulation, Saul is the hybrid product of two contrary "natures," but unlike that formulation, both of those natures are physical and genetic, and they have been united in the only way that we can understand today.

The Christmas story is the first major episode in Luke's gospel, and it is arguably an important factor in the considerable popularity of that gospel among Christians.[27] In addition to taking up a large chunk of Luke's narrative (two of the 24 chapters), the birth story occupies a crucial contextual position at the beginning of the overall story, providing the frame through which the remainder of Luke is often read. Luke does not tell the reader why God chose to produce a half-human offspring, but the Christian understanding usually has something to do with God's love for human beings and his desire that humans be saved from the consequences of sin and for life everlasting in a better world after death. However, Luke's Jesus simulacrum does not say anything like this (but see instead 1:69, 77, 2:11, 30–32, 3:6), although some of the apostles' speeches in Acts tend to develop along these lines.

In stark contrast, *King Rat* suggests that only a god-man could successfully avoid Satan's traps, and that a christological union of two biological natures (that is, a genetic hybrid) might be the only way for God to counter Satan's powers over both divine and human beings. In other words, the birth of the incarnate messiah does not result from divine grace or benevolence, but from God's own struggle to survive. Even gods (and devils) are finite, physical beings. In this light, the gospel of Luke's temptation stories (4:1–13) take on a rather different meaning, as does Jesus's boast that he "saw Satan fall" (10:18) and his betrayal by Judas (who has been possessed by Satan, 22:3). The incarnation of the divine Son does not then so much express God's love for humanity as it indicates that there

26. See Docker (2001). Docker notes that polytheism is anti-canonical (2001: 162, 168).

27. I have occasionally asked my New Testament students which is their favorite gospel, and why. Although I have not kept score over the years, the gospel of Luke is very likely the overall winner, at least among the synoptic gospels, and its Christmas story is a large part of the reason why.

is no limit to God's willingness to use human flesh as a weapon in his age-old war against his supernatural adversary.

Jane Schaberg notes that the possibility of rape in the Christmas stories is often overlooked, and she argues that Luke (and to a lesser extent, Matthew) seeks to mask the taint of illegitimacy associated with the earliest traditions of Jesus's birth (1987: 139, 194). If the gospel of Luke is read intertextually with *King Rat*, then it does indeed narrate a story of rape, but not a story of "natural ... human conception," as Schaberg claims (1987: 74). It is a story of divine rape, and its chief symptoms are Luke's description of Mary's fear and confusion in response to the angel's words – a description that hints at more than it tells – and Luke's non-discussion of Joseph's relationship with Jesus, including his non-reaction to Mary's illegitimate pregnancy. The novel makes explicit what the gospel does not. If Luke is the "gospel for the Gentiles," then one part of Luke's "message" would seem to be that the god of all humanity (probably a Gentile god, although his use of Gabriel as delegate may count against that) has raped a Jewish woman in order to produce a Jewish savior for the Gentiles.

The story of Saul Garamond's conception and birth, and his relationship to his human father, does not directly appear as a unit in *King Rat*. Saul's human father is dead before Miéville's story has begun, but he lives on in Saul's thoughts. His story takes up very little space in the novel, and the reader only gradually becomes aware of it. It appears in retrospective bits and pieces through a scrapbook/diary that Saul's father kept (Miéville 1998: 179–184) as well as in the thoughts and words of Saul, the rat king, and even the Piper. Thus Saul's birth story and his father's story do not serve the same framing function in Miéville's novel that the Christmas story does in the gospel of Luke. Nevertheless, the intertextual play between the stories highlights a profound and disturbing, albeit unwritten, tension at the core of Luke's Christmas story, between Jesus's physical, human father and his spiritual, divine Father. According to Luke's gospel and *King Rat*, read together, there is no place for the human father, who is anyway only the apparent father (3:23), in the work of the true, divine Father and his Son.

The relation between Luke's gospel and *King Rat* is a complex one, featuring significant similarities and dissimilarities. The novel frees the reader from the theological need to identify Luke's one true meaning, and thus it problematizes the idea of "the meaning of Luke." The contrast with the novel also demonstrates that Luke's meaning is determined by its reading context. The gospel of Luke's canonical context in the New Testament, and its juxtaposition there with Matthew and especially John, as well as with Paul's "gospel," has contributed substantially to the traditional Christian concept of the god-man.

The reading lens provided by Miéville's novel opens up an anti-Luke, a non-synoptic, non-Christian gospel that was invisible until Miéville's story "created" Luke as its precursor, resurrecting Luke's story into a secular afterlife beyond the Christian canon. *King Rat* presents the reader with a noncanonical "christological fantasy"[28] or fictional transfiguration of Jesus that stands in significant contrast to the Christian reading of Luke's story. However, it is only possible to read a book such as *King Rat* in tandem with the gospel of Luke if that gospel has already been torn away from the rest of the Bible, and from all of the familiar interpretations that the canonical intertext had helped to attach to it. Freed from the semiotic controls that are provided by the biblical canon and traditional creeds of Christianity, Luke acquires an entirely different meaning.

---

28. The term "christological fantasy" is used by Borges (1962: 106) in reference to his own story, "Three Versions of Judas." See also Aichele 2005: 45-49.

Chapter 6

John Simulates the Anti-simulacrum: Reading Jesus' Writing

Sense appears and is played out at the surface (at least if one knows how to mix it properly) in such a way that it forms letters of dust. It is like a fogged-up window pane on which one can write with one's finger. (Deleuze 1990: 133)

It is comparatively easy at present for the commentator to treat the most widely available text as "virtually John." This is because a single coherent form of text has been chiselled out of the available materials, and the variations from it reduced to a heap of fragments lying at its feet. (D. Parker 2003: 404)

The Word and the World

The gospel of John opens with a hymn that sings the incarnation of the divine Word of light in the midst of the dark, ignorant world (1:1–18), in what is perhaps the closest that any of the gospels comes to what I call in this book the Gospel of Jesus Christ (but see also 3:16–17). It then proceeds to an extended climax during which John's Jesus simulacrum is "lifted up from the earth [in order to] draw all men to myself" (12:32), and then on to a concluding scene in which Jesus as the risen Lord gives final instructions ("feed my lambs, ... tend my sheep, ... follow me," 21:15–19) to his closest disciples, who will from then on be accompanied by "the Spirit of truth, ... [who] dwells with you and will be in you" (14:16–17). From beginning to end, John's gospel presents itself as a "fabric of signs" that has been "preceded by a truth, or a meaning already constituted by and within the element of the logos" (Derrida 1981: 104).[1] John is surely one of the most explicitly logocentric texts ever written.

---

1. Compare Jn 20:30–31, which is discussed further below. See also Moore (1994: 29–31) and Staley (1999: 127–154, especially 130). Moore's book is particularly important in relation to the topic of this chapter. Boyarin (1994) presents a similar, although much more detailed, analysis of logocentrism in the letters of Paul.

This logocentrism is evident throughout the gospel's text: John uses the Greek words, *sēmeion* ("sign") and *logos* ("word"), considerably more than any other biblical gospel. The supernatural Word incarnate in John's Jesus is the pre-textual logos (both in the Greek of John's text and in Jacques Derrida's terminology). That is, this *logos* is both an eternal referent and the *archē* ("beginning," 1:1)[2] to which John's narrative signs (both tales of Jesus's miracles and records of his sayings) continually point. In Derrida's writings, the *archē* is the original, underlying unity from and against which difference arises, and from which all meaning and value derives, according to the onto-theology that has dominated Western thought since Plato. Along with other poststructuralist thinkers such as Gilles Deleuze, Jean-François Lyotard, and Roland Barthes, Derrida has sought to deconstruct this way of thinking, or in other words, to show the precedence of difference over unity, and therefore of the simulacrum over every supposed *archē* or model. In this chapter a similar analysis is applied to the gospel of John.

Throughout the gospel of John an opposition between the mundane and transcendental realms is stressed. The divine Word to which John refers in its prologue does not ever belong to the material, earthly world, but merely passes through it. John's Jesus also utters statements such as

- "He who comes from above is above all; he who is of the earth belongs to the earth, and of the earth he speaks; he who comes from heaven is above all" (3:31).
- "I glorified thee on earth, having accomplished the work which thou gavest me to do; and now, Father, glorify thou me in thy own presence with the glory which I had with thee before the world was made" (17:4–5).

John describes the transfer of the Word from the supernatural world to the natural one, and back again. However, this transfer is a dynamically equivalent translation of the Word, to steal a phrase from the translation studies of Eugene Nida[3] and others, a linguistic transformation in which the spiritual connotations of the eternal Word remain fundamentally undisturbed despite that Word's temporary immersion is signifying matter.

As the incarnation of the Word, John's Jesus simulacrum remains in constant contact with his heavenly Father, the God who is (in) the *archē* of "all things" (1:1–3), and although this Jesus is a fleshy conduit through which God's message is mediated to the human world, there is no distortion

---

2. The Greek word *archē* also initiates Mark's gospel (1:1), but there it does not signify anything transcendental. See further Aichele (2006: 85–104).
3. For example, Nida and Taber (1982).

or static on the line. From the "Olympian perspective" of John's gospel (Staley 1988: 50), the semiotic channel is open and clear, and the message gets through: the translation is accurate and reliable because the meaning (or spirit) is what counts, not the fleshy medium, which is always insignificant for dynamic equivalence. Some recipients may not understand, but the one "who has written these things" (21:24) always understands. If the divine message should fail to reach its human recipients in perfect condition, the fault must lie in those recipients, not in the sender or the semiotic medium. John's Jesus says that "Blessed are those who have not seen and yet believe" (20:29). Those who fail to believe (whether or not they have seen) may not be blessed.

This transfer between worlds is a fantastic one, for what Jn 1:5 calls "the darkness" is very much like the everyday, human world in which we live. It simulates what J. R. R. Tolkien calls the "primary world" (1966: 60). In contrast, the supernatural world of the *archē* is what Tolkien calls a "secondary world" – not secondary in the sense of less important or real, but in the sense that we can only understand it in terms of the primary world. As the man Jesus, the incarnate Word occupies a place in the primary, physical world, but as John frequently emphasizes (for example, 17:14, 16), Jesus never really belongs to this world. Because John's divine Word originates in the supernatural world and eventually returns to it, it is necessarily utopian. This utopianism defines the reality effect of the gospel of John.

This fantastic aspect of the gospel of John[4] draws heavily on the use of irony. To the two worlds or levels of reality correspond two levels of meaning. According to Paul Duke, in John's gospel, "Two worlds have collided in the coming of Jesus, and the inevitable result is the clash of opposition called irony" (1985: 111). Duke describes John's irony as "a *literary device* ... that is used not purely for pleasure or negation but for positive purpose" (1985: 3, his emphasis; see also 100–107). Indeed, John's "literary techniques grow out of and lead back into the philosophical/theological dualism at the heart of the Gospel's thought" (1985: 142).

I agree, but I add that in John's story only the primary world (the "darkness") is simulated directly (through both denotation and connotation). Insofar as the secondary world – the divine world which in John is indeed the more important one and perhaps even the only real one (compare Tolkien 1966: 88–89) – appears at all, it is only through highly

---

4. I discuss the fantastic in the gospel of John somewhat further in Aichele (2006: 75–81, 87–88, 160, and 230–231). I discuss Tolkien's fantasy theory in (2006: 15–30). See also Chapter 4 of this book.

connotative metaphorical or symbolic language, such as "*archē*" or "the light," language which includes irony among various other literary devices. Its simulation is therefore indirect and sometimes obscure. This is crucial to the reality effect of John, and it contrasts to a great deal of fantasy literature (including Tolkien's own Middle Earth stories) in which the secondary world is directly depicted in very explicit and concrete ways, and the primary world is only rarely or indirectly depicted or even not at all.[5] Thus contrary to Duke's claim, the "literary vision" of the gospel of John is not truly "bilevel" (1985: 142). The reader does not "see" John's secondary world nearly as clearly as she sees the primary one.

According to Duke, the gospel of John's irony arises in relation to the simulation of Jesus's identity (1985: 48), and the reader understands this well: "The numerous ironic silences of the Gospel and its rich suggestiveness of language seem to presuppose an audience at least partially conditioned to this mode of expression" (1985: 147, see also 154–155). Thus "Johannine irony is largely an in-house affair" (1985: 151). Despite this, John's disciple simulacra – who should be "in the house" – do not understand, and the reader knows that even their seemingly-sincere words in 16:29–30 ("Ah, now you are speaking plainly, not in any figure! Now we know that you know all things, and need none to question you; by this we believe that you came from God"), which suggest that irony has ended, must themselves be understood ironically (Duke 1985: 57–58).

Duke compares John's simulation of the disciples' misunderstanding of Jesus to that in the gospel of Mark (1985: 60). However, in order for irony to function as a literary device, there can be no dissonance or tension between the implied reader of the narrative and its implied author; I take this to be what Duke means by an "in-house affair." Both the implied reader and the implied author are products of the actual reader's experience of the text (reality effects), and therefore even though irony is an effect of the text, it only becomes "real" when the reader "gets it" – that is, when the virtuality of the story requires it. In other words, successful irony requires the clear transmission of a univocal message (a sort of dynamic equivalence): "an open door from appearance to reality," as Duke says (1985: 49). The gospel of John creates the illusion (reality effect) that the reader stands "above"

---

5. Tolkien vigorously rejected allegorical interpretations of his Middle Earth stories. However, in other cases, highly concrete depictions of a secondary world may themselves have strong symbolic connotations – for example, the fantasy writings of C. S. Lewis, which are often heavily allegorical. Nevertheless, in many cases they do not, or such connotations may be ignored without serious loss – as in *The Wizard of Oz* or *Peter Pan*.

the disciples, closer to the the the secondary world, and thus closer to "the light" – Jesus himself, the divine Word – and it repeatedly stresses the success of its own transmission of the truth. Whether the actual reader "gets the message" may not always be sure, but the implied reader always gets it.

In contrast, Mk 13:14 urges the reader to understand, and that only emphasizes the distance between that gospel's implied reader and author. In the gospel of Mark there is no clear presentation, even symbolically or metaphorically, of who its Jesus simulacrum really is, nor do either the disciples or the implied reader ever understand. In other words, in Mark the reader never understands who Jesus is any better than the disciples do. Mark is also a fantastic text (see Chapter 4 and Aichele 2006), but there is little or no irony in it; sarcasm, perhaps, as in the centurion's words (15:39) but not irony. In addition, no duality of worlds such as the one that undergirds John is evident in the reality effects of Mark's gospel, when read apart from the canon and the Gospel, and even the voices from the sky or cloud in its baptism and transfiguration stories do not clearly come from another world.

According to Mark's last verses, the women at the tomb never told anyone, which implies that either the story never got out and therefore Mark's gospel was never written or else the entire story is a fiction. This is not irony, but rather a dilemma that the very existence of the text of Mark seems to resolve, but in what may be a disagreeable fashion. In contrast, in its final sentence, John's gospel announces that "there are also many other things which Jesus did; were every one of them to be written, I suppose that the world itself could not contain the books that would be written" (21:25). This phrase is frequently regarded as a rhetorical flourish, and indeed it represents a common trope in antique literature.[6] However, if this statement is taken more seriously, then in its last verse the gospel of John connotes the failure of denotation itself. In this way this verse raises the paradoxical self-referentiality that appears in texts such as Mk 16:7–8 to a more explicitly theological level, and thereby it introduces a very sophisticated and subtle irony.[7]

---

6. See Bultmann (1971: 697, n. 2) and Schnackenburg (1982: 335, 374).
7. John 21:22–23 implies a warning to the reader to read carefully. Compare the Introduction and first two sayings of the gospel of Thomas, in which that book describes itself as "secret sayings" and invites the reader to seek and find "the interpretation of these sayings" in order to avoid death and "rule over the All." Other forms of self-referentiality appear also in the synoptic gospels, such as Mark's repeated use of the word "gospel," and Lk. 1:1–4.

John 21:25 does not merely describe the limitations of this one particular book, but it also alludes to the impossibility of ever completely representing an object and therefore the impossibility of representation itself, a theme that has been pursued by numerous modern and postmodern semioticians – that is, a referential incompleteness that characterizes every written text.[8] It is in effect an attempt to by-pass simulation, to connote the *archē*. All writing inevitably separates language from its denoted or connoted referents and threatens the possibility of perfect, clear communication. As a result, every written narrative is a fictional construct, even though few of them makes this an explicit theme. The great irony is thus that any reader would ever take the gospel of John, or any writing, to be a true and reliable message.

This failure of denotation and the resultant paradox may be mitigated by the claim, a bit earlier in John's gospel, that "Jesus did many other signs (*sēmeia*) in the presence of the disciples, which are not written in this book; but these are written that you may believe that Jesus is the Christ, the Son of God, and that believing you may have life in his name" (20:30–31). However, this also means that "life in his name"[9] will have to suffice for the faithful reader, for the incarnate Word itself is no longer present, or rather, it *never was* present in the text, but only as that which "preceded" that which is written (Derrida 1981: 104). Indeed, the Christian life must be lived by the reader in the midst of unrelieved ignorance. The appearance of light in the midst of the dark world, already announced in Jn 1:9, has not brought the darkness to an end, even though "the darkness has [also] not overcome it" (1:5). The two verses at the end of John's Chapter 20 are what some scholars believe to be the original ending of the gospel, and if that was the case, then that earlier version of John was less ironical, although perhaps also a bit less cheery, than the one now included in Bibles, which ends at 21:25.

Only when the gospel of John is separated from the security of its canonical containment (and the Gospel) does the paradox of Jn 21:25 become evident. The intertextual mechanism of the canon of scriptures was developed in part to complete and to conceal the referential incompleteness of texts such as this one. The Bible, regarded as a significant whole, hides the gospel of John's self-proclaimed inadequacy of denotation behind a theological veil of connotations. Writing is always the writing of what Derrida calls "nonpresence" (1973: 62–63, 1976: 303): it is the production of simulacra. Unlike doubting Thomas, who sees and touches

8. See further Derrida (1995: 60–61 and 1981 passim).
9. On the significance of names, see Chapter 4.

the resurrected Jesus's body in Jn 20:26–29, the reader must rely on what John's written text says. The Christian reader believes that she knows what John "really means," not only in 21:25 but also in 20:31 and throughout – and so this great irony is itself ironized – and as a result this reader "knows" that denotation has not truly failed.

Jesus the Geographer

As if the double endings of the gospel of John, both pointing to that gospel's incompleteness, were not enought, the paradoxical incompleteness of John's written simulation of the divine Word appears again, enacted in almost mocking irony, in Jn 7:53–8:11. Scribes and Pharisees bring a woman taken in adultery to Jesus, and they ask him to comment on Mosaic laws that require that she be punished by stoning. Jesus avoids their trap by writing with his finger in the dirt (*katō kupsas tō daktulō kategraphen eis tēn gēn*, 8:6).

> And as they continued to ask him, he stood up and said to them, "Let him who is without sin among you be the first to throw a stone at her." And once more he bent down and wrote with his finger on the ground [*katakupsas egraphen eis tēn gēn*]. But when they heard it, they went away, one by one, beginning with the eldest, and Jesus was left alone with the woman standing before him. (8:7–9)

The Pharisees want to see whether Jesus will interpret Torah, or as they say, "the law [of] Moses," in a way that would be acceptable to them ("This they said to test him, that they might have some charge to bring against him," 8:6). Jesus's reply ducks the legal question. The gospel of John's Jesus simulacrum is engaged here in scriptural eisegesis. According to Deut. 17:6–7, the law is: "On the evidence of two witnesses or of three witnesses he that is to die shall be put to death [by stoning, 17:5]; a person shall not be put to death on the evidence of one witness. The *hand of the witnesses shall be first against him to put him to death*, and afterward the hand of all the people" (emphasis added). John's Jesus significantly re-reads the law, or even offers a new law. According to him, it is not the witnesses who must throw the first stone, but rather one who is sinless. If no one is sinless, then no first stone can be thrown, and thus apparently no stone can be thrown.

Jesus judges the woman, but he does not condemn her. The gospel of John tells the reader that Jesus's judgment is superior to that of the Pharisees (8:15–16), and that it is just (5:30), and therefore it must be so according to some law. John also tells the reader that Jesus judges in terms of a higher law, which is not a law of flesh or of appearance – that is, a law of the simulacrum – but the truth of "right judgment" and "he who sent me," in statements that almost bracket the passage in question (7:24, 8:15–16). This higher law cannot be simulated: this is one of those points at which the gospel of John connotes a secondary world without depicting it. Simulation of the *archē* fails in John 8:7 (as it always must, according to the two endings), and here that term is particularly apt, since *archē* can mean not only "beginning" or "origin" (as in 1:1) but also "sovereignty" or "authority" (Liddell and Scott 1996). The *archē* is beyond simulation; it is the anti-simulacrum.

Although the story of this woman is often read as though Jesus's understanding of the law implies a universal model of forgiveness, his words simply offer an ad hoc, rather forced, and purely practical response to a concrete encounter between two individuals.[10] Furthermore, John's Jesus simulacrum does not command mercy, but instead that the one who throws the stone should be sin-free. However, a legal system that required its judges to be sinless would be quite impractical, for who then would be qualified to judge the sinlessness of the judges? Surely only God, the unsimulatable *archē*. Like the divine Word in John, Jesus's concept of authoritative judgment is utopian. Because of this, Jesus's statement has its strategic place, here in this story, in the Temple and face to face with this woman, but his concept of judgment could never be fully "incarnated," much less universalized.

However, if this is the case, these words of John's Jesus cannot simulate the eternal, divine Word, which according to the prologue is transcendent eternal truth enlightening the dark world, and that would seriously trouble the irony of John's simulation of Jesus. Indeed, in this passage, the other world, the unsimulatable world of the *archē*, is itself suspended in undecidability between an impractical law and no law at all – ironically, perhaps, but again not in the way usually ascribed to the gospel of John.

Therefore, although mercy becomes the effective consequence of Jesus's ruling in Jn 8:7, no law of forgiveness is stated. Indeed, unlike the words of

10. In an email to me, Yvonne Sherwood makes the following point: "Is the story even conceivable as a female Christ forgiving a male adulterer? It seems to me that sexual difference is intrinsic to the story, and earths any abstractions we might deduce from it. I … [am not] just asking the question of what happened to the presumably adulterous man the woman was with, but a broader question about the legacy that this text and others give to us. The whole theology of invective against adulteration of God, via the female, goes back to the OT and continues throughout the NT, it seems" (2 December 2002). The story would also be quite different if instead of concerning a sexual matter, the crime was that of eating shellfish or wearing a garment made of two kinds of cloth.

the Jesus simulacra of Matthew (6:14–15, 18:21–22, 35), and perhaps also Mark (11:25) and Luke (17:3), there is no law of forgiveness in John. Instead, after his resurrection, John's Jesus tells the disciples, "If you forgive the sins of any, they are forgiven; if you retain the sins of any, they are retained" (20:23, compare Mt. 16:19). Forgiveness is binding and cannot be undone, but so also is unforgiveness. However, this remission of sins is not commanded; it is not a matter of obeying some law. Instead, it is the possibility of forgiveness that dictates a law.

Whether the statement of John's Jesus simulacrum in 8:7 is acceptable to his auditors as an interpretation of Torah cannot be determined, because they have become speechless by this point in the story. The translation of this story in the King James Version tells the reader that Jesus's opponents all left because they were "convicted by [their own] conscience(s)" (8:9), picking up on one of the numerous manuscript variants of this awkward text, and strongly implying that at least the opponents (as well as the KJV translators) regard Jesus's words as law. Apparently the darkness of their thoughts has been penetrated by divine light. In contrast, translations of the story in the Revised Standard Version, the Jerusalem Bible, and the New English Bible all omit this phrase, leaving the reason that the opponents left unclear.[11] Has Jesus passed their exegetical test? Has their own self-awareness convinced them that his interpretation of the law of Moses is correct? Or have they simply become tired of Jesus's evasiveness and gone to breakfast?

Apart from this doubtful phrase, there is no irony in Jn 7:53–8:11, either "stable" or "unstable"[12] – that is, no complicity between implied author and implied reader, but also no collision between worlds. Instead a gap opens up in John's text at this point, a gap that the (actual) reader must fill in some way. Jesus's judgment is "right" or "true" because, as John makes clear, he is in living harmony with his Father (see 5:22–27). Who then could be better suited to interpret the Torah? John's Jesus simulacrum is the living Word, and surely he understands the intentions of God, the true author of the Torah, better than any other person. However, on what basis can the reader judge the legal judgment of John's Jesus? If only the one who is attuned to the will of the Father can judge rightly, then how dare the reader make any judgment? If her conscience also convicts her, then she

11. The NEB separates the entire passage, 7:53–8:11, from the main text of John and places the phrase in question in a footnote to the separated passage.
12. Staley (1988: 95, n.1); see also Duke (1985), especially Chapter 7. In his study of irony in John's gospel, Duke never mentions this episode, which is not surprising, as many scholars regard it as not properly Johannine (see below).

accepts Jesus's judgment but also recognizes that she cannot judge. However, if the reader cannot judge, then how can she accept John's judgment that Jesus speaks for God? And if her conscience is clear, then *she* should throw the stone. The reader is trapped, just as the Pharisees are trapped by Jesus in this story, and she is forced to acknowledge her own lack of harmony with the text – her failure to "get it" – and as a result there can be no irony.

Most Christians believe that Jesus is sinless (compare Jn 1:17, 8:46). Indeed, the innocence of Christ is an important component of the Gospel. Why then doesn't John's Jesus simulacrum cast the first stone? His ruling in 8:7 would appear to permit (or even require) him to do so. However, after the Pharisees have left without condemning the woman, Jesus says to her, "Neither do I condemn you; go, and do not sin again" (8:11). Jesus's non-judgment appears again a few verses later in John: "I know whence I have come and whither I am going, but you do not know whence I come or whither I am going. You judge according to the flesh, I judge no one" (8:14–15). This saying ties Jesus's objection to a legal system with sinful judges who judge "according to the flesh" (the simulacrum) to John's paradox of the incarnate Word that exceeds every text (the unsimulatable *archē*), but which "you do not know." Jesus judges no one because he is finally beyond the flesh and beyond the text, in the utopian position of the divine Word.

Nevertheless, Jesus's saying in Jn 8:14–15 continues: "Yet even if I do judge, my judgment is true, for it is not I alone that judge, but I and he who sent me" (8:16, see also 1:17, 5:22–30, 12:45–49). The woman is judged after all, but not "according to the flesh." She receives a purely spiritual judgment, for want of a better description, from the non-textual Word. Has the *archē* then finally been simulated? The woman has indeed sinned ("do not sin again"), but she will not be punished – at least, not this time.

The legal eisegesis of John's Jesus simulacrum is bracketed by the two times that he bends down to write (*katagraphō, graphō*) upon the ground. In the context of the preceding considerations, these two acts of writing become especially interesting. In Jn 7:15, "the Jews" say that Jesus "has learning [*grammata oiden*, knows his letters]" even though "he has never studied," but none of the other gospels' Jesus simulacra ever writes, and the mention of this repeated action in John 8 draws the reader's attention. She wants to know what John's Jesus has written. However, the gospel of John, which often presents Jesus's spoken words at great length in its own writings, here becomes curiously uncommunicative. When Jesus is called upon to comment on the adulterous woman, John tells the reader twice that Jesus stooped to write upon the ground, but it does not say what he wrote – at least, not in Chapter 8. The act of writing is simulated, but not the writings themselves.

Perhaps these writings of John's Jesus are among those "other signs [that he did] in the presence of the disciples, which are not written in this book" (20:30). However, John does not mention that the disciples were present when Jesus wrote in the dirt. "All the people" were there, as well as scribes and Pharisees (8:2-3), but it appears that no one bothered to copy the words down and pass them on. As a result, because the actual reader was not present at the event (like the disciples?), she is excluded from reading that writing. Not unlike Jesus's paradoxical and impractical ruling on the law, and not unlike the written words of the gospel itself, which fail to completely denote their object, Jesus's words in the dirt are unable to signify. John's gospel leaves the reader with merely the signification of signification.

Although the gospel of John never says so, surely the incarnate Word is first and foremost a spoken word, filled with a living breath or spirit that will continue to speak as "the Counselor, the Holy Spirit, whom the Father will send in my name," even when Jesus's body is no longer present (14:25–26) and the Word has returned to the *archē* from whence it came. As in Genesis 1, John's Word is a living voice:

- "For he whom God has sent *utters* the words of God" (3:34).
- "The words that I say to you I do not *speak* on my own authority; but the Father who dwells in me does his works" (14:10).
- "[T]he word which you *hear* is not mine but the Father's who sent me" (14:24, emphases added).

As Derrida says, in reference to Edmund Husserl but using almost Johannine language, "The phenomenological voice would be this spiritual flesh that continues to speak and be present to itself – to hear itself – in the absence of the world" (1973: 16).

This voice appears most often in the gospel of John in the words of Jesus, words that take up a great deal of John's written text. Ultimately, however, this voice is God's "word [*logon*] abiding in you" which offers "life [*zōēn*]," as distinct from "the scriptures [*graphas*]" (5:37–40).[13] The ones who "believe him whom he [God] has sent" – that is, John's Jesus simulacrum – are the ones who hear God's voice (*phōnēn*, Jn 5:37) in the words of that same simulacrum. And if "the words of God" are not heard then "the reason why you do not hear them is that you are not of God" (8:47) – that is, as I

13. *Zōē* in these verses as elsewhere in John is strongly associated with Jesus ("you refuse to come to me that you may have life," 5:40), in striking contrast to its use in Mark. See further Chapter 4.

noted above, the fault lies in the recipient, not in the transmission of the message. This Johannine language is strikingly similar to Paul's distinction between the "written code [*gramma*]" that kills and the "Spirit [that] gives life [*zōopoiei*]" because it writes "not on tablets of stone but on tablets of human hearts" (2 Cor. 3:3, 6). It also echoes Socrates's distinction between the spoken word "written on the soul [*psuchē*] of the hearer together with understanding" and the written word which "can do no more than remind the reader of what he already knows" (Plato 1973: 98 [section 276]), a text that also plays an important role in Derrida's critique of logocentrism (1981: 61–172). In each of these texts, a writing questions the value of writing.

However, in John 8 that Johannine voice is silenced in the silence of writing. There is no failure of simulation for the speaking voice, but for the written text, the very words that John's Jesus writes on the ground, there is no simulation. Jesus writes in silence. Insofar as writing makes noise, it makes only meaningless noises, rustles and scratches and scrapes. What occurs is yet another translation of the Word, a further movement of what is now literal immersion into the physical realm, again and even further transforming the Word. But there can be no dynamic equivalence in the translation of Jesus's written words. Their signifying power comes not from living breath or spirit but rather through unspeakable difference.

Indeed, should the reader even imagine these illegible writings in the dirt to be actual words, signifying characters in Aramaic or Greek or some other human language, or are they better thought of as meaningless doodles or idle cartoons scratched in the dust? Rudolf Schnackenburg lists some of the guesses that scholars have produced regarding what Jesus wrote on the ground (1980b: 165–166). This is probably one of the more ideologically symptomatic products of biblical studies, and perhaps ironical in its own way. The commentators always declare that Jesus wrote something of consequence on the ground, perhaps a quotation from Torah or the Prophets. They never consider that he might have written something silly, unimportant, or nonsensical – something that would not fit comfortably in the Christian canon – or that his "writings" might not have been words at all.

Jesus's earthy inscriptions survive in the text of John 8 only as the written record that there was writing, not a record of the writing itself. It is as though the process of the incarnation of the Word had now reached a further threshold which is also a final terminus and a purely physical text (*gramma*) from which all trace of meaning (*logos*) has been removed or in which no meaning could ever appear – in other words, an asemic text. Only the "edge of language" (Derrida 1995: 60) appears, impossible to decipher. Unlike the utopian referent of the gospel of John's text, both the signifiers and the signifieds of Jesus's written text remain entirely unknown. This is not irony, for irony yields meaning. Instead, this unknown writing forecloses meaning. Can it be coincidence that these two acts of meaningless writing bracket the non-simulation of *archē* in John 8:7?

What Jesus Wrote[14]

Scholars have long noted that the gospel of John's story of the woman taken in adultery presents serious textual problems. The entire passage, Jn 7:53–8:11, is omitted from an impressive list of ancient manuscripts, including nearly all of the oldest ones. In addition, there are numerous textual variations in the manuscripts in which the story appears. Are there any limits to what D. C. Parker (in the second epigraph to this chapter) calls "virtual John"? In some manuscripts this story appears in different places in John's gospel, and in members of manuscript family 13 it appears at the end of Luke 21, where it "fits" quite neatly into Luke's larger narrative.[15]

John 8:1 mentions Jesus going to "the Mount of Olives," followed by "Early in the morning he came again to the temple; all the people came to him, and he sat down and taught them" (8:2). Similarly, the gospel of Luke concludes its account of the apocalyptic discourse with "And every day he [Jesus] was teaching in the temple, but at night he went out and lodged on the mount called Olivet. And early in the morning all the people came to him in the temple to hear him" (21:37–38). It is at this point in the manuscripts noted above that the woman is brought to him. If the story of the adulterous woman is not inserted at this point in Luke's story, the next verse begins a new episode with "Now the feast of Unleavened Bread drew near …" (22:1). Since the story of the woman taken in adultery forms a discrete, self-contained unit, it fits quite neatly into Luke's gospel between 21:38 and 22:1. Conversely, if one deletes Jn 7:53–8:11 from the text of John, there is no disruption of either narrative or discourse in that gospel. The Jesus simulacra of Luke and John are thus effectively interchangeable at these points in their stories (see further Chapter 9), although differences of context in the larger narratives may significantly change the smaller story's meaning, just as location and inclusion or not of this story affects the larger stories.

14. "Jesus Begins to Write" is the gently ironical subtitle of Moore (1992). Although it is true in one sense that no biblical Jesus ever writes, not even John's, in another sense each of the gospels' four Jesus simulacra does nothing but write.
15. See further Brown (1966: 333).

Not only the narrative content but also the language of Jn 7:53–8:11 is arguably more Lukan than Johannine, and in any case the story's language is atypical for the gospel of John. Although the story of the woman caught in adultery is not about forgiveness, it does dovetail nicely with Luke's emphasis on forgiveness (1:77, 3:3, 5:20–24, 6:37, 7:47–49, 11:4, 12:10, 17:3–4, 23:34, 24:47), whereas forgiveness is explicitly mentioned in John only in 20:23, which was discussed above. The metaphysically abstract and often richly metaphorical language that runs throughout John is strikingly absent from this story. Instead it describes a concrete encounter between a specific (albeit unnamed) woman and a specific man, and it is neither a miracle ("sign") nor an occasion of significant teaching – unless 8:7 is after all a law. However, as I noted above, in this story Jesus interprets the law of Moses in response to a single case that has been laid before him, and his statement may not provide a universal law at all, but merely his ad hoc response to that particular challenge. As a result, contrary to the tendency of theologians and preachers to read justice or forgiveness into this story, it may simply be a matter of Jesus outwitting his opponents.

Most modern editions of the Bible print this episode following John 7:52 and before 8:12, sometimes with a footnote to indicate its problematic textual status, but many scholars treat this passage as not truly part of John. The text's history also raises questions about the canonical status of the story – questions that scholars also often ignore. Indeed, they sometimes omit any mention of this story from their discussions of the gospel of John, implying that it is not canonical.[16] The narrative appears to be an addition, an afterthought that remains deeply out of keeping with the rest of the gospel, perhaps inserted into John's text at a later time.[17]

However, no matter how accurate it may be as an account of the history of the gospel's text, the theory that Jn 7:53–8:11 is a later insertion into the larger narrative conveniently rationalizes the incoherence that this story presents – its failure to deliver a clear message – at this point. This theory provides justification for the reader's sense that the story of the woman

---

16. Although Staley 1988 concerns the impact of media changes on understanding of biblical texts, and John 7:53-8:11 explicitly discusses the medium of Jesus's words, in that book Staley pays no attention to that particular text. However, Staley 2005 does address the matter. Duke also pays close attention to the importance of writing in relation to the gospel of John (1985: 148-149), but he too ignores Jn 7:53-8:11. Moore 1994 and Culpepper 1983 also omit any reference to this passage. Bultmann mentions the passage only to exclude it from consideration (1971: 10), and Schnackenburg discusses the passage, but with apologies (1980b: 162).

17. See Schnackenburg 1980b: 170.

taken in adultery does not "belong" to the *archē* of John, and therefore it does not belong in the gospel of John at all. Thus it sanctions the desire to ignore an episode that stands in tension with that gospel's prevailing logocentrism. The reader must decide whether to read this story despite all of its oddity as part of John's larger narrative, or to remove it from the gospel of John and either disregard it altogether or treat it as some hybrid thing, an "orphan text" that is neither canonical nor non-canonical.

Disregarding this story altogether is the path of least resistance. Instead, if we suppose that Jn 7:53–8:11 is not only integral to the narrative of the gospel of John, we see that despite or even because of its disruption of logocentric clarity, it may play a crucial role in the hermeneutic unfolding of the text.

The gospel of John's Chapter 21, the last chapter in that gospel, is another text that may not "belong" in John. Although Chapter 21 does not present the manuscript irregularities of Jn 7:53–8:11, many scholars have argued that this material was also added somewhat later to the text of the gospel.[18] Indeed, if John had ended at 20:29, with the resurrected Jesus reunited with his disciples and saying to the formerly-doubtful Thomas, "Have you believed because you have seen me? Blessed are those who have not seen and yet believe," the result would be satisfyingly ironic, in the sense described by Duke, and the two troublesome endings would not exist.

Instead, this alleged epilogue that forms John 21, with its possibly-allegorical fishing miracle and references to sheep and its forecasts of the fates of Peter and the "beloved disciple," appears bracketed between two pairs of verses that in effect provide two self-referential conclusions to the gospel of John, which were discussed above. Once again, these twin conclusions are:

- Now Jesus did many other signs in the presence of the disciples, which are not written in this book; but these are written that you may believe that Jesus is the Christ, the Son of God, and that believing you may have life in his name. (20:30–31)
- This is the disciple who is bearing witness to these things, and who has written these things; and we know that his testimony is true. But there are also many other things which Jesus did; were every one of them to be written, I suppose that the world itself could not contain the books that would be written. (21:24–25)

18. Staley lists Bultmann, Schnackenburg, and Culpepper among those who make this claim. See also Brown (1970: 1079–1082). Staley himself argues against the claim (1988: 111–116). The manuscript evidence suggests that this material was well established in the gospel of John before 7:53–8:11 was added.

There are even linguistic echoes between "these [things] are written [*tauta de gegraptai*]," in 20:31 and "who has written these things [*ho grapsas tauta*]" in 21:24, and between "the disciple" who bears true witness in 21:24 and "the disciples" in the presence of whom other signs were done in 20:30, and also between the "other signs" of 20:30 and the "other things" of 21:25, both of which are evidently "not written" in this text. The truth-claim of Jn 21:24–25 also reinforces the claim of 20:30–31 that "this book" is written to provide "life in his name" to the believing reader.

The hyperbole of Jn 21:25 calls attention to itself, and also to its first person pronouns. Who is this "I" who supposes (*oimai*) the failure of denotation? Might this "I" denote the same person who is denoted in plural form in the preceding verse: "This is the disciple who is bearing witness to these things, and who has written these things; and *we* know [*oidamen*] that his testimony is true" (21:24, emphasis added)? Rudolf Schnackenburg regards the "we" of Jn 21:24 as an editorial voice that speaks for an entire community (1982: 373–374). Duke does not mention 21:24, but he argues that:

> behind the Fourth Gospel is a strong, corporate literary consciousness … . John's writing follows long spiraling paths with constant allusions to words already spoken or words yet to come. … [I]t is only in a milieu conditioned by the controlled distance of writing that irony can take on the kind of sustained subtlety that it does in the Fourth Gospel. (1985: 148)

As a writing, the gospel of John assures its readers that it too is a "scripture," which like the other scriptures bears witness to Jesus (5:39). In addition, as a result of the language of its two endings, the gospel confirms both its acceptance by the church (especially if "we know" connotes a Johannine community) and its apostolic authority ("this is the disciple"), and these are two of the criteria used to establish canonicity. In other words, in these verses John promotes its own canonical status!

In a somewhat different, but not entirely contrary vein, Jeffrey Staley argues that both "I" and "we" in 21:24–25 are identical to the "beloved disciple," the sometimes purported author and narrator of the gospel of John (1988: 115, see also 39).[19] The third and first person references in these verses refer to the same individual, with the result that in this text John's implied author suddenly and finally becomes explicit,[20] in order to assure the reader that she speaks the truth. Something like this happens also in Jn 19:35: "He who saw it has borne witness – his testimony is true,

19. Compare Lincoln (2002: 11–12).
20. Staley (1988: 39–40, 115). See also Culpepper (1983: 44–49).

and he knows that he tells the truth – that you also may believe." Indeed, truth and truthful testimony are topics of great interest throughout the gospel of John.[21] Staley's argument is plausible, but once again, what if the hyperbole of John 21:25 is not merely a rhetorical flourish? What if denotation really does fail?

If the gospel of John is taken seriously as literary fantasy, then neither the "beloved disciple" or even a Johannine community could know the infinite tales of the deeds of Jesus. However, if "I/we" is neither the disciple nor some community, then what candidates are left? Perhaps Moses is a possibility, for John's Jesus also says, "If you believed Moses, you would believe me, for he wrote of me" (5:46). However, even "Moses" is caught in the incompleteness and finitude stated in 21:25, unless what Jesus calls "Moses" is not an actual Torah or even the virtual Torah but an infinite Torah, God's own Torah, which for John's gospel (if it allows such a thought) would be the divine Word, the unsimulatable *archē*.

Furthermore, if "the disciple" in Jn 21:24 is identical to "I" and "we" in these two verses, as Staley argues, then when "we" confirm the truthfulness of the foregoing gospel ("his testimony"), the text simply confirms its own truthfulness. Likewise, in Jn 8:14, mentioned above as an instance of Johannine logocentrism, Jesus says, "Even if I do bear witness to myself, my testimony is true, for I know whence I have come and whither I am going." This statement may be effective "in-house" rhetoric, but it is surely defective logic, and it even acknowledges that not everyone who bears witness to herself tells the truth. Indeed, in Jn 5:31, Jesus says even more explicitly, "If I bear witness to myself, my testimony is not true" (see also 7:18). Self-authentication may be comforting to those who already accept the authority of the text – the ones to whom its irony should be evident – but it carries no persuasive weight for those who do not.

There is another possible solution to the puzzle of "I" and "we" in Jn 21:24–25. The testimony described in John's two conclusions returns the reader to the question of judgment in 7:53–8:11, and it suggests that there may be a link between the judgments given and withheld in that story and the testimony given (and withheld) in those conclusions. The failure of denotation in the gospel of John is explicitly announced in the two conclusions and overtly enacted when John's Jesus simulacrum writes in the dirt. Denotation fails in John in part because connotation is so powerful throughout this gospel; indeed, in John connotation generally runs rampant over denotation. This results from the two levels or worlds that comprise

---

21. Witness and testimony also play important roles in Derrida (1995).

John's fantastic irony. Denotation also fails in the story of Jesus writing in John 8, but in this story there is no abundance of connotation. Instead, there is a simple deficiency of the referent, resulting from the failure to record what Jesus wrote on the ground.

A further link between the story of the woman taken in adultery and John's two conclusions appears in the topic of writing. The *graphō* of Jesus's writings in 8:6 and 8:8 appears again in 20:30–31 and yet again in 21:24–25. Although *graphō* appears 23 times in the gospel of John (including *katagraphō* in 8:6[22]), five of those instances are in John's two conclusions. Of the remaining 16 appearances of this word in John, 10 denote the Jewish scriptures (for example, "Moses in the law and also the prophets wrote," 1:45). The remaining six instances of *graphō* appear together in another story in which writing figures prominently, but on this occasion John immediately tells the reader what was written.

> Pilate also wrote a title and put it on the cross; it read, "Jesus of Nazareth, the King of the Jews." Many of the Jews read this title, for the place where Jesus was crucified was near the city; and it was written in Hebrew, in Latin, and in Greek. The chief priests of the Jews then said to Pilate, "Do not write, 'The King of the Jews,' but, 'This man said, I am King of the Jews.'" Pilate answered, "What I have written I have written". (19:19–22)

Pilate's response to the priests contrasts ironically to both of John's conclusions.

Although they are tenuous, these intratextual linkages suggest that if Jn 7:53–8:11 is read as integral to the larger story of John, then that gospel does finally show the reader what Jesus wrote in 8:6 and 8:8. However, these words do not appear until Jn 20:30–31 and 21:24–25. In other words, the words of the two conclusions, the brackets that enclose Chapter 21 and that verify and authorize the text of John's gospel, are nothing less than Jesus's written words, missing from Chapter 8. The dirt in which Jesus writes becomes itself the very text of John.

The unnamed disciple, one of the leading candidates for the gospel of John's implied author, makes his first appearance in the gospel in Jn 13:23, well after Chapter 8. Might one of the scribes mentioned in 8:3 have read what Jesus wrote and then become this disciple? An historical argument would be implausible at best, and possibly even ludicrous. However, how else does one account for the fact that the story of Jesus writing wound up

---

22. In the gospel of John, *katagraphō* appears only in 8:6. This is also the only place where this word appears in the entire New Testament. Numerous ancient manuscripts of John have *graphō* instead here.

in John's text and not in Luke? If we suppose that Jn 20:30–31 and 21:24–25 simulate the two signatures of John's Jesus simulacrum, then these verses doubly verify the authority of that gospel, and as a result it is Jesus himself who canonizes John's text. The referent of the first person pronouns in Jn 21:24–25 (in Greek they are not separate pronouns but verbs in the first person) changes, and "I/we" is then not the disciple, as in Staley's reading. Instead, John's Jesus is the one who writes these endings, and the disciple records what Jesus has written in the dirt in the gospel that he has written.

A Dirty Word

Truthful testimony appears yet again in Jn 5:32, where Jesus says that "there is another who bears witness to me, and I know that the testimony which he bears to me is true," anticipating the assertion of the truth of "these things" that "we know" in 21:24. The immediate referent of this "other" would seem to be John the Baptist (see 5:33–36), but the gospel of John itself also "bears witness" to Jesus. If the implied author who writes "I/we" in 21:24–25 is also identified with this other one of 5:32, then these spoken words of John's Jesus also authorize the text of John. The written "I" and "we" who make the claims of John 21:24–25 remain anonymous and thus uncertain, but the only one who could honestly make such claims must be beyond the world and beyond all the books that might be written. Such a being is the anti-simulacrum of the Christian canon – that is, "the Alpha and the Omega, the first and the last, the beginning and the end" of Rev. 22:13. Indeed, another New Testament passage that functions in a similar manner appears near the end of the book of Revelation: "I Jesus have sent my angel to you with this testimony for the churches" (22:16, compare 22:6–8, 18–19). Apart from "I Jesus" in the statement itself, no source is identified for these words, which suddenly interrupt the final comments of the book's narrator, who curiously is also designated as "John."[23]

In other words, if the reader takes the claims of "I/we" at the end of the gospel of John seriously, and not merely as hyperbolic rhetoric, then "I/we" must be none other than the divine Word itself, incarnate and thereby simulated in John's Jesus. The two conclusions correspond to Jesus's two acts of writing in Jn 8:6 and 8:8, and the one who writes "I" and "we" in

---

23. Few if any scholars think now that the same person wrote both the gospel and the Revelation of John. However, given the anonymity of the authors, the similarity of name opens a possibility for connection.

these verses is Jesus himself, who is now directly addressing "you," the reader (see 20:31). John's Jesus simulacrum knows that the disciple's testimony is true – who would know better? – and Jesus is also in the best (or only?) position to suppose that no amount of books could be written to tell all of the things that he himself did (21:24–25, 20:30). John's Jesus simulacrum may be a duplicitous fellow, but he is not necessarily an ironist. He avoids the Pharisees in Chapter 8 by writing words that apparently no one reads, but then he shares those words with the reader at the respective endings of Chapters 20 and 21. The reader is finally allowed to read these words of the Word, and thereby she is included in the believing community, the "strong, corporate literary consciousness" (Duke 1985: 148).

According to this understanding of the gospel of John, Jesus was writing to the reader all along. Perhaps that is the greatest irony of John, whose written, dirty words tell the story of the truth-filled, divine Word. The tension between *graphē* and *logos* is resolved, for now John presents itself to the reader as a message from Jesus himself, signed twice by him. Although this reader is still excluded from knowing the many things that have not been said in the countless books that could have been written about him, that matters little. Jesus himself assures the reader in John's conclusions that she has been given sufficient signs for "life in his name" (20:31).

The reader still ends up with circular self-confirmation, but it is at least more complicated – and therefore both rhetorically and logically more interesting – than if "the disciple" of 21:24 merely announces his own truthfulness. Instead, the gospel of John writes that Jesus writes, and that Jesus is filled with truth (at numerous points, but especially 14:6). Furthermore, what Jesus writes (in the two conclusions) is that John's gospel, as written by "the disciple," tells the truth. Jesus's earthy texts reassure the reader that the gospel has after all succeeded sufficiently – equivalence has been achieved – in its task of signifying the incarnation of the pre-existent Word, even as they announce the inherent finitude and incompleteness of any text. Thus John simultaneously confirms the failure of denotation and assures the reader that this failure is not decisive – indeed, that enough of the divine message has been translated.

Nevertheless, despite the grandiose claims that these two conclusions make, offered in conjunction with spectacular appearances of the resurrected Jesus, what surfaces repeatedly in these conclusions is not the spiritual, eternal Word, the *logos*. Like the account of Jesus writing, these two texts both foreground the physical stuff of the written text (*graphē*), in this case the text of the gospel of John itself. What surfaces is the silent materiality of text: "written [*gegrammena*] in this book," "these are written [*gegraptai*]," "who has written [*grapsas*] these things," and finally the impossibility of writing everything that Jesus did. According to both Jn 20:30–31 and 21:24–25, John's gospel is not "lifted up from the earth" (the primary world) with the crucified and resurrected Jesus (12:32), in order to return to the light of the supernatural *archē* (the secondary world) from which the Word proceeded. Instead, the physicality of its inscription retains John's text in the dark earth of Chapter 8, a tomb that will not empty. John's Jesus simulacrum writes not only on the ground (*eis tēn gēn*), but *of* the ground, of the finite, material text that is unable to denote the infinity of the Word.

The story of the woman taken in adultery is of particular interest because in this text a scripture – that is, this writing that is the gospel of John – tells of another text (another writing) that can never be subdued or controlled, that resists every attempt to read it, not because it is ironical or "bilevel," but simply because the reader cannot see it. However, one important function of a canon is to keep its constituent scriptures in the control of the community that recognizes it – which in the case of the Christian Bible is the Christian churches. The canon subdues the scriptures, making them safe and properly meaningful for their faithful readers. Indeed, most readers (faithful or otherwise) of the Bible are absorbed with the profoundly theological desire to make the text speak clearly, as the Word of God – that is, to privilege that "meaning already constituted by and within the element of the logos." This desire for logocentric understanding is supported and clarified by the intertextual context provided by the canon, over against the meaningless materiality of text. It compels the reader to smooth over the awkwardnesses and incoherences and to tame the wild connotations of biblical texts such as the gospel of John.

Therefore it is not surprising that readers of the gospel of John have not been deterred by the invisibility of Jesus's writings in John 8. Their speculations as to what Jesus actually wrote on the ground may be trivial or even amusing, but they are also telling symptoms of readers' need for control – as are my own. However, if one does not presuppose some sort of canonical coherence among the biblical texts, then my own suggestion is at least no more ludicrous than any of the others.

Schnackenburg claims that Jesus's writing is a "declaration of nothingness," quoting Jer. 17:13 ("those who turn away from thee [God] shall be written in the earth"). For logocentrism, the stuff of writing can never be anything more than a temporary vehicle, "letters of dust" that have no lasting value. Meaning is to be found elsewhere, in the permanence of the *archē* and the *logos*. In contrast, Gilles Deleuze describes "sense" as that which lies on the surfaces of things, "like a fogged-up window pane on which one can write with one's finger," in the first epigraph to this chapter. In John 8, Jesus's senseless letters of dust, written with his finger, threaten to run away with the gospel. When John's Jesus simulacrum writes on the ground, the materiality of written text – the meaningless stuff that makes meaning possible – comes briefly but explicitly into the foreground of this otherwise most "spiritual" and logocentric gospel. These two acts of writing point to texts that the reader cannot read and which are therefore unable to signify.

The gospel of John attempts to simulate that which cannot be simulated. As Stephen Moore says, "The ironic structure that positioned us on a level above these [Johannine] characters depended on our being able to keep the literal and figurative levels clearly separate. ... Irony – which depended on the clean separation of flesh and glory, earthly and heavenly, material and spiritual [...] – now collapses in paradox" (1994: 61–62). The aboriginal Word's appearance in the written (scriptural) words of John's gospel is paradoxical. John's Jesus simulacrum offers to humanity the "eternal life [*zōēn*]" that they have sought in the "scriptures" (*graphas*, 5:39–40). However, the "meaning constituted by the logos" must lie outside of John's text, and indeed, as John explicitly tells the reader, no amount of physical text could possibly contain this meaning. In other words, the Word (*logos*) can never truly be written (*graphē*), or to paraphrase another sacred text, the words that can be written are not the Word.

As Staley says, the story of the adulterous woman "literally brings the rhetorical situation of John 7–8 down to stony earth" (2005: 106).[24] The Word become flesh inscribes the word become dust, and spiritual logos produces dirty written text. The earthy materiality of this semiotic channel interferes with transferral of the logocentric message. The gospel of John's clear, dynamically equivalent transmission of the brilliant divine Word is clouded and obscured in the darkness of the earth, and if it is true that "the darkness has not overcome it" (1:5), it is also true that the darkness is not overcome. John's Jesus simulacrum says, "For judgment I came into this world, that those who do not see may see, and that those who see may become blind" (9:39, compare 20:29). The reader sees, but what she sees is that the writing has been hidden from her.

Even if those writings had survived, as in my supposition above, they would still resist the reader's desire for understanding, as all writing always

24. Another "muddying" of John's logocentrism is described by Moore (1994: 59–62).

does. Any such revival, as yet another translation, is also always a transformation and a betrayal.[25] The dead may be brought back to life, but only at a price, as the story of Lazarus demonstrates (Jn 11:1–44; see also 12:1–18). However, the hermeneutical resurrection of the writings of John's Jesus is not possible. There will be no reading of these dead letters. The living, eternal Word is finally beyond simulation, and this is itself simulated when its written incarnation collides with unreadability.

25. See Derrida (1973, especially 144), and (1981: 61–171).

Part III

CANONICAL REALITY EFFECTS

Chapter 7

The Possibility of Error: *Minority Report* and the Synoptic Gospels

> Isaiah 6:9–10 is a very tricky and difficult text, so it is hardly surprising that it should complicate the Gospel material as well. ... Blindness and insight allow the same event to function in differentiating ways. (Carroll 1997: 109)

> The commentators note in this connection: "The right perception of any matter and a misunderstanding of the same matter do not wholly exclude each other." (Kafka 1958: 69)

In the preceding four chapters of this book, I have explored aspects of the four different Jesus simulacra of the canonical gospels, not in order to produce a complete statement of their differences, which would be impossible, but to add further "flesh" to the rather skeletal survey of differences in Chapter 2 and to depict a somewhat fuller sense of each of them. In addition, and more important, I have sought to illustrate the kinds of reality effects that appear when one reads each of these gospels more or less independently of the semiotic controls provided by the Christian canon and what I call in this book the Gospel of Jesus Christ.

In the remaining four chapters I "reverse the polarity," as it were, to explore how the semiotic effects of canon and the virtuality of the Bible encourage the reader to ignore these and other differences of the gospels' Jesus simulacra and produce instead, both from and against those differences, the single simulacrum of Jesus Christ. In Chapters 7 and 8, my focus is on the so-called synoptic problem, which is itself largely a product of the inclusion of multiple gospels in the New Testament. Readers of the New Testament have long realized that the gospels of Matthew, Mark, and Luke display more similarities to each other than any of them does to the fourth gospel, John. Sometimes they even duplicate large segments of each other verbatim, and as John Sandys-Wunsch says, "if the Synoptic Gospels were answers on separate examination papers, the examiner would immediately assume collusion, and the only problem would be to find out who copied from whom" (2005: 241, see also 242). As a result, these three texts are called the "synoptic gospels": they "see together." The synoptic problem or question of why and how these similarities – and the attendant differences – came about, both historically and theologically, has attracted a great deal of attention for many years.

However, these gospels are not answers to an examination question, and if the reader does not assume that they all answer the same question, or even that they belong together at all, then different problems may arise. If the New Testament canon did not exist in its present form, then surely the synoptic problem would take a very different shape, or perhaps it would not even be a "problem" at all. If there were only one text called a gospel in the Christian Bible – for example, if Marcion had had his way, or if Tatian's harmony had been accepted as the canonical norm, instead of multiple gospels – and especially if that one gospel were reasonably compatible with the "gospel" announced in Paul's letters, then it would be much easier to dismiss the other gospels (if we knew them at all) and their Jesus simulacra as heretical or derivative, as scholars and other readers often do in regard to the surviving non-canonical gospels. The relations between them would be much less interesting.

Even as it is, read simultaneously with the "eyes" of Matthew, Mark, and Luke, the synoptic Jesus is a very blurry figure indeed! In this chapter and the next one, I explore some ways that understanding of the synoptic problem changes when primary attention is focused on differences between the gospels, and on their semiotic multiplicity – their disopticity, as it were. These differences then appear not as effects of some hidden deep process that caused them, but rather as problems to be solved by the reader's own (mis-)understandings – that is, insights which are also blindnesses.[1] What then needs to be explained is not so much differences between the texts as readers' attempts to overcome those differences by explaining them as correlated historical or theological phenomena.

Blindness and Insight

In "The Rhetoric of Blindness," Paul de Man discusses literary scholars whose insights are gained at the cost of a "negative movement that animates the critic's thought, an unstated principle that leads his language away

---

1. "Undoubtedly misunderstanding is always a factual horizon and the finite index of the infinite pole of a sound intelligence. But although the latter is always announced so that language can begin, is not finitude the essential which we can never radically go beyond?" (Derrida 1978: 82).

from its asserted stand, perverting and dissolving his stated commitment" (1983: 103). De Man claims that the tensions that result from this negative movement do not "enter into the synthesizing dynamics of a dialectic."

> It is necessary ... to read beyond some of the more categorical assertions and balance them against other much more tentative utterances that seem to come close, at times, to being contradictory to these assertions. The contradictions, however, never cancel each other out ... the one always [lies] within the other as the sun lies hidden within a shadow, or truth within error. (1983: 102–103)

Critical insight is impossible apart from critical blindness, and thus "'blindness' implies no literary value-judgment" (de Man 1983: 141). Although it is a failure on the part of the critic, some sort of blindness is inescapable. De Man argues that this blindness is inherent in "literary language" and therefore "literature [is] the place where this negative knowledge about the reliability of literary utterance is made available" (1983: 106, see also 1986: 10). He concludes by arguing that the paradox of blindness and insight is "a constitutive part of all literature" (1983: 141, see also 1986: 11).

In a related essay, de Man claims that every reading is an act of criticism and that all language is permeated with theory (1986: 102). Indeed, reading is impossible without interpretation, which he defines as the possibility of error. The struggle of conflicting readings is an unavoidable product of written text. In any act of reading, the text itself is always anticipated and governed by the message that the reader finds there. Thus it would seem that the paradox of blindness and insight is not confined to critical scholarly readings of texts, but is at work whenever texts are read in any way.

> [I]nsight exists only for a reader in the privileged position of being able to observe the blindness as a phenomenon in its own right – the question of his own blindness being one which he is by definition incompetent to ask – and so being able to distinguish between statement and meaning. He has to undo the explicit results of a vision that is able to move toward the light only because, being already blind, it does not have to fear the power of this light. (1983: 106)

As de Man often does, in this chapter I am reading texts as though they read other texts. Stephen Spielberg's movie, *Minority Report* (2002) translates Philip K. Dick's written story, "The Minority Report" (1987), and the resulting intermedial play between the movie and the short story[2]

---

2. Dick's story was originally published in the "pulp" magazine *Fantastic Universe* in 1956. On intermedial translation, see further Chapter 3.

illuminates the play of blindness and insight in the gospel of Mark. This is in turn reflected in Mark's minority status in relation to the other two synoptic gospels, Matthew and Luke.

In the last thirty years, eight movies have been based on different science fiction stories by Dick, who is widely regarded as one of the greatest science fiction writers of the latter half of the twentieth century, and perhaps ever.[3] So far as I know, none of Dick's writings precisely describes de Man's paradox, but his provocative stories are well known for their falsehoods that reveal truths, and truths that become or result in falsehoods – in other words, paradoxes of blindness and insight. Often there is a strong moral dimension to the story as well, and the paradoxes then become paradoxes of freedom and responsibility as well.

Dick's short story, "The Minority Report" is constructed around one such paradox (or "cosmic joke," according to the movie[4]), which is built upon the common opposition between intentions and actions. Is wanting to do something morally equivalent to the deed itself? The gospel of Matthew's Jesus simulacrum suggests that it is: "I say to you that every one who looks at a woman lustfully has already committed adultery with her in his heart" (5:28), although he then proceeds to talk about physical actions that lead to damnation (5:29–30, see also Mt. 18:8–9 and compare Mk 9:42–48). However, even if only physical actions are culpable, at some point in the decision process, something happens to foreclose further choices. Some line is crossed between the desiring of a deed and the doing of it, after which you are no longer free not to act. It is not a question of free will as such – if freedom to choose is an illusion, then so is moral culpability – but rather a question of when is whatever freedom we have truly exercised. In other words, when does the will freely stop being free because it is now committed to some course of action? In other words, at what point does freedom choose to become non-freedom? When does responsibility begin?

Dick's story imagines a near-future world in which, after a nuclear war between Asian nations and the "Western Bloc," social chaos and political paranoia have become pandemic. A new crime-prevention technology has been developed, in which very rare human beings with mutated "precognitive" powers are harnessed to computers in order to predict crimes before they occur. These mutated humans or "precogs" can foresee future events shortly before they happen, but they are unable to distinguish between their visions of the future and present reality, and so in effect they

---

3. A full list of Dick's stories and other writings, and the films derived from them, is available online at Philip K. Dick Trust (1994).
4. All quotations from the movie are from the DVD.

are severely psychotic and unable to function normally (Dick 1987: 325). The precogs are wired with electrodes in teams of three, and their predictions are delivered directly to a computer which compares them to one another. If there is any discrepancy between them, the majority view is regarded as the correct prediction (1987: 337).

Because of this it has become possible to identify, arrest, and imprison people who intend to commit a crime before they have actually done anything wrong. There is no process of law, nor could there be apart from mind-reading. Merely to be identified by at least two precogs as about to commit a crime is sufficient to warrant punishment appropriate to the actual deed. As a result of this "Precrime" program, the crime rate has declined sharply, but at the cost of imprisoning a great many people who have not actually broken any law, although they almost certainly would have if they hadn't been stopped.

However, as Dick's story unfolds it becomes evident that the "majority report" is an illusion, for the precogs always produce three different reports, and although at least two of them always agree on certain details regarding the predicted action, even those two do not share the exact same account of that action (Dick 1987: 347). This is rather like different ordinary people reporting a single event that they have all witnessed, but it also occurs because the precogs correctly anticipate not only potential events in the larger world, but also the effects of each other's reports on those future events as well. As with Heisenberg's Uncertainty Principle, the act of observation changes the observed event. Each precognition is itself an event that adds to the causal nexus and thus changes the possible future.

Something like this may happen whenever someone learns that others know things that are important to her. For example, if I discover that you know that I am about to do something, that discovery may change what I do, or how or when I do it. If I know that my behavior has been predicted, I may change my choices and commitments and the consequent behaviors. Knowledge of the precognition has at least as much impact on my behavior as any other knowledge would. This also happens when a potential criminal becomes aware that her crime has been foreseen, as happens in both Dick's story and Spielberg's movie. Deferral of the crime transforms the clairvoyant insight into error. Insight arises from the possibility of error, but in that very upsurge it becomes a new blindness. This establishes the possibility of "multiple futures" (Dick 1987: 337).

As a result, the precog mechanism is deeply flawed. Yet although this flaw is revealed at the end of Dick's story, the Precrime police system survives thanks largely to the efforts of Precrime Commissioner John Anderton, the story's principal character. Grave doubts have been raised about the system's reliability, but this insight is covered up so that the status quo can be maintained. "You'll be a good police officer. You believe in the status quo," Anderton tells Ed Witwer, his rival and successor in the police agency (Dick 1987: 347). Dick's stories are rich in ironies of this sort, and they often end on a note of paranoid bitterness.

All of the film versions of Dick's written stories, like many movies based on written texts, take considerable liberties with those stories. This is inevitable in any translation between writing and film, and a highly "literal" film translation of a written story would be practically impossible, for reasons that were discussed in Chapter 3. Following Walter Benjamin, de Man also speaks of translation as an act of criticism: "translation canonizes its own version more than the original was canonical. That the original was not purely canonical is clear from the fact that it demands translation; it cannot be definitive since it can be translated" (1986: 82).

Spielberg's movie differs from Dick's story in ways too numerous to be completely listed here, and indeed, this movie takes many more liberties with its written "source text" than Pier Paolo Pasolini does in his film translation of the gospel of Matthew. Not only is there the necessity of audio and visual depiction of written characters, events, and places, which is always far more detailed than in the written text, but in order to save the conceptual paradoxes at the heart of Dick's stories, directors and screenwriters deviate widely from his narratives (and from each other) in other respects, producing what might be considered to be quite different stories. In this process, these movies consistently de-ironize Dick's stories and the paranoid aspect may disappear or be changed.[5]

In addition, Hollywood films tend to divide their characters into relatively unambiguous good guys and bad guys. In contrast, the protagonists of Dick's stories are often flawed and even rather unpleasant, and his character Anderton is no exception. Spielberg splits Dick's protagonist, Anderton, into two characters, Detective John Anderton and Precrime Director Lamar Burgess (who also partially replaces Dick's sinister character, General Leopold Kaplan), with the result that Spielberg's Anderton simulacrum is a much more attractive and admirable character, wracked with grief for his young son, who was abducted in pre-Precrime days and is presumed dead. In contrast, Dick's Anderton is an older man (like Burgess), and no son is mentioned.

---

5. For another instance, compare Ridley Scott's movie, *Blade Runner* (1982), which translates Dick's 1968 novel, *Do Androids Dream of Electronic Sheep?* (1982).

Indeed, apart from John Anderton's name and the Precrime concept – and with it, Dick's paradox – there are few similarities between the movie and the short story. The post-nuclear, paranoid, socially-oppressive aspects of the world of Dick's story largely disappear from the film. In addition, the Precrime program is abandoned at the end of Spielberg's movie, when Anderton, with the help of his estranged wife and one of the precogs, reveals that Burgess has abused his powers and used the Precrime system not only to convict completely innocent people but also to conceal crimes of his own. The precognitive mutants are then released from their involuntary servitude and allowed to live more-or-less normal human lives, again unlike Dick's story. Blindness is replaced by insight, and darkness by light. Truth and justice prevail in *Minority Report*, as they usually do in Hollywood's narrative worlds, and totalitarian efficiency gives way to humanistic justice.

To See but Not Perceive

Perhaps the most striking difference between Dick's story and Spielberg's movie is the simulation of the precogs themselves. In both accounts, there are two males and one female. Dick's description of them is vivid and disturbing:

> In the gloomy half-darkness the three idiots sat babbling. Every incoherent utterance, every random syllable, was analyzed, compared, reassembled in the form of visual symbols. ... All day long the idiots babbled, imprisoned in their special high-backed chairs, held in one rigid position by metal bands, and bundles of wiring, clamps. ... Their minds were dull, confused, lost in shadows. ... The three gibbering, fumbling creatures, with their enlarged heads and wasted bodies, were contemplating the future. The analytical machinery was recording prophecies, and as the three precog idiots talked, the machinery carefully listened. (1987: 325)

In this case, there is no lack of detailed description in the written text. Dick's Anderton describes the precogs as "deformed and retarded. ... Especially the girl, there. Donna is forty-five years old. But she looks about ten. The talent absorbs everything." The room where they are kept is called the "monkey block." There is no hint that anyone considers the mutants to be worth treating as human beings. People are revolted at the sight of the ugly and degraded precogs, and no one objects to their enslavement by the police.

In contrast, in Spielberg's movie, the precogs are not "babbling idiots." Instead the movie's precogs generally say very little, and they otherwise appear to be physically attractive and mentally normal young adults. The female precog, Agatha,[6] even plays a crucial role in the story, and she acts with intelligence as she helps Anderton to unmask Burgess and the blindness of Precrime. The precogs can speak – indeed, the first word in the movie is spoken by Agatha, who says the word, "murder" – but they usually float silently in a sensory deprivation tank, drugged and connected via sensor wires from their heads to an elaborate computer apparatus that records their intuitions as digital videos. In contrast to the precogs in Dick's story, their mental experience is not a paranoid one, in which some other consciousness wholly consumes their own, but rather it is a schizophrenic one, in which they are unable at times to distinguish between their actual experience and future events experienced by others. "Is this now?" Agatha asks Anderton as she looks around when he separates her from the other precogs and takes her from the Precrime unit.

Unlike Dick's story, in the movie the precog simulacra form a "hive mind" that "sees" the exact same future at the same time and are "never wrong." They are perfectly synoptic. "But occasionally they do disagree," Iris Hineman, the scientist who discovered the precogs' abilities, tells Anderton. Hence the rather rare minority reports. "Insignificant variables" in their precognitions open up the possibility of an "alternate future," and once again, because of these variables, interpretation is required, introducing the possibility of error.

According to the movie, the precogs are not genetic mutations but rather the congenitally deformed children of addicts to a mind-altering drug. Spielberg's Anderton tells his FBI adversary, Danny Witwer, "try not to think of them as human," but he is unable to follow his own advice. Compassion for the precogs is emphasized in the lengthy interview between Anderton and Hineman, which has no counterpart in Dick's story. The precogs' psychic condition is in effect an enslavement to the murderous plans of others, and thus it is not a talent but rather a "curse," as Hineman says. Comments of a tour guide at the Precrime building, another scene that appears in the movie only, also stress widespread recognition that the precognitives are fully human, albeit seriously handicapped, persons. After

6. The name changes from Donna to Agatha and from Ed to Danny Witwer are among many tiny detail changes that also define differences of the simulacra. Anderton's wife, who is Lisa in Dick's story, becomes Lara in Spielberg's movie. These differences cannot be explained as necessities of intermedial translation. Spielberg's transformation of the marital relations between the Andertons (bad in both stories, but in the film strained by the loss of their son) is also consistent with the movie's general "lightening" of Dick's story.

they are released from their police captivity at the end of the movie, the three precogs are shown living peacefully together in a cottage that is evidently far away from the rest of the human world. They are not in exile, but rather a place where they can think their own thoughts, relatively free of precognitive visions: reading books, surrounded by piles of books, and apparently no longer synoptic.

Another crucial difference between Dick's story and Spielberg's movie concerns the importance of eyes, visual images, and the act (or lack) of seeing.[7] Despite its nearly continuous and intense action, the movie provides a good example of what Gilles Deleuze calls the dominance of the perception-image (1986: 70, see Chapter 3). "The eyes of the nation are upon us," Burgess tells Anderton. In a movie, we might expect the visual to play a prominent role, as it does in *Minority Report*, although Deleuze shows that that is not always the case. Indeed, we need to be cautious about this cinematic sense of visibility. As Roland Barthes says:

> the cinema has a power which at first glance the Photograph does not have: the screen (as Bazin has remarked) is not a frame but a hideout; the man or woman who emerges from it continues living: a "blind field" constantly doubles our partial vision. (Barthes 1981: 55–57)

Intriguingly, in Spielberg's movie, Anderton hides out from the police after his eye transplant surgery behind the screen of a movie theater: a blind field indeed!

However, it is somewhat surprising that references to eyes, images, and seeing are rather sparse in a written story that is about clairvoyance – that is, blindness and insight – and yet that is the case in Dick's story, despite its richness of visual detail. Indeed, exactly what the precogs themselves "see" is never described by Dick, and whether or to what degree they are self-aware at all is not clear. The recorded crime predictions take the form of "visual symbols" that are derived from computerized analyses of the precogs' oral "babbling," but it is not explained what these symbols are or how they are derived.

In perhaps the most important scene in which sight is foregrounded in Dick's story, when Anderton kills Kaplan in order to deliberately fulfill a faked majority report and thereby falsely justify the Precrime program, a crowd of witnesses struggles to view Kaplan's dead body. "The incident, occurring before their very *eyes*, was incomprehensible. It would take time for acceptance to replace *blind* terror" (1987: 352, emphasis added; see also

---

7. Eyes and photographs also figure prominently in Scott's movie (1982), but not in its "source text" (Dick 1982).

350–351). Indeed, it is blindness and not (in)sight that predominates throughout "The Minority Report." In the penultimate sentence, Anderton advises Witwer, "better keep your eyes open" (1987: 354). As in many of Dick's stories, the reality effect is a paranoid one, in which occasional glimpses of truth do little more than emphasize the prevailing darkness; it is a bleak universe in which redemptive knowledge is rare or of little value.

In contrast, Spielberg's movie makes it clear that each precog is self-aware, but she also "sees" in her mind's eye what other persons see or will soon see with their physical eyes. These "previsions" are not mind readings, but rather experiences of something that has not happened, but will soon happen – an especially vivid and accurate premonition. This clairvoyant vision is then downloaded directly from the precog's consciousness and stored in computer files that must be viewed in turn by the Precrime police in order to anticipate and prevent the crime that would otherwise occur. As one of the cops says, "we see what they see." However, like normal vision, the prevision is "partial vision," as Barthes says, and it may be deceptive. In this way the previsions enact the paradox of blindness and insight. These visual precog recordings are "played back" on the movie screen at several points in the film, including the public revelation of Director Burgess's crime, as "seen" in a minority report from the precog, Agatha. This witnessing of a murder is far from incomprehensible, and the large crowd that watches the playback of Agatha's recorded prevision in the movie's final scenes immediately understands and accepts what has happened, unlike in Dick's story.

Eyes, images, and references to seeing also appear in many other important ways in Spielberg's movie. One of the first images in the film is an extreme close-up of Agatha's right eye, just before she says the word, "murder." Somewhat later, she asks Anderton, "Can you see?" and she repeats this question to him twice, later in the movie. Anderton in turn says, "How could I not have seen this?" He indulges his personal grief by watching holographic recordings of his missing son and estranged wife while consuming an illegal drug called "Clarity," which he buys from a blind dealer. The drug also causes him to re-visualize the moment when his son was abducted. Later, while fleeing from the Precrime police, Anderton avoids the omnipresent retinal scanners (perhaps the movie's sole suggestion of a police state[8]) by having his eyes surgically replaced with a dead man's. Later still, Agatha helps Anderton avoid the police by using

---

8. In Dick's story, the machines scan brain waves, but they are more easily avoided than the movie's retinal scanners (see Dick 1987: 336). Although Spielberg's narrative world is sunnier than Dick's is, it is no utopia.

her precog abilities to determine the policemen's line of sight – that is, by seeing what they will see, and thus implying that the movie's precogs have conscious control over their powers.

Limited Visibility

Despite or even because of the many differences that characterize this movie's intermedial translation of its written source text, a kind of reciprocity appears between the written and cinematic texts. The oppressive paranoia of Dick's cynical reality effects highlights and even complements the redemptive schizophrenia of Spielberg's more hopeful story, and vice versa, like "[f]ragments of a vessel which are to be glued together" (Benjamin 1968: 78). Benjamin speaks of the tangential point at which the original text and its translation touch one another, not a transfer of meaning but rather the appearance of what he calls "pure language" (1968: 80), or what de Man calls "the materiality of the signifier" or "literary language" (1986: 10–11). The tensions between these two texts both expose and trouble the tenuous connections between language and meaning.

The emphasis on eyes and seeing in the movie illuminates the written story's darkness, even as the cynical bitterness of the short story contrasts to the movie's "Hollywood ending." The darkness that permeates Dick's story is not agnosticism: there is no doubt in it about truth or falsehood (as there is in many of his stories), and the falsehood of Precrime prevails in "The Minority Report" because it is politically convenient. The world is a seriously damaged place, and paranoia triumphs because "they" really are out to get you. Nevertheless, the reader knows the truth about the falsehood of Precrime, and to recognize the blindness of others is to have some insight. In contrast, the visuality that drives Spielberg's movie is an opposed form of belief: the truth emerges because people's eyes are open, even though blindness remains (for example, the disappearance of Anderton's son remains unsolved). The world truly is a good place, for even the insanity of the precogs can be treated humanely, and sanity will triumph. What was hidden will come to light, and everyone will know the truth. Both stories offer examples of what Deleuze calls the "small form" of the action-image (1986: 160), although Dick's story is the better example, for the larger situation in it does not change.

This tension between Dick's story and Spielberg's movie identifies opposing poles of a single ideological spectrum. At either of these extremes, there is escape from the possibility of error. A distribution of the biblical gospels may be plotted along this spectrum. Closest to Spielberg's end of the spectrum lies the gospel of John, for which "The light shines in the darkness, and the darkness has not overcome it" (1:5) and "No one has ever seen God; the only Son, who is in the bosom of the Father, he has made him known" (1:18). A bit further into the range of the spectrum, in the stories of both Matthew and Luke, blindness is certainly a problem and a significant factor, but in each of them insight finally triumphs. The endings of all three of these gospels emphasize seeing and understanding (Mt. 28:7, 17; Lk. 24:31, 45; Jn 20:6–7, 25, 29).

In contrast, for Dick's cynical gnosticism, the light at best only flickers in the darkness, and the story ends on a note of grim despair. No gospel lies near Dick's end of the spectrum, but at some middle point between the extremes of blindness and insight, and therefore best exemplifying de Man's paradox, lies the gospel of Mark. Mark's reality effects echo most strongly the translation-tension that is evident between Dick's story and Spielberg's movie, in a space where neither hope nor irony dominates and where error is always possible, and perhaps even ubiquitous. For Mark's story, insight is blindness, and blindness is insight. As de Man says (although not about Mark), "The contradictions ... never cancel each other out ... the one always [lies] within the other as the sun lies hidden within a shadow, or truth within error" (1983: 102–103).

As a result, there is a tension within the New Testament between the gospel of Mark and the other three gospels, and while the paradox of blindness and insight is not the only theme or topic through which this tension becomes manifest (some others are noted below), it is one important index of the gospels' differences. More specifically, among the synoptic gospels, what Mark "sees" or allows to be seen becomes on this matter as on many others a "minority report" which is often overlooked in favor of the "majority report" presented by Matthew and Luke. In other words, these two gospels are sometimes "syn-optic" with each other but not so (or less so) with Mark, while majority combinations that include Mark are much less common or significant. I do not refer here to the "major" or "minor agreements" between Matthew and Luke against Mark. That is a separate matter, and will be considered in the next chapter, although it surely influences and is influenced by the matter at hand.

The gospel of Mark's paradox of blindness and insight appears in words for eye (*ophthalmos, omma*), blindness (*tuphlos*), and sight (*blepō, oraō, eidō, theōreō*), but also knowledge or understanding (*noeō, suniēmi, gignōskō*), and variants on these words. However, the paradox does not appear in the fact that Mark uses these words – indeed, they tend to appear more frequently in Matthew, Luke, or John than they do in Mark, which is perhaps not surprising, given their more "hopeful" endings – but rather in the ways that Mark uses them. Stephen Moore even describes Luke as "the gospel of the look" (1992: 85, 111–116), but Luke's "look" is quite different from Mark's, as Moore also makes clear. There is no blindness in it. Mark foregrounds its own fictionality more than either of the other synoptic gospels do, and its language emphasizes "the material, phenomenal aspects of the signifier." As a result, Mark is in de Man's terms more "literary" than the other gospels (1986: 10).[9] Mark's gospel points to its own referential illusions or reality effects, and this distinctive self-referentiality manifests the paradox of blindness and insight.

One crucial site of this paradox is Mk 4:11–12, where Mark's Jesus simulacrum says to his disciples, alluding to LXX Isa. 6:9–10, "for those outside everything is in parables; so that [*hina*] they may indeed see [*blepontes bleposin*, 'seeing they see'] but not perceive [*idōsin*], and may indeed hear but not understand [*suniōsin*]; lest they should turn again, and be forgiven." The parables of Mark's Jesus function to keep outsiders blind even though "seeing they see." In contrast, insiders such as the disciples have been "given the secret of the kingdom of God" (4:11) and everything has been explained to them (4:34), and therefore they should see – that is, understand.[10] However, as Mk 4:13 suggests, despite this the disciples do not understand: "Do you not understand [*oidate*] this parable? How then will you understand [*gnōsesthe*] all the parables?" Jesus's disciples remain unable to "see" throughout the gospel of Mark's story.

In contrast, Matthew and Luke each make small, and different, adjustments to the use of Isaiah's language by their respective Jesus simulacra, and either the tension between "seeing" and "not perceiving" or else the disciples' non-understanding does not appear. The gospel of Matthew's Jesus simulacrum says, "I speak to them in parables, because [*hoti*] seeing they do not see [*blepontes ou blepousin*], and hearing they do not hear, nor do they understand [*suniousin*]. ... But blessed are your eyes, for they see [*blepousin*] ..." (13:13, 16). This use of "because [*hoti*]" significantly changes the sense of Isaiah's saying, and as a result, the parables help the stupid outsiders to understand, as the disciples already do. Indeed, the disciples have "been given *to know* [*gnōnai*] the secrets of the kingdom" (13:11, emphasis added), a small but significant contrast to Mk 4:13, for

9. "The self-reflecting mirror-effect by means of which a work of fiction asserts, by its very existence, its separation from empirical reality, its divergence, as a sign, from a meaning that depends for its existence on the constitutive activity of this sign, characterizes the work of literature in its essence" (de Man 1983: 17).

10. See further Kermode (1979: 23–47).

"know" in this saying serves to underline the disciples' comprehension of the parables – they have not merely been given them – in Matthew (see also Chapter 8).

The gospel of Luke's Jesus says, " To you it has been given to know [*gnōnai*] the secrets of the kingdom of God" (8:10), as in Matthew, and he also does not chastise the disciples for not understanding the parable. However, Luke's Jesus then continues, "for others they are in parables, so that [*hina*] seeing they may not see [*blepontes mē blepōsin*], and hearing they may not understand [*suniōsin*]," which is closer to Mark. Nevertheless, although the words of Luke's Jesus about the outsiders maintain the sense of Isaiah better than the words of Matthew's Jesus do, the Markan "seeing they may see but not perceive" language, which is closest to Isaiah and which nicely expresses the paradox, does not appear.

The paradox appears again in Mk 8:17–18, where Jesus again speaks to the disciples: "Do you not yet perceive [*noeite*] or understand [*suniete*]? ... Having eyes [*ophthalmous*] do you not see [*blepete*], and having ears do you not hear?" Again the paradox appears, now in the form of a question. Luke's Jesus simulacrum does not ask these questions, and Matthew's Jesus merely asks why the disciples do not perceive (*noeite*, 16:9, 11). Just a few verses later in Mark (8:22–26), Jesus has difficulty healing an unnamed blind man (*tuphlon*). He spits on the man's eyes (*ommata*), and the man is then able to see but his vision is distorted. As he says, "I see [*blepō*] men; but they look like trees, walking" (8:24). Then Jesus touches his eyes (*ophthalmous*), and the man "looked intently [*dieblepsin*] and was restored, and saw [*eneblepen*] everything clearly" (8:25). Neither Matthew's nor Luke's Jesus performs such a miracle (but compare Jn 9:1–7). This man in Mark is apparently one of "those outside," for Jesus eventually sends him away.

This story of restored sight is followed immediately in the gospel of Mark by Jesus's hostile confrontation at Caesarea Philippi with the disciples over the question of his identity (8:27–33). In this story, Jesus sees the disciples (*idōn*, 8:33) but they apparently cannot "see" him, for after Peter's so-called "confession," Jesus orders them to "tell no one about him" (8:29–30). This episode, after the preceding story of a blind man who sees even though he is an outsider, further emphasizes the blindness of the insider disciples, and this suggests that Jesus silences them because none of them understands who he is, and thus also that "the Christ" is not the right answer.

In contrast, the disciple simulacra in Mt. 16:13–23 and in Lk. 9:18–22 have no difficulty "seeing" Jesus and understanding him. In response to

Peter, Matthew's Jesus even says, "Blessed are you, Simon Bar-Jona! For flesh and blood has not revealed this to you, but my Father who is in heaven" (16:17), and he commands the disciples to "tell no one that *he was the Christ*" (16:20, emphasis added). Luke's Jesus tells the disciples to "tell *this* to no one" (9:21, emphasis added), again more like Mark, but even that tiny difference suggests that Peter's reply, "The Christ of God," is the correct answer (as the gospel of Luke also makes clear elsewhere), unlike in Mark. In addition, in Luke there is no exchange of rebukes as there is in Mark, and no "Get behind me, Satan!" as in Mk 8:33 and Mt. 16:23.

Other outsider simulacra in the gospel of Mark, like the blind man of Bethsaida, have little difficulty seeing Jesus. Both the woman with the hemorrhage and the Syrophoenician woman should be blind according to Mk 4:11–12, but they are not. Indeed, in these stories Jesus is the blind one. The hemorrhaging woman's unclean touch causes Jesus to look around (*perieblepeto idein*, 5:32) for her. She causes *him* to see, just as she initiates the miracle. Jesus merely perceives (*epignous*, 5:30) that something has happened. In this case, the comparable stories in Matthew and Luke have much in common with Mark. In Mt. 9:20–22, Jesus sees (*idōn*, 9:22) the woman, and in Lk. 8:43–48, Jesus perceives (*egnōn*) that power has gone out from him after which the woman sees (*idousa*) that she has been detected.

However, serious divergences appear again between Matthew's and Mark's stories of the Gentile women, and Luke has no comparable story. There is no explicit seeing in the gospel of Mark's story of the Syrophoenician woman, but her clever reply to Jesus's aphorism is perhaps the clearest instance of de Man's concept of blindness and insight anywhere in the gospels.

> And he said to her, "Let the children first be fed, for it is not right to take the children's bread and throw it to the dogs." But she answered him, "Yes, Lord; yet even the dogs under the table eat the children's crumbs." (7:27–28)

She sees what he doesn't, in his own words, and then he sees what she has seen. It is the unnamed woman's words, not Jesus's, that effect the miracle, as he says ("For this saying you may go your way," 7:29). In contrast, in the story in Mt. 15:21–28, the Canaanite woman speaks significantly different words, concerning crumbs from the masters' table, not the children's crumbs, and her words do not produce the miracle, but instead it is Jesus's reward to her for her faith ("Be it done for you as you desire," Mt. 15:28). I argue in Chapter 4 that Jesus's child-language in passages such as this one in Mark's gospel signifies quite differently from similar language in Matthew.

In Mk 10:46–52, Jesus heals another blind man (*tuphlos*, 10:46), Bartimaeus, this time merely by speaking to him, although his words in 10:52 ("*your* faith has made you well," emphasis added) suggest that Bartimaeus, like the Syrophoenician woman and the woman with the hemorrhage, has performed the cure, and not Jesus. It is what blind Bartimaeus "sees" that enables him to see. In this case, Bartimaeus follows Jesus. The corresponding stories in Mt. 20:29–34 and Lk. 18:35–43 have numerous differences, and both indicate that Jesus, not the man, has performed the cure, although Lk. 18:42 suggests both possibilities ("Receive your sight; your faith has made you well," compare Mt. 20:32, 34).

Another Markan outsider who sees clearly is the scribe in 12:28–34. There is no indication that the unnamed scribe is testing Jesus, and he sees "that he [Jesus] answered them [Sadducees] well," while Jesus in turn sees "that he [the scribe] answered wisely" (*idōn*, 12:28, 34). He is even "not far from the kingdom of God." This scribe stands in striking contrast to the disciples at Caesarea Philippi, and indeed nothing like this mutual seeing ever happens between Jesus and his disciples in the gospel of Mark. Nor does anything like it appear in the other gospels (but see Lk. 20:39). In Mt. 22:34–40, it is a lawyer who asks Jesus which commandment is the greatest, but this is "to test him," and there is no language of seeing. In Lk. 10:25–29, a lawyer "put him [Jesus] to the test" by asking, "what shall I do to inherit eternal life?" and again there is no explicit language of seeing.

Throughout the gospel of Mark there is no change in the overall blindness of Jesus's disciples. They abandon Jesus when he is arrested, and when he is on trial, Peter refuses to recognize him: "I do not know [*oida*] this man of whom you speak" (14:71, see also 14:68). Despite minor differences, both Matthew's and Luke's Peter simulacra use similar words to deny their respective Jesuses. Perhaps this is sheer cowardice, but cowardice can take the form of blindness. Nevertheless, in the larger context of Mark's story, where sight is often troubled by blindness, Peter's denial can be attributed in part at least to his ongoing uncertainties about Jesus, whereas that is not an option for either Matthew's or Luke's Peter, each of whom has already made it clear that he knows who Jesus is.

The reader might be tempted by the sequence of episodes in the gospel of Mark to wonder if Jesus himself moves from blindness to insight as the story unfolds. The degree to which Mark's Jesus simulacrum ever sees any truth, or even whether there is a truth to be seen in Mark, is uncertain at best. Whether Jesus hears the voices from the sky at his baptism or transfiguration (1:11, 9:7) is not said, and the outcome of his temptation by Satan (1:13) is also doubtful. He receives no reply from God to his repeated prayers in Gethsemane (14:35–41) and he dies abandoned (15:34). What he has "seen," or whether he has seen anything, remains unknown. Matthew's and Luke's Jesuses also receive no answers to their prayers on the Mount of Olives, unless we count Lk. 22:43 ("and there appeared [*ōphthē*] to him an angel from heaven, strengthening him"), which does not appear in most of the oldest manuscripts (see further Chapters 5 and 9). However, there is never any doubt throughout their respective stories that both Matthew's and Luke's Jesus simulacra see the truth clearly and without any blindness. Thus there is also no evident movement from blindness to insight for each of them, but for quite different reasons.

According to the gospel of Mark, the women followers of Jesus observe (*theōrousai*, 15:40) his crucifixion from a distance. They see (*etheōroun*, 15:47) where Jesus was buried, and on Easter they see (*anablepsasai theōrousin*, 16:4) the stone rolled away from the door. This repetition of *theōreō* may suggest a more "critical" activity, in de Man's sense, perhaps that these female disciples are watching closely in these episodes, in effect reading crucial texts. As if in anticipation of de Man's remarks, their "theoretical" activity is necessarily associated with blindness: the dead body's disappearance and the strange young man's rumor of its resurrection and a possible future meeting, which the gospel of Mark does not depict. Mark's women disciples both witness and fail to witness the resurrection. They see (*eidon*) the young man who tells them to "see [*ide*] the place where they laid him" and that "you will see [*opsesthe*] him [Jesus in Galilee], as he told you" (Mk 16:5–7). But they tell no one (16:8).

In similar episodes, the gospel of Matthew uses *theōreō* in 27:55 and 28:1 but not in 27:61, and Luke has *oraō* in 23:49, *theaomai* in 23:55, and no verb of sight for the discovery that the stone has been removed. In addition, Matthew has no verb of sight in 28:3, but *eidon* appears in 28:6 and *oraō* in 28:7, and Lk. 24:3–8 has no verb of sight. However, sight continues to play important roles in both of these gospels' Easter stories, and although blindness also occurs ("some doubted," Mt. 28:17; "these words seemed to them an idle tale, and they did not believe them," "their eyes were kept from recognizing him," "they still disbelieved for joy," Lk. 24:11, 16, 41), both gospels conclude with triumphal encounters between disciples and the risen Jesus.

Despite the glut of seeing at the very end of Mark's story, the resurrected Jesus is not seen. Mark's resurrection event, if one can call it that, does not result in faith, joy, or proclamation, but rather in amazement verging on madness, fear, flight, and silence. The story was never told. The gospel of Mark is at this point not far from the blindness that permeates Dick's story, with perhaps only the strange young man's apparently frightening final words in 16:6–7, promising a meeting with Jesus that never happens in Mark, to offer a glimmer of insight. However, Mark's gospel also differs from "The Minority Report," for while Dick's story clearly indicates that the truth has been covered up, exactly what is the truth is not clear in Mark. The gospel maintains the paradox to a degree that the short story does not.

The women at the tomb in the gospel of Mark experience something like what Barthes calls the vertigo of the photograph. Barthes describes the reality effect of the photographic image as a sort of resurrection:

> the Photograph *astonishes* me, with an astonishment which endures and renews itself, inexhaustibly. ... Photography has something to do with resurrection. ... This distortion between certainty and oblivion gave me a kind of vertigo. (1981: 82, 85, his emphasis)

This is Deleuze's "vertigo of the simulacrum" (1990: 262), the oscillation between virtual certainty and actual oblivion that forms a "crystal-image" (1989: 82; see further Chapter 2). Barthes argues that this vertigo cannot be produced by the cinema, which is too much like ordinary experience, but only by the still photograph (1981: 89–90),[11] and indeed, this vertigo does not appear in *Minority Report*. The women at the tomb in Mark's gospel see something that astonishes them (16:8), even though what they see does not settle anything. Instead it leaves them with an unanswered (and perhaps unanswerable) question; it is a moment of insightful blindness and blind insight. Perhaps this is the meaning of resurrection in Mark's gospel.

As I noted above, the resurrection stories of Matthew's and Luke's Jesus simulacra, despite their many differences, lead to conclusions of glory-filled insight at the ends of their respective gospels. In each of these stories, despite moments of blindness, the disciple simulacra see and even worship their respective Jesuses (Mt. 28:9, 17; Lk. 24:31, 38–39, 45). Differences between the simulacra are numerous in these two stories, but both stories agree that sight and insight have triumphed over blindness. The longer ending of Mark (16:9–20), often regarded as a later addition to that gospel and especially similar to Luke's ending, also turns the deep uncertainty of Mk 16:6–8 and elsewhere into clear sight (16:9, 12, 14), troubled only by passing moments of blindness (16:11, 13). The Jesus simulacrum who appears in this ending ("the Lord Jesus," 16:19) is quite different from the one who dies abandoned by God in Mark 15:34 (see further Chapter 2),

---

11. However, see Deleuze's remarks on the "photogramme" as an extreme of the cinematic image (1986: 84–86).

and he condemns doubt (16:14, 16) and "confirms the message" of his apostles (16:20), not unlike the Jesus simulacra of Mt. 28:20 and Lk. 24:49 (see also Acts 1:8).

Synoptic Minority Report

The gospels of Matthew and Luke differ significantly and at many points from each other, and I have explored some of these differences in Chapters 2, 3, and 5 of this book. However, despite these differences, the majority reports among the synoptic gospels between Matthew and Luke are more numerous and more weighty semiotically than any majority reports in which Mark is involved. For example, Matthew and Luke narrate two quite different Christmas stories, as well as different accounts of the deaths and resurrections of their Jesus simulacra. Yet both of these gospels have Christmas stories that feature a virgin birth and other miracles, and they both have accounts of resurrection appearances of a triumphant Jesus, whereas Mark has neither birth nor resurrection appearance.

Likewise in Dick's story, although the two precog reports that are identified as the majority report differ from each other in ways that turn out to be quite meaningful, they are regarded as sufficiently similar to one another to be treated as though they were in agreement (1987: 337), and therefore as decisive. In Spielberg's movie the two majority reports are described as identical. I am not suggesting that either Dick or Spielberg had in mind an allegorical relation between the three precog reports and the three synoptic gospels. Nevertheless, every story is a precog report of sorts, for as Barthes says, "the general structure of narrative ... appears as essentially *predictive*" (1986: 142, his emphasis). The word "synoptic" even draws upon a visual metaphor. In both Dick's and Spielberg's stories, each of the three crime previsions is a simulacrum, a "precession of the model" (Baudrillard 1994: 16) which is absorbed for crime prevention purposes into yet another simulacrum, the majority report. Likewise, although the three synoptic gospels each have their own differences of the simulacrum, according to Christian belief they all simulate a single coherent story. As texts, the gospels are far from unanimous, but for Christian readers, they project just one virtuality, the single reality effect that is the story of Jesus.

Many of the differences that separate the gospels of Matthew and Luke from Mark are indeed small. Nevertheless, in addition to these small differences, the synoptic majority report of Matthew and Luke also outweighs the Markan minority report in regard to larger, less easily ignored features of the stories. My focus in this chapter is on de Man's paradox of blindness and insight as one important feature that distinguishes the gospel of Mark as the minority report among the synoptic gospels. This paradox is one among several narrative themes or topics concerning which Mark's report differs consistently both textually and meaningfully from the reports presented by Matthew and Luke.

Some of these other topics also reflect the paradox of blindness and insight. One of these topics is the well-known "messianic secret" in Mark. However, the messianic secret is not truly a feature of the gospel of Mark, but instead it is a product of the reader's desire, like that of Mark's Peter simulacrum (8:29), for Jesus to be the Christ. Mark simply does not agree with the majority report of Matthew and Luke (as well as John) that Jesus clearly is the Christ. Yet Mark's blindness in regard to Jesus's messianic status is also Mark's insight. Indeed, Mark explicitly requires insight from the reader: "let the reader understand [*ho anaginōskōn noietō*]" (13:14), and thanks to the role of de Man's paradox in Mark's gospel, this phrase means something quite different there than it does in Mt. 24:15. There is no messianic secret in Mark, but instead there is a significant and provocative divergence from the majority report, for which Jesus is the Christ.

In other words, the gospel of Mark's Jesus simulacrum has no secret identity. If Mark were not read in juxtaposition with the other New Testament gospels – that is, as a book that belongs together in the canon with Matthew, Luke, and John (and Paul) – this alleged secret would not exist. Mark's presentation of Jesus's relation to the Christ provokes blindness and insight throughout the story, not only on the part of Jesus's followers and opponents within the story, but also on the part of readers who read that story as though it were a version of Matthew or Luke.[12] In those gospels, it is quite clear that each of their respective Jesus simulacra is indeed the Christ, and even more (for example, Mt. 16:16–20, 28:9; Lk. 2:11, 4:41, 24:26). These readers want to be followers who see, not blind opponents.

Another topic on which the gospel of Mark diverges from the synoptic majority report concerns the relation of Jesus to the son of man. However, in this case, the question does not concern the identity of Jesus so much as it does that of the son of man. Like the Jesuses of the other gospels, Mark's Jesus simulacrum tells a story about the son of man. Mark's Jesus may be *a* son of man, but he is explicitly not the only one, as one of his sayings describes multiple sons of men (3:28, see Chapters 2 and 4). If the son of man sayings of Mark's Jesus all belong to a single story, then this saying

12. For example, Moloney (2002: 163).

infects all of the son of man sayings in that story with its multiplicity – and if these sayings do not all belong to a single story, then Mark's Jesus still talks about multiple sons of men. In contrast, both Mt. 12:32 and Lk. 12:10, again despite small differences, make it clear that there is only one, unique son of man, who is almost certainly Jesus (see also Jn 8:28, 9:35–37).

A rather different sort of minority report appears in Mark's abrupt ending at 16:8. This theologically troubling ending is treated by interpreters as a hermeneutical problem to be solved by theories of either textual mutilation or "what the reader already knows." These solutions bring Mark's insufficiencies from the standpoint of Christian theology more into alignment with the more "synoptic" endings of the gospels of Matthew and Luke, whose own substantial differences are again ignored because either of their endings is far more preferable to the Christian reader than is Mark's ending. It appears that soon after Mark was written, Christians were already trying to find theological insight hidden in the blindness with which Mark ends at 16:8. Yet both the longer and the shorter added endings of Mark have proven to be unnecessary, because Matthew and Luke provide stories that are far more theologically satisfactory from beginning to end than does Mark.

According to the prevailing understanding of the "history of the synoptic tradition" (see further Chapter 8), much of the gospel of Mark was absorbed into Matthew and Luke, in varying ways. However, the unknown canonizers of the New Testament also chose to include Mark in the Bible as a separate text, despite its evident variations from the majority report. Perhaps the canonizers wanted to include a diverse range of reports, and they deliberately included Mark *because* it was a valuable minority report. Something like this is sometimes suggested by present-day defenders of the canon who also wish to celebrate the diversity of perspectives within the Bible. Yet this idea is not mentioned by ancient Christians as a reason for reading Mark, and furthermore, other "diverse" gospels such as Thomas or Peter, with more evident apostolic credentials than Mark's, were not included in the Bible. Indeed, it is only in recent times and only among some Christians that the diversity of the biblical texts has become valuable.

The Christian canon of the scriptures makes desirable and even perhaps necessary the synoptic reading of Matthew, Mark, and Luke, a reading in which diversity has no place. Even though the gospel of John is evidently a very different thing, harmonizing[13] readings of the four gospels are also

---

13. The shift in metaphor from the realm of sight (synopsis) to sound (harmony) does not seem to change the overall point.

widespread, not only in the everyday practice of Christians, but in appropriations of "the story of Jesus" in popular culture (see further Chapter 10). If the gospel of Mark's minority report is (or was) at all valuable within the canonical context, its greatest merit has been as a foil against which the "Jewish" Matthew and the "Gentile" Luke, each of them more popular than Mark in the early churches and still today, would seem to have more in common with each other. In this way, Mark's divergences help to emphasize the "unanimity" of the majority report.

Because of this, once the churches rejected the strategy of a single gospel account (proposed in different ways by both Marcion and Tatian) and recognized both Matthew and Luke along with John as desirable scriptures, then inclusion of Mark in addition to them might have seemed like a good idea. The canonical illusion of three books that are "synoptic" because they seem to tell slightly different versions of the same story would make it possible for the biblical canon to "naturalize" an orthodox Christian reading of Mark, one in which de Man's paradox does not appear because the canon blinds the reader to the blindness in Mark, leaving only insight apparent.

This is how the gospel of Mark also contributes to the virtuality of the Bible (see Chapter 1). The Christian canon encourages readers to read Mark as though it belongs with the other two synoptic gospels, as though it *should be* part of the Bible, and therefore as though its deviations from the other gospels are finally just acceptable minor quirks – in other words, not at all like the unacceptable deviations from the majority report that appear in non-canonical gospels such as Thomas or Peter. Yet Mark's blindness and insight, apart from the controls provided for it by its canonical status, are no more "orthodox" than are aspects of the gospels of Peter or Thomas. If Mark were not in the Christian canon, its deviations from Matthew and Luke would be more evident, and more significant. It might even be regarded as heretical, as Thomas often is, and the number of scholars and other readers who regard Mark as secondary or derivative, as only a few do now, would likely be much larger.[14]

The word "synoptic" applied to the gospels of Matthew, Mark, and Luke is not merely a convenient shorthand to acknowledge evident textual similarities, but it often reflects belief in important historical relationships

14. Although some scholars disagree, non-canonical gospels such as Thomas or Peter are often read as secondary and derivative from the canonical gospels, which among other things reduces the need to trace or explain "synoptic" relations that include them. For many centuries, the gospel of Mark was also regarded as derivative from Matthew, and its deviations were dismissed for that reason. See further Chapter 8.

between those texts that lead back ultimately to a single point of origin, which is the "historical Jesus," another simulacrum developed by modern biblical scholars. The historical Jesus never appears in the Bible, but he is supposed as the original reality of which the gospels' stories are more or less correct representations: the model which precedes its copies. Thus the designation, "synoptic," also carries important theological overtones. The canon forces the focus of the three gospels' "eyes."

Perhaps more important, the differences between the two "majority" reports provided by the gospels of Matthew and Luke would stand out more clearly if Mark were not in the New Testament, and the inclusion of both of them in the canon would then be less tolerable. It is easy to overlook the numerous differences between Matthew and Luke because their differences from Mark are much greater, and the net result in either case is more congenial to Christian faith. However, these differences which seem relatively small in the current canonical context might very well seem much larger and more troubling in the absence of Mark. This is the "blindness" of the majority report. Mark's minority report makes the illusion of a majority report possible and grounds its truth as such. It provides the proof, as it were, that none of these stories is the entire Gospel, and that they are each at best "the Gospel According to ... ." At the same time, the synoptic majority report overwhelms Mark's minority report, and thus Mark's report has been "lost" in the Bible even more effectively than the precog Agatha's report is lost in Spielberg's *Minority Report*, because Mark has remained in plain sight all the while.

Chapter 8

Fantasy and the Synoptic Problem: Q and the "Minor Agreements" Against Mark

> History alone institutes the legibility of a writing; as for its Being, writing derives that not from its meaning (from its communicative function) but from the rage, the tenderness, or the rigor with which its strokes and curves are drawn. (Barthes 1985: 220)

> The concept of the "definitive text" corresponds only to religion or exhaustion. (Borges 2000: 69)

In Chapter 7, I explored how the gospel of Mark functions as a "minority report" in relation to the "majority reports" of Matthew and Luke, with special reference to the paradox of blindness and insight. The Markan minority report supports even in its difference an illusion of synoptic agreement between the gospels. In this chapter, I examine some specific aspects of textual "agreements" (an aspect of their majority reports) of Matthew and Luke against Mark in relation to questions of literary fantasy and the canonical control of semiosis.

Similarities between the synoptic gospels are particularly evident in the material that follows the birth stories – which are themselves rather different – at the beginnings of Matthew and Luke. Mark has no birth story, and its beginning is quite abrupt (1:1–3). Similarities in the narratives continue until the passion and resurrection accounts that conclude each of the gospels, where there are again considerable differences between the three stories. Much of this similar material in what Aristotle would call the "middle" of each story (1967: 30) appears in all three gospels, but a considerable amount appears only in Matthew and Luke. However, even in this similar material, the synoptic Jesus is a rather blurry figure, as I mentioned in Chapter 7. If the reader could only figure out how to adjust the fractured "eyesight" offered by the gospels of Matthew, Mark, and Luke – the right combinations of corrective lenses, as it were – then perhaps

Jesus would come into better focus. This indeed appears to be the desire of many readers, including New Testament scholars.

The synoptic problem and its various solutions all belong primarily to study of the "history of the synoptic tradition," the efforts by biblical scholars during the last two centuries or so to reconstruct the formation of these New Testament books in the early centuries of the Common Era. In contrast, my own interests in the Bible have been formed by postmodern semiotics, literary theory, and the philosophy of language, and by attention to theological dimensions of narrative structure. What then might I have to offer to this discussion? In *The Case Against Q*, Mark Goodacre suggests that "narrative criticism" may have something to offer to understanding of the synoptic problem (2002: 17), and several chapters of his book are devoted to this possibility. Taking Goodacre's suggestion as an invitation, in this chapter I offer an alternative, postmodern approach to consideration of the so-called "minor agreements" against Mark, as well as to the hypothesis that a long lost text was the source for significant blocks of non-Markan material that Matthew and Luke seem to share in common. My approach may have implications for the history of the synoptic tradition, but that is neither my starting point nor my primary concern. I do not ignore the synoptic problem or wish it away, but I redefine the terms of the problem.

Synoptic Optometry

The synoptic problem has led modern biblical scholars to various hypotheses, such as the idea that the gospel of Mark was written first, the idea that Mark was then drawn upon and modified by Matthew and Luke, which were otherwise written independently of one another, and the idea (correlative to the second idea) that another text in addition to Mark was also drawn upon by both Matthew and Luke. Scholars call this hypothetical text "Q," from the German word *Quelle* (= source), and they construct or reconstruct Q by working backward from the synoptic texts. In the following, I draw upon the definition of the text of Q that appears in the *Q – Thomas Reader* (Kloppenborg *et al.* 1990: 35–74). These scholars sometimes even talk as if they have an actual ancient manuscript of Q in front of them, and they proceed to theorize about the "Q community" and the historical formation of the text of Q (for example, Kloppenborg 1987).

The Q theory makes sense of the fact that the gospels of Matthew and Luke have similar material that Mark does not have. However, this theory is often treated as proven, despite the additional fact that apart from the texts of Matthew and Luke, there is no evidence that this document ever existed, and despite the availability of other plausible theories to explain these similarities between Matthew and Luke, such as Austin Farrar's hypothesis that Luke's text was produced by creative rewriting of Matthew as well as of Mark. One of the great ironies of New Testament studies today is that a great deal of effort is spent in studying the text of Q, which may very well never have existed, while other effort is spent in denying the historical value of another text that certainly does exist today, the so-called "Secret Gospel of Mark."[1] Whether or not the Secret Gospel is a forgery, as many claim, the degree of these scholarly investments (both for Q and against the Secret Gospel) is symptomatic of ideological investments that play large roles in New Testament studies.

No text resembling Q has ever been found, nor is there any indisputable reference to such a text in ancient writings that still exist.[2] Another serious difficulty faced by the Q hypothesis is a large number of "minor agreements" between the gospels of Matthew and Luke, in contrast to Mark, which appear in passages that are not usually thought to be included in Q. The exact number of minor agreements is difficult to specify because of manuscript variations and also because of disagreements between scholars regarding what counts as "agreement."[3] These minor agreements range from one to five or six additional, different, or missing words, and thus simply adding these agreements to the accepted "edition" of Q will not do. That they exist strongly implies that Matthew and Luke were not composed independently, as most proponents of the Q hypothesis claim, but rather that (most probably) the author of Luke was both familiar with and rewrote parts of Matthew – and if some parts, then why not others?

One important different between the gospel of Mark and the other two synoptic gospels concerns the element of the fantastic in their respective stories. In Chapter 4, I noted the significant role that literary fantasy plays in the narrative logic of Mark. Tzvetan Todorov defines the fantastic as hesitation between marvelous (supernatural) and uncanny (strange but nevertheless natural) explanations for events that occur in a story (1973: 31–33, see also 41–57). The genres of the marvelous and the uncanny imply

1. The text of the Secret Gospel may be found in Cameron (1982: 69–71). The dispute is summarized in Crossan (1985: 100–103), and although this dispute has "evolved" in the last 25 years, the basic positions remain the same.
2. There are many references in the ancient Christian writings to gospels and other texts that are otherwise unknown today. The question is whether any of these texts might be Q.
3. See further Goodacre (2002: 152–153, n.2), and especially Tuckett (1991).

two different and incompatible understandings of reality, and fantastic hesitation appears in the narrative whenever reference to one or the other reality cannot be decided. Fantasy is thus very much a matter of reality effect. The fantastic is intrinsic to the illusions of literary realism itself, and that realism is the product of the modernist distinction between the real and the fantastic.[4]

According to Todorov, this fantastic undecidability is experienced by characters in the story, who are not sure what sort of world they inhabit, but also by the story's implied reader, who is not sure what sort of story it is. Todorov argues that fantastic hesitation cannot be sustained, and if it is not resolved by the narrative itself in one direction or the other, then it will be decided by the actual reader (1973: 41–44). Furthermore, fantastic disruption of the narrative's reference to reality corresponds to a linguistic ambiguity between the "poetic" and the "allegorical." The fantastic is both fictional (not simply poetic) and literal (not simply allegorical, 1973: 58–74). In other words, the fantastic narrative does denote something beyond itself, and that denotation is not entirely absorbed by symbolic connotations, such as a hidden message or deeper meaning.

When the fantastic plays a significant structural role in any story, then that text becomes what Roland Barthes calls a writerly text, or "text of bliss" (see further Chapters 2 and 4). The writerly is not the same as the fantastic, but it contributes to fantastic hesitation. Bliss refers to "an excess of the text, to what in it exceeds any (social) function and any (structural) functioning" (Barthes 1975: 19). In a text of bliss, semiosis flows freely and with little control, and thus the writerly text "make[s] the reader no longer a consumer, but a producer of the text" (1974: 4). Conflict over meaning seems to be built into the act of reading such a text, which is in effect all surface, a surface that reflects parabolically upon itself and never opens up to refer unambiguously to extratextual truth. Instead, reference is "split" (Jakobson 1987: 85) or divided between what Roman Jakobson calls the poetic function of language, its "self-focusing character" (Eco 1979: 90), and what Jakobson calls the referential function, its ability to denote some extratextual reality. Because they are neither poetic nor allegorical, fantastic texts often feature split reference.

Fantasy as defined in this way is fundamental to both the structural formation and the component units of the gospel of Mark. In Mark's story, meaning is disrupted and reference breaks down because the flow of semiosis is uncontrolled. Split reference is frequently evident in Mark, and it both

---

4. See further Aichele (2006: 15–30).

makes Mark a writerly text and contributes strongly to the fantastic in Mark. It also means that Mark's "eyesight" is doubled, and this surely adds to the blurring of Mark's Jesus simulacrum. Because Mark's gospel never resolves the hesitation between the uncanny and the marvelous, it is a fantastic text from beginning to end. The fantastic in Mark's stories exceeds even the spectacular death and resurrection stories of the non-canonical gospel of Peter. However, Mark's canonical status and location in the Bible tend to restrain its fantastic semiosis and conceal it from actual readers. As a result, many fantastic aspects of Mark can only be uncovered by "removing" that gospel from the canon – that is, by post-canonical readings of Mark's story, such as the one in Chapter 4.

Fantastic semiosis also plays a large role in many significant differences between Mark and the other two synoptic gospels. Todorov's theory implies that narratives can be compared to each other in terms of the degree to which each one slides over into the genre of the marvelous or the uncanny. The gospel of Mark's component narrative units are consistently more fantastic than corresponding stories in Matthew or Luke. The writerly, fantastic, uncontrolled semiosis that runs throughout Mark contrasts sharply to consistent tendencies in both Matthew and Luke to contain the semiosis in their stories by defining them as uncanny or (more often) as marvelous, and thereby to clarify the distinct identities of their respective Jesus simulacra. In other words, the gospels of Matthew and Luke each have relatively good "eyesight," even though they do not "see" the same thing: that is, their respective reality effects are not as ambiguous as Mark's are, but they are also not the same. Both Matthew and Luke tend to be what Barthes calls readerly texts ("texts of pleasure"): they explain their mysteries, and their christologies are more explicit, more fully developed, and less paradoxical than Mark's christology. In other words, stories in both Matthew and Luke are consistently less fantastic than stories in Mark, or not fantastic at all.

Markan priority is not crucial to my argument about the gospel of Mark and fantasy, but insofar as some assumption about priority may be necessary in discussions of textual relations between the gospels, I continue to assume it. However, I will return to this matter at the end of this chapter. Those who argue that Mark was derived from Matthew, or Matthew and Luke, explain (away) Mark's writerly semiosis as the results of editing,[5] but the fantastic is not merely an occasional awkwardness in the text of Mark. There is no unambiguous revelation of the story's referent in Mark, and

---

5. For example, see Farmer (1993).

perhaps it is because of this "deficiency" that Matthew and Luke both offer alternatives to Mark in which similar material is presented in ways that denote more clearly and less fantastically. If we must talk about priority and derivation, then I think that it is much more likely that Matthew and Luke each removed or neutralized fantastic material that they found in Mark, sometimes in different ways and therefore simulating significantly different Jesuses, than it is that Mark took relatively non-fantastical material from either Matthew or Luke (or both of them) and then repeatedly gave it a fantastic twist.

The fantastic resists the univocality demanded by belief, and belief also rejects fantastic aspects of narratives – that is, it de-fantasizes them, transforming them into narratives of either the uncanny or the marvelous. As Todorov says, fantasy requires *near* belief, which is neither belief nor disbelief (1973: 31), and this is again a matter of reality effect. Why would Mark's gospel consistently tell stories that are *harder* to believe, precisely because they are fantastic? If Mark is derivative from Matthew or Luke, or both of them, this question must be answered. However, if Mark was written first, then the writing of gospels such as Matthew or Luke, in which the fantastic tends to be neutralized in favor of Christian plausibility, makes sense. Nevertheless, I have no answer for the equally difficult historical question of why Mark's fantastical text was written at all. Perhaps whoever wrote this gospel was not a Christian in any sense that we can understand today.

The history of the synoptic tradition would be much simpler (and less controversial) if there had been no gospel of Mark to disturb it. Indeed, if that were the case – that is, if Mark had been denied admission to the canon, or had not survived, or even had never been written – would anyone then doubt that Matthew had been written first, or imagine that there had ever been a text such as Q? In such a case, if Mark were known at all, it might be regarded as a stunted, clearly inadequate version of Matthew – as it was for many centuries, before the theory of Markan priority became prominent, and still is by some scholars. Nevertheless, the gospel of Mark was admitted to the New Testament canon. Early Christians neutralized its fantasy by adding more readerly endings to it and, more important, by juxtaposing it in that canon to the other gospels and to Paul's letters. I will say more about this in Chapter 9.

Supposing once again a single historical trajectory connecting the gospels, the fantastic semiosis that lies on the surface of Mark is neutralized and contained by the rewritings offered in Matthew and Luke, resulting in narrative readerliness and explicit christologies. The fantastic then re-emerges in the gospel of John, but as a deep conceptual framework for the narrative as a whole. Thus John also simulates a fantastic Jesus, but a much different Jesus than Mark does. Just as Mark may have created the gospel genre, John radically transforms it, perhaps even in response to the taming of Markan fantasy by Matthew and Luke.

However, this results in a theological sublimation of the fantastic in John's story, so that instead of threatening the reader's beliefs, as Mark's story does, it encourages belief (see Chapter 6). As a result, the gospel of John's fantasy Jesus has always been popular with Christian readers, while Mark's fantasy Jesus has not. Indeed, Mark has always been the least popular of the canonical gospels, because fantastic aspects of its story have been the most threatening to faith. In contrast, Matthew and especially Luke (with its sequel, Acts) in combination with John have provided significant scriptural support for institutionalized orthodoxy in the Christian churches – that is, the Gospel of Jesus Christ (see Chapter 9).

Evangelical Hypermetropia

In previous writings, I have treated Q as though it were an actual text, although the Q hypothesis has not been crucial to my argument. My interests in Q have never been primarily concerned with its historical value, but rather in its usefulness as a way to think about textual and literary relations between the synoptic gospels. However, my views have shifted from largely uncritical acceptance of the Q hypothesis to skepticism, both because there is no historical evidence for such a text apart from the similarities between the gospels of Matthew and Luke but also for the rather a-historical reasons detailed below, which led me to think that some version of the Farrar hypothesis is at least as plausible as the Q hypothesis, or even more so. "Q-talk" continues to be a useful, although potentially misleading, shorthand for points where the gospels of Matthew and Luke "agree" in differing from Mark, but it is no more than that.

In contrast to Q, the gospel of Mark definitely exists, and although the text of Mark that appears in modern Bibles may not be the same as whatever the authors of Matthew or Luke drew upon, nevertheless it serves as a more-or-less independent text against which similar texts from those other gospels can be compared. However, no such independent text of Q is known today. Furthermore, the text of Q as it is derived from Matthew and Luke is a highly "oral text" (Kelber 1983: 185) that has not evidently been seriously affected by its transcription into writing. In contrast, Mark's narrative ambiguities may arise from the writing down of oral traditions, a "distanciation of words from meaning" (Kelber 1983: 74) in which the writerliness, and especially split reference, inherent to some degree in all writing makes evident the reader's lack of understanding (this is even noted in Mk 13:14). Werner Kelber argues that the gospel of Mark's creation of "the form of written gospel" had in effect deconstructed the "oral, prophetic function" of the sayings genre, and this deconstruction then made it possible for Matthew and Luke to "appropriate" the sayings in Q (1983: 208).

As hypothesized, the text of Q resembles that of the non-canonical gospel of Thomas, and the existence and form of this gospel is sometimes cited as support for the plausibility of Q. Like Q, Thomas is a list of sayings of Jesus, with little or no narrative thread to connect them. Neither Q nor Thomas has a birth or passion story, and Q contains only one miracle story while Thomas has none. Q and Thomas even include some similar sayings, and at least some of the material in Thomas may even predate the biblical gospels, as Q would have to.

Nevertheless, although the gospel of Thomas is in many ways quite different from any of the synoptic gospels, it does display something like the writerly self-referentiality of Mark. According to Thomas's introduction, it is composed of "secret sayings which the living Jesus *spoke* and which Didymos Judas Thomas *wrote down*" (Cameron 1982: 25, emphases added). In other words, Thomas makes explicit from the very beginning that it is a written, not an oral, text. The next two sayings in Thomas continue this self-referentiality by stressing the need to seek and find the interpretation of the written sayings. Nothing like this appears in Q. Narrative structure, and especially what Barthes calls the weaving of codes (1974: 14–21), plays important but differing roles in the element of the fantastic in Thomas and Mark. In Mark's narrative, the semiotic codes are paradoxical, but in Thomas's seeming lack of narrative they are insufficient or contradictory, and this is an important difference, but in each case the result is fantastic hesitation. However, the apparently random sequence of the sayings of Thomas's Jesus is more fantastic than Q's more orderly collection of material,[6] and the lack of an extended narrative context in Thomas makes indeterminate the referent of the sayings. Therefore the sayings of Thomas's Jesus simulacrum appear more enigmatic, bizarre, and "heretical" than corresponding sayings, including sayings attributed to Q, that appear in narrative contexts such as the biblical gospels.

In addition, in both Thomas and Mark, the fantastic appears in component units of the texts. In contrast, there is no evidence in Matthew

---

6. See Goodacre (2002: 184–185) and Kloppenborg (1987: 88–93).

or Luke that any supposed Q material resulted from written transformations of oral material such as those that may have influenced either Thomas's or Mark's fantasy. Q as it is currently accepted has little fantastic material in its component units, and the relatively non-fantastic quality of Q is highlighted by its differences from Thomas. Thomas also typically includes within each saying less explanatory material, such as allegorizing commentary or fragments of narrative, than does Q. The parabolic sayings of Q's Jesus simulacrum tend in some cases toward the marvelous and in other cases toward the uncanny, but generic indeterminacy is not maintained, and therefore the sayings are not fantastic. Thomas is therefore more fantastic than Q both in its overall apparent lack of order and in the content and expression of its component units.

Similarly, although the ambiguous relation in Q between its Jesus simulacrum and the son of man is fantastic, the story that Q's Jesus tells of the son of man is divided in both the sequence of the sayings and in their reference on one hand to an uncanny human being who lives and is despised in this present moment (Lk. 6:22, 7:34, 9:58),[7] and on the other to a marvelous heavenly being who will appear in some future time (Lk. 11:30, 12:8, 10, 40, 17:24, 26, 30).[8] Q's son of man is not fantastic, for Q's sequence presents in effect a double story, featuring two distinct son of man simulacra. There is no hesitation between them. The gospel of Matthew's sequence of these son of man sayings is less straightforward than is Luke's, thereby producing an element of hesitation, but Q proponents usually argue that Luke probably reproduces Q's sequence.

In contrast, each of the gospel of Mark's son of man sayings is more paradoxical and fantastic than any of those identified as Q, because Mark's narrative structure weaves all of the Markan sayings into a single fantastic son of man story.[9] In other words, Q (especially in Luke) cleanly separates two stories, featuring distinct son of man simulacra, but Mark (and to a lesser degree, Matthew) tells a single story of a son of man (or sons of men in Mark) that oscillates between the uncanny and the marvelous. Only two of the alleged Q son of man sayings "overlap" in any way with Markan son of man sayings. Luke 12:8[10] and Mk 8:38 are both marvelous sayings, for these son of man simulacra are conjoined with "angels of God/holy angels" and the "glory of his Father." However, Lk. 12:10 and Mt. 12:32 are also both

---

7. The corresponding passages in Matthew are 5:11, 11:19, and 8:20.
8. The corresponding passages in Matthew are 12:40, 10:32, 12:32, 24:44, 27, 37, and 39.
9. See Aichele (2001: 151–172, 2006: 203–221), and Chapter 4 of this book.
10. The phrase "son of man" does not appear in Mt. 10:32, although "men" does.

marvelous (the son of man is a possible object of blasphemy, like the spirit of God), but Mk 3:28 is not only uncanny but arguably the prime ingredient in the fantastic mix that forms the son of man story of Mark's Jesus (the plural sons of men are sinners and blasphemers).

Other sayings in the hypothetical Q collection also "overlap" with material in the gospel of Mark, and these passages are known as "major agreements" against Mark.[11] In these overlaps, direct comparisons between supposed Q texts and Mark are possible. It is not surprising that these major agreements tend to be less fantastic than the corresponding Markan material. For example, Lk. 3:7–9 and Mt. 3:7–10 each present a John the Baptist simulacrum who is a firebrand prophet and therefore likely forerunner of Jesus, who is clearly the messiah in each of those gospels. This agreement is then followed (or interrupted) by words that are similar to Mk 1:7–8, "After me comes he who is mightier than I, the thong of whose sandals I am not worthy to stoop down and untie. I have baptized you with water; but he will baptize you with the Holy Spirit" (compare Lk. 3:16; Mt. 3:11). The theologically specific phrase "the Holy Spirit" in this English translation transforms the vaguer, anarthrous phrase *pneumati hagiō* ("holy spirit," but also "pure breath") of the Greek texts. As a result, the marvelous or supernatural aspect connoted by the English text is not necessarily connoted by the Greek.

Perhaps because of this, an agreement between Matthew and Luke against Mark adds "and with fire" to the end of those sentences, and this ends the ambiguity of *pneumati hagiō* by emphasizing the marvelous. Kloppenborg *et al.* treat this agreement between Mt. 3:11 and Lk. 3:16 as part of the succeeding major agreement (1990: 36). However, Frans Neirynck lists the phrase, "and with fire," in these verses as a minor agreement (1992a: 32; see also 1974: 57) – that is, not from Q. Apparently there is some disagreement about whether or not these words derive from Q or from Matthew.[12] This in turn suggests uncertainty regarding the extent of Q, which is hardly surprising in these overlaps. However, if these words are considered to be a minor agreement, then this compatibility of major and minor agreements (note the repetitions of "fire") to form a larger narrative and conceptual unit also raises doubts about the Q hypothesis, suggesting that the distinction between major and minor agreements is itself merely an artifact of the Q hypothesis. For those who reject Q, there is neither major nor minor, only agreements of Matthew and Luke against Mark.

---

11. For a partial list, see Kelber (1983: 208).
12. See further Goodacre (2000: 52, 181–182).

These verses then continue in the major agreement between Lk. 3:17 and Mt. 3:12, with John the Baptist describing the coming mightier one as follows: "His winnowing fork is in his hand, to clear his threshing floor, and to gather the wheat into his granary, but the chaff he will burn with unquenchable fire." These words echo John's own preaching in the agreement between Lk. 3:7–9 and Mt. 3:7–10, and again the word "fire" appears. The allegorical connotations of these further sayings in the gospels of Matthew and Luke are supernatural: that is, the one to come will not simply be a mightier human being, as Mark's story allows, but a marvelous one who brings divine judgment.

According to Todorov, the marvelous (supernatural) is not itself fantastic, but the fantastic occurs at points of undecidability between the marvelous and the uncanny. Because of this, the supernatural Jesuses implied by these sayings in the gospels of Matthew or Luke are not fantastic. In contrast, Mark's Jesus may well be the mightier one announced by John the Baptist, but that does not clarify his supernatural status. He may merely be an uncanny mighty one. Any supernatural qualities of Mark's Jesus simulacrum remain uncertain at best, for Mark tells of no miraculous Christmas story and no miraculous resurrection appearances, unlike both Matthew and Luke. This uncertainty contributes to the fantastic. Later in Mark, Jesus's relation to John the Baptist continues to be ambiguous (1:14, 9:9–13, 11:27–33, see also 6:14–16), and Jesus is not clearly superior to John, in contrast to the Jesuses of Matthew and Luke.

Another major agreement occurs between Lk. 4:1–13 and Mt. 4:1–11, where detailed temptation stories are presented in very similar ways. The marvelous or supernatural element in these stories is prominent. In contrast, Mark's entire temptation story consists only of a few words in 1:12–13, "The Spirit immediately drove him out into the wilderness. And he was in the wilderness forty days, tempted by Satan; and he was with the wild beasts; and the angels ministered to him." The gospel of Mark never explicitly states that Jesus has defeated Satan or successfully resisted his temptations, and so when Jesus is charged with being possessed by Beelzebul in 3:22, the semiotic possibility that this is a correct judgment remains open, and this produces fantastic hesitation. The highly detailed triple temptation accounts attributed to Q state explicitly that Jesus has defeated Satan (Mt. 4:4, 7, 10; Lk. 4:4, 8, 12), and thus in both Matthew and Luke the Beelzebul possession charge, when it occurs (Mt. 12:24; Lk. 11:15), must be mistaken.

This narrative logic is further augmented by another major agreement, this time between Lk. 11:19–20 and Mt. 12:27–28, in which each Jesus simulacrum states that "if it is by the finger [Matthew: spirit] of God that I cast out demons, then the kingdom of God has come upon you." The reader of either Matthew's or Luke's gospel already knows, thanks to their respective birth and baptism stories, that that gospel's Jesus is indeed imbued with the spirit of God, and as a result, there is no fantastic hesitation about either gospel's conditional statement. In contrast, no statement like this appears in the gospel of Mark, and although Mark's Jesus has remarkable powers (walking on the sea, quieting a storm, feeding many people with just a little food), it is never clear what the source of those powers is.

Yet another major agreement against Mark occurs between Lk. 13:18–19 and Mt. 13:31–32. In this case there can be little or no de-fantasizing, for the mustard seed parable of Mark's Jesus (4:31–32) is not particularly fantastic, although the Greek of the text is "broken" (Taylor 1953: 270) and the exaggerated smallness of the seed and largeness of "the greatest of all shrubs" seem whimsical. Nevertheless, the growth of the mustard plant in the gospel of Mark's parable is a natural phenomenon, even though it is uncanny as Jesus describes it. In contrast, the parable in the major agreement exaggerates the plant even further into a tree, with "birds of the air [*ouranou*]" nesting in its branches, rather than nesting in the shrub's shade, as in Mark. This makes these parables of Matthew and Luke more amenable than Mark's parable to another allegorizing, supernatural reading, in which heaven's birds (perhaps Christians, or the saints) dwell in heaven's tree, and this is most explicit in the parable of Matthew's Jesus simulacrum, which compares the mustard plant to "the kingdom of heaven [*ouranōn*]."

As I noted above, fantastic semiosis is prominent and significant at different levels of the narrative in the gospels of Mark and John, but much weaker throughout Matthew and Luke. If we suppose the existence of Q and the textual history in which it plays a part, then Q apparently consisted of a non-fantastic collection that was drawn upon by Matthew and Luke as those gospels each de-fantasized material that they appropriated from Mark. In different ways, Matthew and Luke both restrict the flow of semiosis as they "normalize" (or we might even say Christianize) the genre of narrative gospel, and the presence and influence of alleged Q material in each of them is one important factor among others that makes those gospels non-fantastic.

Evangelical Myopia

Some Q proponents have argued that the minor agreements were derived from an otherwise unknown version of the gospel of Mark. If that were the case, then that missing version of Mark would also tend to direct semiosis toward the marvelous, much as the existing added endings of Mark do (see Chapter 7), and the existing, fantastic text of Mark that ends at 16:8 would still present a puzzle. No complete manuscripts of any gospels, and few fragments, have survived from the first three centuries CE, when the texts were written. During this period the gospel texts were apparently still quite "fluid," and it is highly probable that various versions of Mark and the other biblical gospels were known prior to canonization.[13] In addition to the existing multiple endings of Mark, the "Secret Gospel of Mark" offers evidence of what may be one or two other versions of Mark. In this respect, to treat the minor agreements as further evidence of a different Mark makes sense.

However, to support acceptance of one hypothetical text, Q, by supposing the existence of another one is to pile supposition upon supposition, a doubtful procedure at best and unnecessary in this case, since other, simpler hypotheses are available. If the Precrime police in Steven Spielberg's movie, *Minority Report* (2002, see further Chapter 7), were to infer from two existing majority reports that a missing, third majority report must have existed as a variant of an existing minority report, that would not be unlike this hypothetical lost version of Mark. It would eliminate any troubling disparity.

As Goodacre observes, study of the minor agreements focuses on the smallest units of meaning, and one consequence of this is that the reader may lose sight of larger signifying features such as narrative structures (2002: 16–17, 188–189). These structures would include (although Goodacre does not mention them) writerliness, self-referentiality, and the fantastic. At the same time, the understanding of minor agreements as "sense units" (Tuckett 1993: 124) privileges signified meaning over against textual signifiers, and it therefore has serious consequences for what is counted as an agreement. Most of the following examples are taken from Neirynck's list of 43 "significant agreements" (1993a: 32–33, 1993b: 229–230), which draws from earlier lists by J. C. Hawkins, E. D. Burton, and M.-J. Lagrange. These agreements are significant according to Neirynck because their existence cannot be explained in a manner consistent with the Q hypothesis. However, they also tend to be significant in the sense of "meaningful" – that is, many of these agreements have distinct effects on semiosis.

---

13. In Chapter 6 I noted instances of similar textual fluidity in the gospels of Luke and John.

Perhaps the most widely discussed of the minor agreements appears between Mt. 26:68 and Lk. 22:64 and adds six words (five words in Greek: *tis estin ho paisas se*), "Who is it that struck you?" to the single word, "Prophesy!" which is spoken to Jesus after his conviction by the council in Mk 14:65.[14] This verbatim agreement is particularly important because of its unusually large number of words, making it very unlikely that the writers of the gospels of Matthew and Luke each came up with it independently, and also because it is situated in their passion narratives, which do not appear in reconstructions of Q.

As in the major agreement concerning the mustard seed parable that was discussed above, the story in Mark's gospel is not fantastic. Instead it describes the all-too-familiar situation of a convicted prisoner who is mocked and tormented by his accusers. This particular prisoner has previously been perceived as a threat and a danger (Mk 11:18, 12:12), and he has been arrested under violent circumstances (14:43–48) and then convicted of blasphemy (14:64). Jesus is eventually crucified by the Romans, who release a murderer and insurrectionist instead of him (15:7–15). This story suggests that Jesus's enemies view him as a rather bad man. The command to prophesy in Mark seems little more than the triumphant crowing of Jesus's opponents and not unlike the taunting that he endures later in that gospel at the hands of soldiers and again on the cross (15:18–19, 26, 29–32, 36, 39).

These taunts and insults have often been interpreted by Mark's readers as irony[15]: that is, the gospel of Mark presents the enemies of Jesus as inadvertently speaking the truth about him. However, just as it is not clear that Mark's Jesus is the messiah or son of God, so it is also not clear that he is a prophet (see 6:4, 8:28, 11:32), and it is precisely this latter ambiguity that this minor agreement clarifies. It is as though Matthew and Luke each feels a need to take the taunt seriously – but irony taken seriously is not very effective irony. What is merely a mocking command in Mark becomes in both Matthew and Luke a demand that Jesus perform a supernatural trick and display for his tormentors his prophetic power. Since both Matthew and Luke make it clear as early as their birth stories and then again elsewhere that each of their Jesus simulacra truly is the son of God by way of the Holy Spirit, the reader of either gospel already knows that its Jesus simulacrum could indeed say who had struck him if he wanted to,

---

14. Unlike Matthew and Mark, Luke situates this event immediately after Jesus's arrest and before the council trial.

15. For example, Moloney (2002: 306).

and so this question provided by the minor agreement produces the irony. None of this is the case in Mark. With this addition, Matthew and Luke each bring the story of the humiliation of their respective Jesuses more into line with their larger narratives of the marvelous son of God.

A related situation appears in the minor agreement between Mt. 27:40 and Lk. 23:35. Here the words, "if he is the Christ of God, his Chosen One," in Luke and "If you are the Son of God," in Matthew appear in addition to the taunt of those watching the crucifixion in Mk 15:30, "save yourself, and come down from the cross!" The gospel of Mark's Jesus simulacrum does have powers over nature (to still a storm, to feed multitudes with little food, to walk on water), but it is not clear that he has power over human activities such as his own crucifixion. Mark's larger story gives the reader no reason to think that Jesus could get down from the cross, and so the taunt in that text is again simply an expression of hatred.[16] In contrast, Matthew and Luke have both told their readers quite clearly that each of their Jesus simulacra is the supernaturally-conceived Son of God, and thus the qualification added to the taunt again becomes inadvertently ironical, for the reader of either story already knows that its Jesus is choosing not to save himself, or at least that he needs no saving. In addition, each of the other two synoptic Jesuses has explicitly rejected Satan's invitation to throw himself from the top of the Temple (Mt. 4:5–7; Lk. 4: 9–12), and this may inform the reader's understanding of these sayings at the crucifixion. However, Mark does not provide details about the temptation.[17]

Other minor agreements differ from more fantastic Markan texts. The agreement between Mt. 3:16 and Lk. 3:22 identifies the dove at the baptism as "the Spirit of God/Holy Spirit" (with the article in the Greek text of Luke), and thus it reinforces the allegorical understanding of the major agreements discussed in the previous section regarding John the Baptist and his preaching about a coming mightier one. Each of these baptized Jesuses is indeed a supernaturally mighty one. As I noted earlier, the intratextual compatibility of these major and minor agreements to form larger units raises serious doubts about the Q hypothesis. In addition, this agreement clarifies what is fantastically ambiguous in the gospel of Mark, where the "Spirit [*pneuma*] descending upon [Jesus] like a dove" (1:10) is not clearly identified as coming from God. Mark's lack of clarity about this spirit persists, since it is also not stated in Mark that Jesus defeats Satan in

---

16. Note also the contrast between Mk 15:32 and Jn 20:25–27.

17. Additional minor agreements depicting marvelous events in contrast to what seem in Mark to be natural events appear between Mt. 14:14 and Lk. 9:11, and Mt. 16:16 and Lk. 9:20.

the wilderness (see above) and he is later accused of being possessed by Beelzebul (3:22). Mark never clearly identifies the spirit of its Jesus simulacrum, and "the Holy Spirit" does not belong uniquely to Mark's Jesus.[18]

The minor agreement between Mt. 26:64 and Lk. 22:69 specifies that the reign of a supernatural son of man commences "hereafter/from now on [*ap' arti/apo tou nun*]," in the life and death of this Jesus simulacrum, or perhaps even in these very words. Once again this minor agreement is consistent with Q, as it would fit nicely into Q's second story of the son of man, or perhaps even serve as a transition of sorts from the first story to the second one, if it were not located in the passion stories. Mark 14:62 also describes a son of man, using similar words to Matthew, except that "you will see" this son of man in some uncertain future. In addition, although the saying of Mark's Jesus is also marvelous, the larger Markan story of the son of man in which it is embedded is fantastic. Jesus may be *a* son of man in Mark's gospel, but if so he is one of many (see 3:28), and whether he is the one that "you will see ... seated at the right hand of Power, and coming with the clouds of heaven" is not clear.

In Mark's transfiguration story, Jesus is metamorphosed and "his garments became glistening, intensely white, as no fuller on earth could bleach them" (9:2–3), but there is no mention of his face. Although the appearance of Elijah with Moses (9:4) describes a marvelous event, the remainder of Mark's transfiguration story is fantastic. In contrast, the minor agreement between Mt. 17:2 ("and [Jesus's] face shone like the sun, and his garments became white as light") and Lk. 9:29 ("the appearance of [Jesus's] countenance was altered, and his raiment became dazzling [*eksastraptōn*] white") describes the altered face of each of their Jesuses[19] in addition to exaggerating even further the brightness of their clothing. It appears as though both Matthew and Luke want to emphasize the supernatural quality of the story.

These stories are usually called "transfiguration" stories and translated accordingly, even though the Greek word used in Matthew and Mark is *metemorphōthē*. The gospel of Luke uses merely *egeneto ... heteron* ("was altered").[20] Does "metamorphosed" have too many "pagan" connotations

18. Compare Mk 3:29 to 13:11, and contrast Mt. 10:20. See also Aichele (2006: 55–56).
19. On the "face of Christ" see Deleuze and Guattari (1987: 167–191). In the resurrection scene of the gospel of Peter, the head of Jesus as he is led from the tomb is described as "overpassing the heavens" (10:40, Cameron 1982: 80).
20. See Taylor (1953: 389).

for Christian sensibilities, and is this perhaps why Luke does not use the term? Although Luke's Emmaus road story (24:13–31) may also imply such a transformation, here too the term is not used. Matthew's language is more vivid than Luke's in both the transfiguration agreement and the Easter agreement discussed below, and again it may be that Luke is avoiding the use of dangerously pagan terminology.

Similarly, in the minor agreement between Mt. 28:3 and Lk. 24:4 the words, "like lightning/dazzling [*hōs astrapē/astraptousē*]," are used to describe the appearance or clothing of the angel or men at the tomb on Easter.[21] In contrast, the Easter scene in Mark is highly fantastic, for one can imagine uncanny as well as marvelous explanations for the mysterious young man's presence in the otherwise empty tomb (16:5), but his robe is simply "white," like Jesus's garments in Mark 9:3, and lacking even the hyperbole of "as no fuller on earth could bleach them." In this way Mark's narrative leaves open the semiotic decision regarding the man's identity. The appearance (unique to Mark) of a similar and equally mysterious young man at the scene of Jesus's betrayal (14:51–52) does nothing to clarify this matter. The scene in the tomb at the very end of Mark's story is crucial, and again it seems as though this fantastic undecidability is not a good thing, for the more detailed descriptions in Matthew and Luke both strongly suggest the supernatural identity of the tomb's occupant(s), which is even more explicit in Mt. 28:2 ("an angel of the Lord"). Thereby the hesitation ends.

This is further reinforced by the minor agreement between Mt. 28:8 and Lk. 24:9, where instead of saying "nothing to any one" as in Mk 16:8, the women report (*apaggeilai/apēggeilan*) to the disciples, eliminating the paradox of the story that was never told at the end of the gospel of Mark. In addition, instead of the fear of the women as they flee the tomb in Mk 16:8, Matthew's women disciples depart with "fear and great joy" (28:8), and no fear is mentioned in Lk. 24:9. Another example of this reduction of fear appears in the minor agreement between Mt. 8:27 and Lk. 8:25, "the men marveled/they were afraid, and they marveled [*hoi ... anthrōpoi ethaumasan/ phobēthentes ... ethaumasan*]," in contrast to Mk 4:41, "they were filled with awe [*ephobēthēsan phobon megan*, 'feared great fear']." Marveling replaces or at least counterbalances fear, and Matthew and Luke often narrate little or no fear when comparable Markan passages tell of fear.

---

21. Similarly in the gospel of Peter, two men come from the sky "in a great brightness" to resurrect Jesus, and on Easter the women see a young man in a "brightly shining robe" in the tomb (9:36, 13:55; Cameron 1982: 80–81).

Fear in the synoptic gospels is often not of supernatural things or events but of the fantastic unknown. Here the role of narrative structure in augmenting or diminishing fantastic semiosis is especially evident.

Another shift from the fantastic to the marvelous is less pronounced but still suggested by the minor agreement between Mt. 13:11 and Lk. 8:10, according to which the disciples are not merely "given the secret of the kingdom of God" as in Mk 4:11, but they are "given *to know* [*gnōnai*] the secrets of the kingdom of God [Matthew: heaven]" (emphasis added). This minor agreement implies that the disciples have achieved understanding of, or perhaps even entry into, the kingdom of God; they are adepts in the divine secret. The reader of either Matthew or Luke also knows secrets: namely, that Jesus is truly the son of God, that since his resurrection he dwells in heaven at the side of God (for example, Mt. 28:18; Lk. 1:32–33), and that he brings salvation from sin (for example, Mt. 1:21, Lk. 1:68).

In contrast, the gospel of Mark tells its reader no such secrets (even if "son of God" is included in 1:1, as in some manuscripts), and the kingdom remains a mystery. Furthermore, to be given a secret that you do not understand (see 4:11), as is the case for the disciples throughout Mark, is not the same as to know the secret, which implies that you understand it. I may have been given the formula for mass-energy equivalence, $E = mc^2$, but that does not mean that I recognize or understand it. Mark's reader has also been given a secret "formula," which is the text of Mark itself, but she does not understand it, and this is made explicit in 13:14 ("let the reader understand [*noeitō*]"). Mark marks its own writerliness, and like the disciples, the reader remains "outside."

Many of the minor agreements have little or no evident impact on fantastic semiosis in either Matthew's or Luke's stories. For example, the minor agreement between Mt. 26:75 and Lk. 22:62, "And [Peter] went out and wept bitterly," says a good deal more than Mk 14:72, "And he broke down and wept," but both Mark and the agreement describe ordinary events. The negative agreement between Mt. 14:19 and Lk. 9:16 arises from the absence of material similar to Mk 6:41, "and he divided the two fish among them all." However, fish are mentioned earlier in the feeding stories of Mt. 14:15–21 and Lk. 9:12–17, as they are again in the second feeding stories in Mk 8:7 and Mt. 15:34, 36. The same is true for the word "great" in both Mt. 24:21 and Lk. 21:23, in addition to words that also appear in Mk 13:19. The apocalyptic tribulations of "those days" will be marvelous in any case, and the addition of this word does not affect their supernatural status.

These differences of detail neither result in nor diminish fantastic hesitation.[22]

However, some agreements in this latter category have what might be called indirect impact on the fantastic. Michael Goulder speaks of the minor agreements as responding to a "need to explain" (1993: 158). The effect of such differences is to "smooth" the account and fill in small narrative gaps, and thereby improve the realism. These small semiotic differences make the gospels of Matthew and Luke more readerly than Mark – that is, less disruptive of understanding, or more helpful to the reader. In these ways, they direct the story's semiosis. For example, Mt. 26:50 and Lk. 22:48 agree in adding the words "Jesus said to him" to the account of Judas's kiss which appears in Mk 14:45, and Mt. 27:54 and Lk. 23:47 have "what took/ had taken place" instead of "thus" in Mk 15:39. Likewise, the agreement between Mt. 10:1 ("to cast them out, and to heal every disease and every infirmity") and Lk. 9:1 ("to cure diseases") details and thus eliminates any ambiguity of "authority over the unclean spirits" in Mk 6:7.[23]

Neirynck describes such changes as "stylistic improvements" (1993a: 27), and he notes that "phenomena of literary style cover a great deal of the coincidences between Matthew and Luke against Mark" (1974: 199). Neirynck provides detailed lists of many of these stylistic changes, of various types. For example, the frequent replacement of *kai* ("and") in Mark by *de* ("but") in Matthew and often also Luke (see Neirynck 1974: 203–204) has no impact on denotation, since both words are logical copulas, but this difference may affect connotation. "He is poor and he works hard" has the same truth value as "he is poor but he works hard," but different overtones. Such stylistic differences may not affect fantastic semiosis very much, but any aid to the reader's understanding counteracts writerly obscurity.

As with the major agreements, among the minor agreements many of the differences from existing texts of the gospel of Mark are quite small, but they are not insignificant. Similarly, in Spielberg's movie, *Minority*

---

22. Other fantastically "neutral" agreements include Mt. 3:5 and Lk. 3:3, Mt. 9:7 and Lk. 5:25, Mt. 9:16 and Lk. 5:36, Mt. 12:4 and Lk. 6:4, Mt. 12:9 and Lk. 6:6, Mt. 13:10 and Lk. 8:9, Mt. 9:18 and Lk. 8:41, Mt. 10:10 and Lk. 9:3, Mt. 14:13 and Lk. 9:11, Mt. 19:29 and Lk. 18:30, Mt. 21:17 and Lk. 21:37, Mt. 26:74 and Lk. 22:60, and Mt. 27:59 and Lk. 23:53.

23. Other agreements that provide clarity or help to maintain narrative continuity occur between Mt. 8:2 and Lk. 5:12, Mt. 9:2 and Lk. 5:18, Mt. 9:17 and Lk. 5:37, Mt. 12:1 and Lk. 6:1, Mt. 9:20 and Lk. 8:44, Mt. 14:1 and Lk. 9:7, Mt. 17:5 and Lk. 9:34, Mt. 17:17 and Lk. 9:41, Mt. 21:23 and Lk. 20:1, and Mt. 28:1 and Lk. 23:54.

Report, tiny differences of detail between the majority and minority prevision reports correspond to large differences of denotation and connotation. Just as alleged Q material in both Matthew and Luke consistently tends to be non-fantastic, often directing semiosis toward the marvelous, in contrast to Mark's fantastic undecidability, so also their minor agreements against Mark are non-fantastic and have the same reality effect, or else they have no great impact on semiosis. As a result, the general tendency of both the major and minor agreements is to make both Matthew and Luke more readerly, in contrast to Mark, which is writerly throughout and constantly makes meaning a problem.

The net effect of both Q, whether it actually existed or is merely a modern product of synoptic differences and similarities, and the minor agreements is to replace material that is fantastic and more writerly in the gospel of Mark with material that is marvelous and more readerly in Matthew and Luke. In other words, both the major and minor agreements, whatever historical, redactional phenomena they may evidence textually, work to much the same semiotic effect, controlling the connotations of passages in Matthew and Luke that are otherwise similar to Mark and yielding non-fantastic material that is otherwise similar to fantastic material in Mark's story. From this perspective, there is no difference between the literary or reality effects of the alleged Q document and the minor agreements.

A Different Difference

The hypotheses of Markan priority, the independence of Matthew and Luke, and the existence of Q all imply particular understandings of the early formation and beliefs of Christian communities, and ultimately of Jesus as a unique historical individual, the supposed single referent of the various stories in the gospels. Alternative hypotheses such as those of Farrar or William Farmer (updating J. J. Griesbach's "two gospel" theory) necessarily imply somewhat different understandings of these matters. These historical and theological understandings influence scholars when they choose between hypotheses, just as they also influence the ways that the gospels are read today.

Each of these attempts to reconstruct the history of the synoptic tradition also entails a modernist concept of history itself (that is, of historical reality) as linear, coherent, rational, and meaningful. It is often supposed that there had to be unique autographs of the various biblical writings, even though none are known today, and that each of these autographs corresponds in some special way to an author's intention that entirely defines its meaning, and so likewise there had to have been some single unique point at which the writing process began and which led ultimately, in clearly definable ways, to production of the gospels as they are now known. The text's author may be understood either as an individual or as a collectivity, such as "the Matthean community," and the further complication provided by hypothesized multiple sources or redactors (as well as later copyists) does not alter the fundamental logic of this view of history and the correlated search for a point of origin.

According to this concept of history, each of the gospels was produced for understandable reasons, and they all belong somehow within a variegated but ultimately coherent field of tradition that emanates from one man and his first followers. In other words, history must be a unified whole. One consequence of this way of thinking is the concept that the synoptic gospels "obviously" belong together, and so they must be related closely to one another. They are all somehow versions of one story. The thought that three authors independently and purely coincidentally produced three quite similar stories about three different characters named Jesus – that is, yielding three distinct Jesus simulacra, not just three versions of one story – is completely unacceptable. It is also unthinkable that these stories would describe different Judases, Marys, Galilees, Jerusalems, etc. – even different Gods.

Many Christians may believe that three authors independently produced these three stories, but that due to divine inspiration the gospels all speak one truth, the Gospel of Jesus Christ. This would not be coincidence, and it would still yield three versions of just one story. In another age, such belief might be quite natural (that is, ideologically acceptable). However, the natural tendency today is to think that the synoptic gospels must be historically and theologically related to each other. In other words, their production of a single reality effect is a result of human activity. By tracing the textual relations between these books, modern scholars seek to restore the original version of each one of them and thus move closer to identifying and understanding its proper meaning, and eventually that of the whole series. As Neirynck says:

> The minor agreements force us again and again to study each passage in light of the whole Gospel, and this has been, it seems to me, most profitable to our comprehension of the three Synoptic Gospels (1993a: 62).[24]

Ideological dimensions of this modern concept of history appear not only in its exclusions but also in its conflicting results. The more "philosophical"

---

24. See also Tuckett (1993: 137) and Farmer (1993: 206–207).

or "ethical" Jesus simulacrum of Q may make it a more palatable first gospel than Mark to theologically liberal Christians, while the more "prophetic" or even "apocalyptic" Jesus simulacrum of Matthew, which is the first gospel according to the two gospel theory (as well as the older Augustinian view), perhaps appeals more as the first gospel to conservative Christians. One ideological benefit of the Q hypothesis is rejection of Matthean priority without full acceptance of Markan priority – for after all, Q was supposedly written earlier than Mark. Mark's ambiguous Jesus simulacrum has never been very appealing to Christians, but if Q is not supposed then Markan priority may serve as a compromise, especially if Mark can be "repaired" by supposing a lost original, of which the existing manuscripts are bungled copies. Such "repairs" to Mark also allow the supposition of a more theologically appealing Jesus.

However, if there were no Christian creeds or New Testament canon, or even further, if Christianity had died out centuries ago,[25] would readers of the gospels today (if there still were any) be tempted to trace their relations? Would Matthew, Mark, and Luke be so obviously synoptic? Belief in the Bible as the single, coherent "Word of God" – that is, the virtuality of the Bible – together with the canonical sequence of multiple gospels press readers to seek some sort of unitary, linear order. Modern scholars rearrange the gospel sequence in the name of historical accuracy, but they do not question the need for a meaningful sequence. As Barthes's epigraph to this chapter implies, these writings are defined in terms of their legibility, which is their meaning, and not in terms of the "strokes and curves" of their signifiers. However, the understanding that results from this modern concept of history in conjunction with acceptance of the virtuality of the Bible focuses primary attention on similarities between the gospels, their so-called "shared" or "parallel" material, and the great many cataloged differences[26] between the gospels are valued chiefly as symptoms or evidence that change has occurred.

For the onto-theological metaphysics of modernism, which is essential to this concept of history, sameness is prior to difference, and difference arises only as disturbance of primal unity. In contrast, for postmodern thought, difference or multiplicity is ontologically prior to sameness or similarity, which arises as the violent rejection or refusal of difference.[27] For

25. For an imaginative but plausible "alternate history" in which Christianity effectively dies out due to the plagues in Europe, see Robinson (2002). Robinson's novel does not tell what happens to the Bible.
26. Thanks to the considerable labors of Neirynck and others.
27. For example, see Derrida (1976) and Deleuze (1994).

a postmodern approach, the reality effects of the gospels of Matthew, Mark, and Luke become less "synoptic" with one another, and perhaps more so with other texts. Other synoptic opportunities for the gospels become more apparent, both in the Bible and in the larger ancient world. The gospel of Mark may have more in common with similarly fantastic, writerly texts in the Jewish scriptures, such as Job or Jonah, than it does with perhaps any other New Testament text, not so much at the level of the signifier, but in relation to questions of semiosis. Other aspects of Matthew or John may also align them significantly with other material from those scriptures. In addition, numerous readers have noted intertextual affinities between Luke (and to a lesser extent Mark) and pagan Hellenistic literature. In Chapter 9, I explore another alternate synopticity, this one between Luke and John and against Matthew or Mark. These often overlooked similarities between Luke and John, together with the letters of Paul, contribute significantly to the simulation of Jesus Christ in the Gospel. Although a different sort of synoptic problem appears in this case, many scholars who examine the matter treat it in much the same way – that is, as an historical question of originality and derivation. I do not.

In addition, as I noted in Chapter 1, intertextuality is not a function of an author's intention, but rather a relation between the text's signifiers and the reader. Meaning is always and only stretched between texts, as they are brought together in the various understandings of actual readers, and thus meaning is always the product of eisegesis. There is no reason why intertextual readings of the gospels should be confined to ancient Mediterranean texts. Once we break free from the modernist concept of history as a meaningful, linear whole, a much wider range of semiotic relationships becomes conceivable. Whatever actually happened in the past is only accessible through the many stories (fictions) that we today either create or accept from others – including stories such as the gospels – and as a result there are many divergent and inconsistent histories. Freed from canonical control, the gospels' semiosis becomes unlimited, and then the synoptic problem takes on a very different form indeed.

Chapter 9

LUKE AND JOHN, AND THE SIMULATION OF CHRIST

Interpretation is our modern way of believing and of being pious. (Deleuze and Guattari 1983: 171)

[T]he similarities – and dissimilarities – between the theologies of the two evangelists [Luke and John] constitute ... an exceedingly interesting subject. (Bailey 1963: viii)

A Different Synopsis

I noted in Chapter 2 that within the New Testament each of the four stories in the gospels of Matthew, Mark, Luke, and John simulates a character named Jesus who is followed by some disciples. Each of these Jesuses talks about the kingdom of God and performs miracles, and each of them is crucified by the Romans and raised from the dead. Yet despite interesting similarities between the four gospels' stories and their Jesuses, neither the stories nor the characters in them are the same. Important differences and even contradictions appear between these stories, and therefore they all cannot be true and they all cannot refer to the same person named Jesus. Instead, the name of Jesus serves as a hook in each story on which it hangs diverse predicates, and as a result each of these Jesuses is a distinct reality effect. These four Jesuses are four distinct simulacra or virtual beings, the ideological products of the reader's attempts to decode the texts. They are "models of a real without origin or reality" (Baudrillard 1994: 1), not different replicas of a single original model. I have sketched some aspects of these differing reality effects in Chapters 3 through 6.

Despite this, Christians and indeed most readers do not understand the gospels in this way. Instead they read the gospels as four versions of a single story, which is the Gospel of Jesus Christ, or even as four chapters of a single larger whole, which is the Bible. One of the more important functions of the Christian Bible is to restrain the semiosis of its constituent texts and thereby to support the Christian churches' theological claims. The Bible does this by forming an intertextual network through which texts within that canonical network are interpreted in relation to other texts within the network. In addition to the four Jesuses of the gospels, distinct Jesus simulacra appear elsewhere in the New Testament. Furthermore, texts from outside of the canon, such as theological proclamations, sermons, and creeds, also play important roles in the churches' interpretation of the Bible. All of these texts are usually understood as though they referred to a single Jesus Christ.

Nevertheless, it is the intertextuality within the biblical canon, as the "Word of God," that establishes the core framework for the control of biblical meaning. In particular, in terms of my interests in this book, the canon is crucial to the definition of the Christian understanding of Christ. I do not deny that there are (or always have been) in the churches many different understandings of Christ: a quick Google search on "jesus christ," or a review of the history of Christian thought, will confirm as much, Nor do I deny that the Bible functions differently in different Christian denominations and communities. Nevertheless, insofar as any understanding of Christ becomes part of Christian discourse – that is, not just a matter of private experience – it refers in some way to biblical texts. In addition, although texts of the Christian Old Testament (the Jewish scriptures as appropriated into the Christian Bible) play an important role in this definition, the texts of the New Testament are doubly decisive, both in relation to each other and in the ways in which they control Christian understanding of Old Testament texts through their citations of "the scriptures." Therefore the New Testament texts have the more powerful canonical function for Christians.

The canon of the New Testament makes possible or at least assists significantly in the construction of the singular Jesus Christ simulacrum of Christianity, and thus in the formation of the Gospel and the virtual Bible. As described in Chapters 7 and 8, the "majority report" presented by the synoptic gospels contributes in important ways to the Gospel. However, an essential ingredient in this construction of the Christ simulacrum is what John Bailey calls in the second epigraph of this chapter the "exceedingly interesting subject" of similarities between the respective "theologies," or more specifically for my purposes here, the Jesus simulacra of the gospels of Luke and John.[1]

---

1. See also Schnackenburg (1980a: 32). For a helpful review of scholarship on the relationship between Luke and John, see Smith (1990).

The gospels of Luke and John play especially important roles in this construction of the Gospel of Jesus Christ. The cumulative reality effect of those complementary and even harmonious simulations within the larger intertextual structure that is the canon of the New Testament – that is, how Luke and John are read in combination within the New Testament – contributes substantially to the Christian concept of "Jesus Christ" that I sketched at the end of Chapter 2. There are curious and important affinities between Luke and John, and because of them Luke is compatible with John in ways that neither Matthew nor Mark are – indeed, in ways that overwhelm and obscure differences and similarities that appear in those other gospels, when all four books are read together within the canonical intertext. Bailey even claims that John's author was "stimulated" by "his" reading of Luke into writing the gospel of John (1963: 114). Dwight Moody Smith argues that "Luke shows a strong tendency to depart from, alter, or omit the Markan (or Markan/Matthean) tradition, which he follows for much of his Gospel, at those points where it is contradicted or otherwise called into question by the Fourth Gospel" (Smith 1990: 100), and Lamar Cribbs agrees. Indeed, the "synopsis" between these two gospels is far more important to the Christian ideology than is the better-known synopsis between Matthew, Mark, and Luke.

This compatibility between the gospels of Luke and John is augmented considerably by Luke's sequel, the Acts of the Apostles. As in Chapters 2 and 5, in this chapter I treat Luke and Acts as two volumes of a single work, and I regard the Jesus simulacrum that appears briefly and intermittently in the book of Acts as identical to that of Luke. The inclusion in the New Testament of the Acts of the Apostles further reinforces the intertextual christology of Luke and John, as well as serving as a valuable link between those gospels and the letters of Paul. One might likewise regard the Johannine letters as a sort of supplement to the gospel of John, but in these letters the Jesus simulacrum is already well on its way to being absorbed into Jesus Christ, as happens in most of the New Testament epistles.

As Bailey notes, the gospel of John sometimes anticipates in its story of Jesus what the book of Acts narrates as the formation of the church (1963: 105). For example, in John Jesus announces that "the Counselor" or "Spirit of truth" will "be with you forever" and "teach you all things" (14:16–17, 26), in effect completing that otherwise incomplete gospel (20:30, 21:25; see Chapter 6) and guaranteeing successful comprehension of its meaning (16:12–15). John's resurrected Jesus breathes on the disciples, and this breath is the "Holy Spirit" which he gives to them (20:22). If the spirit of John's resurrected Jesus is the Counselor of 14:16–17, "whom the world cannot receive," then the disciple simulacra in John 20 must be able to "receive the Holy Spirit" because they too are no longer "of the world" (15:19, 17:14–16). Similarly, in the Acts of the Apostles, the Holy Spirit arrives during the Pentecost meeting and transforms the gathered followers of Jesus into the church, guaranteeing that differences of language will not hinder the proclamation of the apostles' message to "every nation under heaven" (2:5).[2] In each case a divine spirit arrives or will arrive after the post-resurrection departure of Jesus to secure the successful delivery of the message. Nothing like this appears in either Matthew or Mark.

In addition, the word *Ioudaios* ("Jew") is used much more often in either the gospel of John (71 times) or the Acts of the Apostles (79 times) than it is in the remainder of the New Testament (40 times, with five in Matthew, seven in Mark, and five in Luke). Unlike Matthew or Mark (or Luke), in both John and Acts, "the Jews" are usually enemies of Jesus or of the early church. Given the contribution of this phrase in these texts to the long history of Christian antisemitism, these are hardly innocent descriptions. Smith notes that in comparison to the synoptic gospels, "John's Jesus is a more distinctly Christian figure who stands over against 'the Jews'" (1990: 234), and this description also applies well to the Jesus of the book of Acts, far better than it would to the Jesus simulacra of either Matthew or Mark (or Luke alone). Pierson Parker notes other connections between John and Acts.[3]

Scholars have been so taken by the synoptic problem that they have sometimes ignored or downplayed other potential relationships between the gospels. The non-canonical gospel of Thomas, which may have been written much earlier than any biblical gospel, includes parables of Jesus that are similar to those in the synoptic gospels (but missing in John) as well as "I am" sayings of Jesus that are similar to "I am" sayings in John (but missing in the synoptics).[4] In addition, both John and Mark simulate fantastic Jesuses, in strong contrast to either Matthew or Luke, although the fantastic undecidability of the identity of the Jesus simulacrum and his relation to God functions quite differently in John than it does in Mark (see further Chapter 8). Mark and John are not particularly "synoptic." However, the contents of two other non-canonical gospels, Egerton Papyrus 2 and the "secret gospel of Mark," both imply that by the second century

---

2. See Schnackenburg (1982: 136, 325–326, 359–360), and Bultmann (1971: 692–693).
3. Described in Smith (1990: 97–99).
4. Smith compares John to the non-canonical gospels *vis-à-vis* the synoptics (1990: 192–193, 236–237).

some Christians were producing texts that contained elements from both Mark and John.

It is well known that there are curious similarities between the gospel of John and the synoptic gospels, but much of the focus of this scholarship has been on John's dependence upon (or independence from) either Luke or Mark. In other words, was John's author aware of either Luke or Mark? Smith argues that "Apart from its ancient, canonical setting, John's independence is obvious enough" (1990: 189).[5] Others maintain that John's author knew some version of Luke, or that Luke as we know it now was revised by an editor who was familiar with the gospel of John. Speculations regarding John's historical dependence upon or independence from the other gospels have ideological or theological dimensions not unlike the speculations regarding Q and the minor agreements (see Chapter 8). However, this is not my concern here. As in previous chapters of this book, I am not particularly interested in hypothetical historical trajectories, underlying oral traditions, or probabilities of influence between any of the gospels, and I do not argue that compatibility between Luke and John is intentional on the part or either author.

What does interest me in this chapter is how and what these gospels "see together." Instead of speculating about trajectories, I explore the effects that result from this synopsis between the gospels of Luke and John within the canonical structure. These intertextual effects take different forms.[6] Apart from the simulation of Jesus, there are other concepts or language in regard to which Luke and John have evident affinities, and which distinguish the two of them from either Matthew or Mark. These include, among others, the Holy Spirit, the sisters Mary and Martha, and the use of the important verb, *graphō* ("write"), but they will not be directly addressed here.

Coded Realities

In *S/Z*, Roland Barthes describes five codes in relation to which he reads Honoré de Balzac's novella, *Sarrasine* (1974: 19–20). Each code is a "voice

---

5. See also Brown (1966: xliv–xlvii).

6. For lists of connections between Luke and John, see P. Parker (1960: 99–100), Brown (1966: xlvi–xlvii), Schnackenburg (1980a: 30–34), and Smith (1990: 85–87). Perhaps the most complete survey is that of Cribbs (1979), who identifies numerous verbal parallels, common items of factual information, sequential agreements, and other strong indications of connection between Luke and John. See also Smith (1990: 100–101), discussing the work of Cribbs, and (105–108), discussing the work of Robert Maddox.

out of which the text is woven" (1974: 21) through the process of reading it. These codes are not embedded "in" the text but are brought to it by the reader – that is, they belong to the intertextual network, not the text itself, and thus the coded "voice" is always that of the reader, not the author. The codes themselves interweave with one another in complex ways to produce a meaningful narrative, or as Barthes says:

> The five codes create a kind of network, a *topos* through which the entire text passes (or rather, in passing, becomes text). ... The code is a perspective of quotations, a mirage of structures; we know only its departures and returns; the units which have resulted from it ... are themselves, always, ventures out of the text, ... so many fragments of something that has always been *already* read, seen, done, experienced. (1974: 20, his emphasis)

In the order in which I discuss them here, these five codes are the semic, hermeneutic, proairetic, symbolic, and cultural codes, to use Barthes's terminology.[7] I define them further below. Although Barthes limits his study to these five codes, there is no reason to think that they are the only ones, or that other readers might not draw upon other codes.[8] One important feature of Barthes's analysis (which complicates my discussion) is that often multiple codes apply to a single textual unit or "lexia," interweaving like the elements of a musical score (1974: 21). Barthes even says that "This analogy can be carried even further. We can attribute to two lines of the polyphonic table (the hermeneutic and the proairetic [codes]) the same tonal determination that melody and harmony have in classical music" (1974: 29–30). In the following I draw upon these five codes, but unlike Barthes I do not use these codes as Barthes does to explore in depth the "polyphony" of a single text, but instead to identify points of shared "melody" or significant "harmony" *between* two texts, the gospels of Luke and John. As intertextual phenomena, the codes are well suited to reading several texts at once. Given the theological implications of the canon, the ways that John and Luke play (with) these codes allow them to collaborate almost seamlessly in the Christian ideology.

7. These codes correlate loosely to three of the first four of Aristotle's elements of tragedy (1967: 25–58). The semic code corresponds to what Aristotle calls the language, and the hermeneutic code corresponds to the thought or message, although the symbolic and cultural codes also contribute to this element. The proairetic code corresponds to the Aristotelian plot. No code corresponds closely to Aristotle's concept of character, although each of them may impact upon character.
8. For a Barthesian reading of the gospel of Mark that draws upon additional codes, see Belo (1981).

The semic code or code of the semes concerns the potential for meaning already present in the signifier (Barthes 1974: 19), which Barthes elsewhere calls "signifiance" or the "obtuse meaning" of a "signifier without signified" (1985: 43, 55). Already at the level of the signifier – that is, insofar as the reader understands it to be a signifier, and not just a meaningless object – the ideological control of meaning appears. The other codes have more to do with the signified, or the denotation and connotation of reality. The code of the semes interweaves with these other codes in the simulation of characters, actions, and events in a narrative (diegesis[9]). If the hermeneutic and proairetic codes correspond, as Barthes says, to harmony and melody in music, then the code of the semes concerns significant aspects of the notes themselves (such as pitch, timbre, or loudness).

The gospels of Luke and John both describe Jesus in narrative (diegesis) as "the Lord" (*kurios*: Lk. 2:11, 7:13; Jn 6:23,[10] 11:2). In contrast, in Matthew Jesus is never referred to in diegesis as "the Lord," and this phrase is always reserved for God. No matter how closely Matthew's Jesus simulacrum may be associated with God prior to his death, he is not God, at least not until he is resurrected, when the disciples worship him (28:17). The term "Lord" also does not appear in Mark's diegesis prior to the added endings. Mark refers to Jesus in diegesis as "the Lord" only in the longer added ending (16:19–20), which is quite different in style and content than Mk 1:1–16:8 but similar to the ending of Luke. As I noted in Chapter 2, the multiple endings of Mark produce multiple gospels of Mark, each with its own Jesus simulacrum.

In other words, only in Luke and John does the text in effect announce that Jesus is the Lord, not necessarily as an explicit theme, but simply by their (nearly identical) narrative discourse. In contrast, in each of the four gospels, various characters speak the word, "Lord" (*kurios*). However, because neither Matthew nor Mark uses *kurios* to describe its Jesus simulacrum in diegesis, each of them requires the reader to decide whether characters who speak in this way have chosen the best term. The imitation of spoken or written words in a narrative (mimesis) relates more to the

9. Mimesis is the representation of discourse, for words can only truly imitate words, although when written words "imitate" spoken words, strange things may happen (see Chapter 1). Diegesis is the representation of everything other than words: actions, descriptions, etc. Mimesis and diegesis stand at two extremes of a continuum, with many intermediate points: indirect discourse, narrated thoughts or feelings, etc. See Chatman (1978: 146–262).

10. *Kurios* is missing from this verse in the oldest manuscripts of John, but it does appear in Codex Bezae Cantabrigiensis.

simulation of characters, and here the semic code interweaves with Barthes's hermeneutic, cultural, and symbolic codes.

For example, when Mark's Jesus tells the cured demoniac to "Go home to your friends, and tell them how much the Lord has done for you, and how he has had mercy on you" (5:19, contrast Lk. 8:39), the reader must decide whether *kurios* refers in this saying to Jesus himself or to God (see Mk 1:3). Matthew's Jesus simulacrum even says, "Not every one who says to me, 'Lord, Lord,' shall enter the kingdom of heaven, but he who does the will of my Father who is in heaven" (7:21, see also 22–23). In contrast, Luke's Jesus says, "Why do you call me 'Lord, Lord,' and not do what I tell you?" (6:46). Although these two sayings are superficially similar – they are both attributed to Q (see Chapter 8) – the difference of meaning between them is considerable. Matthew's Jesus suggests that simply calling him "Lord" is by itself of no value, but obedience to God ("my Father who is in heaven") is what counts. Luke's Jesus says that recognition of his lordship should be accompanied by obedience to himself.

Something like this also appears in another affinity of the signifier between Luke-Acts and John, when various characters describe each of their Jesus simulacra as the "Savior" (*sōtēr*, Lk. 2:11; Jn 4:42; Acts 5:31, 13:23). The word "salvation" (*sōtēria*) is also used several times in Luke and Acts, and in Jn 4:22. Matthew does not use either term, while *sōtēria* appears only in the shorter added ending of Mark, and *sōtēr* not at all in Mark.

Semic resonances extend also to words and phrases that the gospels of Luke and John do not use, but that do appear in Matthew or Mark. According to Smith, "In not a few cases the agreement [between Luke and John] is a matter of a common silence or suppression of information, or departures from what we find in the other Gospels" (1990: 86), and he lists several of these agreements of silence.[11] In other words, it may be significant that Luke and John both *do not* say something that one or both of the other biblical gospels says. Neither Luke nor John contains anything like Jesus's difficult saying in Mk 3:28, with its christologically troublesome plural phrase, "sons of men." Matthew 12:31–32, although otherwise similar to the saying in Mark, also does not contain the plural phrase. Given the importance of the "son of man" in the words of the various Jesus simulacra, and in Christian understanding of those words and of Jesus, this is a significant difference.

Furthermore, unlike the gospels of Matthew and Mark, neither John nor Luke uses the noun "gospel" (*euaggelion*) at all. In Lk. 8:1, Jesus is

---

11. See also Cribbs (1979: 232–234).

"preaching and bringing the good news [*kērussōn kai euaggelizomenos*],"
but the comparable verse in Mt. 9:35 has "preaching the gospel [*kērussōn
to euaggelion*]." Since *euaggelion* is a very important word in the New
Testament and in Christian thought, the non-appearance of this word in
these two gospels is striking. That they may wish to reserve this word for
something else is hinted in the book of Acts, which uses the term *euaggelion*
twice: in 15:7, Peter uses the word to describe his preaching to the Gentiles,
and in 20:24, Paul mentions "the gospel of the grace of God" as that which
he "testifies to." For the Acts of the Apostles, *euaggelion* is announced by
apostles: it is an "act of the apostles." It is also well on its way to becoming
the ideology of the Christian church – that is, what I have called in this
book the Gospel. By avoiding the use of "gospel" as in Matthew or Mark,
both Luke and John open up space for the Gospel.

There is one more semic connection between the gospels of Luke and
John, this time in the form of a manuscript puzzle. John 7:53–8:11, the
story of the woman taken in adultery, appears in modern printed texts of
John, which either include the text in the position indicated by those verse
numbers or else print it in a footnote that follows Jn 7:52. However, in some
manuscripts of John this passage appears in other locations in that gospel,
and most important for my purposes here, in members of the medieval
manuscript family 13 this passage appears at the end of Luke 21, where it
fits quite neatly into Luke's narrative (see further Chapter 6). This evidence
suggests that this passage at one time slid back and forth between these
two gospels. This raises further questions about not only their historical
but more importantly their ideological relationship, and also about the
extent of the text of each of these gospels.[12] The story's proper textual
location is vague; there a porousness on the boundary between Luke and
John which amounts to a softness in the canon. In addition, although the
gospel of John's seemingly redundant Chapter 21 does not appear in any
manuscripts of Luke, it too has resonances with Luke, and it may well have
been added on to John.[13]

Other intertextual effects between the gospels of Luke and John reach
beyond the level of the signifier and further into fields of the signified.
Barthes's hermeneutic code treats the story as an answer to one or more

12. See also Smith (1990: 189–190) and Brown (1966: 335–336). A similar question
    arises about the multiple endings of Mark: all three ending possibilities are
    included in most modern printed editions of Mark, but which ending is the
    "canonical" one?
13. See Bailey (1963: 12–17) and Brown (1970: 1079–1082). John 21 is also discussed
    more fully in Chapter 6.

questions, or as he says, "the various (formal) terms by which an enigma can be distinguished, suggested, formulated, held in suspense, and finally disclosed" (1974: 19). The hermeneutic code both raises a question and delays (but usually finally gives) an answer to it.

One ideologically important question that drives each of the gospels is the question of Jesus's identity. The gospels of Luke and John give very similar responses to this question, in contrast to Matthew or Mark. Not only is Jesus "the Lord" and "the Savior" in both Luke and John, but Jesus and his divine Father appear to be in complete harmony; indeed, they are so closely aligned as to be nearly indistinguishable. Luke's Jesus says, "he who rejects me rejects him who sent me" (10:16), and John's Jesus even says, "I and the Father are one" (10:30, see also 12:44–45). Neither Matthew nor Mark has comparable sayings. The saying in Mk 9:37, "whoever receives me, receives not me but him who sent me," is not equivalent because an important and unresolved question throughout Mark concerns who sent Jesus (3:21–22, 11:27–33). Matthew 10:40, Lk. 9:48, and Jn 13:20 are similar to the saying in Mark, but in Matthew, Luke, and John the divine origins of their Jesus simulacra are clear from the start of each story, and thus they signify differently. In other words, Mk 9:37 functions quite differently in relation to the larger hermeneutic structure of that gospel, unless one reads Mark in the light of Luke or John – that is, as directed by the canon.

In the gospels of Luke and John, each of their respective Jesus simulacra describes the Temple as "my Father's house," and each of these Jesuses knows from the story's beginning that he belongs in it (Lk. 2:49; Jn 2:16, 14:2, with some variation in the Greek). Here semic, symbolic, and cultural codes are also in play. The capitalization of "Father" is an artifact of translation, but it emphasizes that the phrase does not connote Joseph's house. Instead the phrase is used by Luke's and John's Jesus simulacra to refer to the Temple in Jerusalem (except Jn 14:2, where it appears to refer to heaven, although this may suggest a heavenly Temple). Neither Matthew nor Mark uses the phrase "Father's house" at all. In addition, both Luke and John develop other implications of the concept of Jesus as the son of God in ways that are striking similar to each other and quite different from anything in either Matthew or Mark. Both Lk. 4:22 and Jn 6:42 explicitly raise the question of Jesus's status as "son of Joseph" (see also Lk. 3:23 and Jn 1:45), but neither Mark nor Matthew ever uses this phrase, either. In each of these similarities between Luke and John, either Jesus's role as God's divine son is emphasized or his role as Joseph's human son is diminished (see further Chapter 5). Again symbolic and cultural codes are in play.

The gospels of Matthew and Mark do include references to their Jesuses as "the son of God," but the significance of that phrase is less clear in each of those stories. "Son of God" may connote the king of Israel (as in Ps. 2:7), or any Israelite (as in Isa. 63:8). Matthew's Christmas story is cryptic compared to Luke's Christmas story, especially in relation to Jesus's paternity. It consists only of "before [Mary and Joseph] came together she was found to be with child of the Holy Spirit" (Mt. 1:18). Matthew's emphasis on Joseph and his all-too-human reaction to Mary's mysterious pregnancy downplays the divine element in Jesus's birth, when compared to Luke. In addition, although Matthew's Jesus simulacrum often refers to God as "my Father," he also frequently calls God "your [or our] Father." In Mark, there is no Christmas story and Jesus is described as the "son of Mary" (6:3), a phrase that implies that his father is unknown. Although Mark's Jesus does speak about (and to) the "Father," he never calls God "my Father," but he says "your Father" in 11:25. It is not at all clear that Jesus is "the Son" of "his/the Father" in Mk 8:38 and 13:32.

Another hermeneutic question concerns the story's truthfulness and reliability, and this too is an important focus of both Luke and John. The gospel of Luke's preface (1:1–4) creates an appearance of historical reliability, and John is obsessed throughout with the question of its own truth – for example, "This is the disciple who is bearing witness to these things, and who has written these things; and we know that his testimony is true" (21:24). Both gospels stress the value of the "witness," as does the book of Acts.[14] In contrast, neither Matthew nor Mark grounds its story in the reliability of a witness. The continuing relevance of the story beyond its end is also emphasized in both Luke and John. The appearances of a resurrected Jesus, who sends "the promise of my Father upon you" (Lk. 24:49, plus the discourse and apotheosis of Acts 1), or who blesses those "who have not seen and yet believe" (Jn 20:29), open the endings of both Luke and John toward a decisive but already-decided future, in which each of these gospels as the revelation of the truth about Jesus will play an important part (Jn 20:31). Matthew also implies a greater, Christian future (16:18–19, 28:19–20), but again this is somewhat more cryptic, and Mark offers only unfulfilled foretellings of an encounter with the resurrected Jesus in Galilee (14:28, 16:7).

Other intertextual effects appear at the level of the action or events of the story, which Barthes calls the proairetic code. Barthes claims that "the proairetic sequence is never more than the result of an artifice of reading:

14. See also Lincoln (2002: 12).

... its basis is therefore more empirical than rational, and it is useless to attempt to force it into a statutory order" (1974: 19). The code of actions is often interlaced in the gospels, as in other narratives, with the hermeneutic code as well as with the remaining two codes of the signified: the code of the symbol, "the place for multivalence and for reversibility ... making depth and secrecy problematic," and the cultural codes, or "references to a science or body of knowledge" (Barthes 1974: 19–20). Each of these codes concerns connotations, connections to the range of the reader's experience, perhaps in the form of hidden meanings or allegories, or perhaps in the form of historical, geographical, mythical, practical, or other types of knowledge specific to some community.

This weaving of codes is evident in both Matthew's and Luke's birth stories, each of which makes it explicit that its Jesus simulacrum is not only spiritually but physically the son of God. Thereby Mark's derogatory phrase, "son of Mary" (6:3), which does not appear in any other biblical gospel, is neutralized even as possible metaphoric connotations of "son of God" are controlled or even eliminated. Nevertheless, important differences between Matthew's and Luke's Christmas stories run contrary to Christian harmonizing tendencies. In contrast to Matthew, Luke elaborates the supernatural dimension of Jesus's conception (1:11–20, 26–38), and this resonates strongly with John's opening story of supernatural incarnation (1:1–18, see Chapter 5). This complementarity between the gospels of Luke and John serves a single, larger understanding in Christian thought. Otherwise, Luke's and John's stories would describe two distinct events, and that would be troublesome theologically. It may even be that this complementarity makes it easier for readers to overlook, as they often do, the evident differences in birth stories between Luke and Matthew (as well as the lack of a story in Mark) – in effect, they become a sort of "majority report."

As a result, in both the gospels of Luke and John, Jesus is really God's son, not Joseph's son, and the less forceful quality of Matthew's claim in this regard can be overlooked. Although John's prologue is not usually thought of as a Christmas story, it emphasizes the divine *archē* of the Word that becomes flesh in Jesus Christ, and if Mary's impregnation according to Luke is understood as a miracle analogous to God's creation of the universe in Genesis 1, as Raymond Brown suggests (1993: 314, 531) – that is, if God does not use physical semen to impregnate Mary (again, see Chapter 5) – then there is a great deal of compatibility between Luke and John here, since Jn 1:1–3 is an afterlife of Genesis 1. A Genesis reading of Luke's birth story is also supported by Luke's genealogy for Jesus, which traces his lineage through Joseph ("as was supposed," 3:23) back to "Adam, the Son of God" (3:38). Perhaps an ironical point of the downplaying of Joseph in Lk. 3:23 is that Jesus's true lineage runs through Mary and the Holy Spirit, and thus he is the son of God in a non-metaphoric way that no normal human being could ever be, not even Adam. As a result, Genesis 1–3 serves as a third text, a further intertext between the opening scenes of Luke and John, functioning in quite different ways in each gospel and yet uniting them with each other and distinguishing them both from either Matthew or Mark.

The gospel of Luke's supernatural fetus is then something more like John's Word, who "was in the beginning with God" and who was God (1:1–2). Although nothing in Luke's birth story implies the Johannine pre-existence of the divine Word, which itself is not physical "flesh," nevertheless that Word "became flesh [*sarx egeneto*] and dwelt among us, full of grace and truth" (1:14). Becoming flesh, the Word is manifested as "the only Son from the Father," Jesus Christ (1:17–18). When cultural and hermeneutic codes are also brought into play, Gabriel's claim in Luke 1:35 that the spirit of God will overcome Mary and impregnate her with "the Son of God" can fit fairly comfortably into John's mythic hymn of the incarnation of the divine Word.

According to Christian belief, the primeval, divine Word becomes flesh in Mary's womb due to the action of the spirit of God. As I noted in Chapter 5, commentators get nervous at the thought that God had intercourse with Mary, physically injecting supernatural seed into her womb. Nevertheless, if Luke's "holy spirit" (without the definite article in the Greek text) could be a divine, creative agent such as the gospel of John's pre-existent Word, that was in the beginning with God, and that was God (Jn 1:1–2), then in effect, the Word is that seed. This suggests that Jesus's allegorical interpretation of the sower parable in Lk. 8:11–15 ("The seed is the word of God," contrast Mk 4:14; Mt. 13:19) connects that parable to the gospel of John. Mary is the "good soil" *par excellence*! Comparable sower parables and interpretations also appear in Matthew and Mark, but those gospels lack anything like John's prologue or Luke's dialogue between Gabriel and Mary in their narrative contexts.

According to the gospel of John, "That which is born of the flesh is flesh, and that which is born of the Spirit is spirit" (3:6).[15] John does not provide

---

15. John 20:22 and (possibly) 1 Pet. 1:23 hint at a spiritual conception of each Christian. In addition, 1 Peter's "imperishable seed," conjoined with the "living and abiding word of God," has overtones of the *logos spermatikos* of the Stoics (see also Ja. 1:21).

a story of spiritual impregnation as such, but it describes an aboriginal, transcendent Word through which "*all things* were made [*panta ... egeneto*]" (1:3, emphasis added) and which therefore is implicitly not itself a "thing." For John, the Word and the world are two fundamentally different orders of reality (see Chapter 6). The Word is "the light" (1:4–5, 9) that enters into the dark world. Here too John may not be far from Luke: "Therefore be careful lest the light in you be darkness. If then your whole body is full of light, having no part dark, it will be wholly bright, as when a lamp with its rays gives you light" (11:35–36, compare 22:53). These words in Luke continue the saying in 11:33–34, in which Jesus speaks of the eye as the "lamp of the body" – "when your eye is sound, your whole body is full of light" – and a similar saying appears in Mt. 6:22–23. Both of these sayings are usually identified as coming from Q, and they suggest that the light comes from outside – that is, from the external world – and illuminates the interior of the body. However, the additional words in Lk. 11:35–36 are "Johannine" – that is, in those words as in the gospel of John, the light does not come from outside but it is "in you" (see Jn 14:17, 20, 15:4, 7). It comes from another world, the world beyond the world. Here symbolic and cultural codes are in play.

According to this weaving together of the gospels of Luke and John, the Word of light comes into the dark world (John 1:4–10) when the non-physical divine spirit miraculously impregnates the physical human woman (Lk. 1:35–38). This intertextual weaving of Luke's and John's stories has been going on since at least the second century, well before either the doctrine of the Trinity or the Christian canon were established.[16] According to the non-canonical Protevangelium of James,

> And he [Joseph] went to the place of the cave, and behold a dark [bright] cloud overshadowed the cave. And the midwife said: "My soul is magnified to-day, for my eyes have seen wonderful things; for salvation is born to Israel." And immediately the cloud disappeared from the cave, and a great light appeared, so that our eyes could not bear it. A short time afterwards that light withdrew until the child appeared, and it went and took the breast of its mother Mary. (19:2; Cameron 1982: 118)

Jane Schaberg quotes *Epistula Apostolorum* 3, "the word, which became flesh through the holy virgin Mary, was carried (conceived) in her womb by the Holy Spirit," which also suggests such a blending of Luke and John, as do the Christian additions to the *Sibylline Oracles*.[17] In a medieval text,

16. See Dunn (1980: 42, 50–51), and Brown (1993: 314, n.48). For a recent, postmodern weaving of these texts, see Moore (1992: 116–120).
17. Schaberg (1987: 180–181, 190).

"The Birth of Jesus," Mary is impregnated by the Holy Spirit and gives birth to light, which then becomes "outwardly an infant."[18]

To be sure, this weaving of Luke's and John's stories requires some theological sleight-of-hand, for in Christian trinitarian language, the Holy Spirit is the Third Person of the Trinity and the Word is the Second Person. However, in the daily life of the churches, and of most Christians, such distinctions may not matter, especially in today's post-Neoplatonic world. Even though the gospel of John never mentions Mary by name, its story of incarnation nicely complements the supernatural special effects of Luke's Mary-centered story. Luke's account of Jesus's birth is both more concrete and less overtly theological than John's hymn of the Word's incarnation, which never describes specifically how the Word becomes flesh. In turn, the fleshy "pagan" overtones of Luke's Christmas story are neutralized when read in light of John's monotheistic, spiritualized prologue. The combination of the two stories asserts that contrary realities – divine, transcendent spirit and physical, human flesh – have joined together in a mysterious and marvelous fashion, so that they are both essential characteristics of the being that results. This is not far from the Gospel of Christ as the incarnate savior deity, and not far from what eventually emerges as "orthodox" christological dogma: "two natures without confusion, change, division, or separation ... in one person and one hypostasis," as the fifth century Council of Chalcedon confessed.

The proairetic compatibility between the gospels of Luke and John extends beyond their birth and incarnation stories. Both gospels emphasize a connection between Jesus and John the Baptist at the beginnings of their stories. According to John's gospel, John the Baptist is sent by God to "bear witness to the light, that all might believe through him" (1:7, see also 1:15, 19–20), and in Luke, John the Baptist's father, Zechariah, prophesies that he will "give light to those who sit in darkness and in the shadow of death" (1:79, alluding to Isa. 9:2). In each case, the John the Baptist simulacrum functions as a theological index pointing toward Jesus (see also Lk. 1:41–44), even as his secondary status in relation to Jesus is emphasized. Matthew also downplays John in relation to Jesus (see 3:14–15). However, in Matthew, the "light" does not appear until John is arrested and Jesus withdraws, when Isa. 9:2 is more explicitly quoted (in 4:16) with different overtones.

In the gospel of John, the Baptist himself denies that he is Elijah or a prophet (1:21), and the angel in Lk. 1:17 announces that John will go "in the spirit and power of Elijah," comparing him to Elijah but also

18. For "The Birth of Jesus," see Cartlidge and Dungan (1980: 104–106).

distinguishing him from Elijah. In contrast, Matthew's Jesus specifically affirms ("if you are willing to accept it") that John the Baptist is Elijah (11:13–14, see also 17:11–12), and Mark's Jesus also suggests this (9:12–13). The final words of both gospels' Jesuses are thought by bystanders to be directed to Elijah (Mk 15:36; Mt. 27:47, 49), but in Luke and John the final words are quite different. The gospel of Mark begins with Jesus coming to be baptized by John, and it also emphasizes a connection between the two men until John's death, and perhaps even beyond (see 6:14–16). Isaiah is again quoted (40:3, in Mk 1:3) but without mention of light. However, unlike Luke or John, in Mark specific details of the connection between John and Jesus are never clear. Mark's Jesus may be John's "mightier one" (1:7), but Jesus may also think that John is not only Elijah but the "son of man" (9:12–13). Both symbolic and cultural codes again operate in relation to these texts.

The similarities between the three synoptic gospels, and their differences from the gospel of John, are most evident in the middle of each gospel's story. The complementarity between the gospels of Luke and John is strongest at the beginnings and endings of their stories. However, at a few intermediate points, they again contrast sharply to the other two canonical gospels. Bailey notes that neither Luke's Jesus nor John's Jesus ever passes through Gentile territory (another "common silence" among the signifiers), in contrast to stories in Mark and Matthew (1963: 108, n.1). Bailey attributes this difference to Luke's and John's rejection of the implications of the stories of the Syrophoenician or Canaanite woman in Mk 7:24–30 and Mt. 15:21–28 – that is, that Jesus was interested mainly (or only) in the Jewish people – in which case the hermeneutic code is involved along with proairetic and cultural codes. The more universal Jesus simulacrum of either Luke-Acts or John correlates to each one's presentation of "the Jews" as opponents of Jesus. Indeed, "Luke and John agree that the Jews' failure to give heed to Jesus is of a piece with their failure to heed Moses and the prophets (cf. Lk. 16:29–31 and Jn 5:46–47). … In both John and Luke, 'Israel' as a theme is closely related to Christology" (Smith 1990: 108, summarizing Maddox's views).

In addition, in neither Luke nor John is there a significant conjunction of the cursing of the fig tree and the cleansing of the Temple, as there is (although in different ways) in Matthew and Mark. The gospel of John has nothing comparable to the cursing of the tree, and Luke has instead a parable of a fig tree in which the tree is not destroyed but spared for another year (13:6–9, echoed in Jn 15:2). The result in either case is a narrative whose reality effect is not disturbed by the juxtaposition of Jesus's violence in the Temple to a tree that is miraculously withered for no good reason, "for it was not the season for figs" (Mk 11:13). This phrase does not appear in Matthew, and so the cursing of the tree by Matthew's Jesus is less irrational than it is in Mark. Nevertheless, in contrast to the juxtaposition of stories in both Matthew and Mark, the Jesus simulacra of both Luke and John are untouched by the stain of irrational cursing. Furthermore, both Luke and John have distinctively declared the Jewish Temple to be Jesus's "Father's house," and so in each of these cases there can be no impropriety in the cleansing of it by its true Owner, the universal Lord.

The Passion(s) of Jesus Christ

The gospel of John's passion story has much in common with each of the synoptic gospels. However, nearly all of the "common traditions" that Bailey identifies as shared by Luke and John are found in their passion, crucifixion, and post-resurrection stories,[19] and since the crucifixion and resurrection of Christ also form the core of Paul's "gospel," it is in this "common" material that the Gospel has deep roots (see further Chapter 10). Bailey argues that John uses Luke as a source for its passion narrative "to a far greater degree" than it uses Mk (1963: 20), and Cribbs correspondingly claims that Luke's passion story "possesses a sizable quantity of material that the third evangelist shares only with John ... in virtually every pericope in which their passion/resurrection traditions overlap" (1979: 242). Furthermore, "Luke's degree of verbal/factual/sequential agreement with Matthew/Mark *is much lower* in these three chapters [Luke 22–24] than it is in most other sections of his gospel" (Cribbs 1979: 241, his emphasis).

The gospels of Luke and John each separate the story of the anointing of Jesus from Judas's betrayal, and each of them attributes that betrayal to the influence of Satan (*eisēlthen ... satanas*, Lk. 22:3; Jn 13:27).[20] Semic, hermeneutic, and cultural codes are relevant here. The actions of the respective Judas simulacra, which are not explained in either Matthew or Mark, are presented in both Luke and John as the workings of a supernatural power, and this further emphasizes the supernatural status of their Jesus simulacra. It appears that for these gospels, mere human machinations are not enough to kill Jesus. In addition, neither Luke nor John refers to the scriptures when Jesus is arrested – another significant "common silence." In contrast, both Mk 14:49 and Mt. 26:56 (see also Mk 14:21, 27 and Mt.

19. See also Smith (1990: 3), Schnackenburg (1982: 37–39), and Cribbs (1979: 219, 237, 241–250).
20. See Bailey (1963: 29–31) and Schnackenburg (1980a: 31, 1980b: 78, 1982: 31).

26:24, 31) refer to fulfillment of the scriptures in connection with the arrest of Jesus, and this implies that the arrest is the will of God or the unfolding of some foretold destiny that condemns Jesus. Satan has no part in it.

In the garden and before he is arrested, John's Jesus, "knowing all that was to befall him" (18:4), is apparently quite willing to drink the "cup" that is given to him by "the Father" (18:11) – in other words, God wills Jesus's death, but Jesus accepts the divine will without qualm. In addition, he carefully orchestrates his own arrest: he steps forward to identify himself to those who have come to arrest him, and they are apparently thunderstruck (18:6). Similarly, Luke's Jesus shows no signs of distress prior to his arrest, unless one includes the doubtful Lk. 22:44, "And being in an agony he prayed more earnestly; and his sweat became like great drops of blood falling down upon the ground" (contrast Mt. 26:37–39; Mk 14:33–36). This statement follows immediately upon the equally doubtful Luke 22:43,[21] in which Jesus is strengthened by "an angel from heaven." There is no angelic visit during the Gethsemane stories of Matthew or Mark,[22] but this may be another link to John, for when John's Jesus arrives in Jerusalem, the crowd hears a voice from heaven, which is identified as that of an angel. Jesus comments that "This voice has come for your sake, not for mine" (12:27–30). Although each of the three synoptic Jesus simulacra prays that God "remove this cup" (Mk 14:36; Lk. 22:42, compare Mt. 26:39) of impending death prior to his arrest, even so, Luke's gospel comes much closer to John.

In each of the four gospels, it is the Roman official, Pilate, the representative of imperial, universal rule, who orders the crucifixion. However, the gospels of Luke and John each do more to minimize Pilate's responsibility for Jesus's execution than do either Matthew or Mark. In Mt. 27:14 and Mk 15:5, each Pilate simulacrum "wondered greatly/wondered" at Jesus's non-reply to the charges, and he later asks the crowd, "what evil has he done?" (Mt. 27:23, see also 17–19; Mk 15:14, see also 10). He does not pronounce Jesus to be innocent, although his hand-washing which leads to the self-condemnation of "all the people" in Mt. 27:24–25 may imply as

21. Luke 22:43–44 does not appear in the oldest manuscripts, but like Jn 6:23 (see note 10 above), it is found in Codex Bezae Cantabrigiensis. This is yet another textual site where the boundaries of the canon blur, and perhaps another Jesus simulacrum appears.
22. All three synoptics locate the scene before the arrest on the Mount of Olives, but Luke does not mention a garden. Another "common silence" in Luke and John is the lack of the name "Gethsemane."

much. In contrast, Luke's Pilate says explicitly, "I find no crime in this man" (23:4, see also 23:14–16, 22), and John's Pilate, after a philosophical discussion with Jesus, also says, "I find no crime in him" (18:38). Here cultural codes are especially significant.

Each of the Jesus simulacra of the gospels of Luke and John clearly knows from the story's beginning what his fate will be, both on earth and in heaven. Neither of these Jesuses is reluctant to die. As I noted above, Matthew's and Mark's Jesuses are less eager to die, and each of them seems compelled by some scriptural force. However, both Luke's and John's Jesus simulacra willingly offer themselves as vicarious sacrifices, and although this voluntary sacrifice may seem inconsistent with Satan's action through Judas, both of these features are essential to the Gospel story of Christ as the one who defeats the powers of evil and thereby saves. Nevertheless, one consequence of this is that Luke and John both put Jesus and Satan on the same "side" in their support for the crucifixion, while neither the scriptures nor the Romans (Pilate) are held responsible. Another consequence is that Jesus's betrayal by Judas is illusory in both Luke and John, although for the Satan-possessed Judas, the betrayal leads anyway (in Christian thought) to damnation or worse. In Matthew and Mark, Judas's betrayal seems more a matter of his choice, even though it also remains more mysterious.

Both Luke's and John's Jesus simulacra are calm and assured as they approach their deaths. In the gospel of Luke, Jesus is composed and forgiving when nailed to the cross, and he promises to be with the faithful thief "today in paradise" (Lk. 23:43, see also 23:34 and Jn 19:26–27).[23] In John, the crucified Jesus calmly completes the task for which he has come in order to fulfill the scriptures (19:24, 28, 36–37). Each of these Jesuses is comfortable on the cross and dies knowing full well that he will be rescued from the grave. The final words of Luke's Jesus are "Father, into thy hands I commit my spirit!" (23:46), and John's Jesus says serenely, "It is finished" (19:30). Luke and John put different last words in the mouths of their Jesus simulacra, but in each case the words connote closeness to God.[24] Despite the textual variations, again there is a kind of complementarity between Luke and John, especially when compared to the contrary and theologically difficult final phrase that appears in both Mt. 27:46 and Mk 15:34, "my God, why hast thou forsaken me?" Hermeneutic and cultural codes are in play here.

23. See also Brown (1970: 906).
24. See Schnackenburg (1982: 284–285) and Bultmann (1971: 673–674, 677).

Although the post-resurrection stories of John and Luke-Acts are once again different from each other, each of them underlines Jesus's supernatural power and avoids the brevity and general lack of detail of Matthew's Easter story as well as Mark's disturbing final scene, from which the resurrected Jesus is absent. For both Luke and John, "The death of Jesus marks a crucial turning point, for he thenceforth enters into his glory" (Smith 1990: 108). Rudolf Schnackenburg's summary of the gospel of John applies equally well to Luke-Acts: "The earthly Jesus is understood as the Christ who continues to be present in his community" (1980a: 43). Although one might also say as much of Matthew, these themes are not as well developed in that gospel, and not at all in Mark, except in the added endings. It is only in Luke and John that

> by virtue of his resurrection and exaltation Jesus the man of the Spirit became
> Lord of the Spirit; the one whose ministry was uniquely empowered by the
> (eschatological) Spirit became by his resurrection the one who bestowed the
> Spirit on others; or more precisely, by his resurrection he began to share in
> God's prerogative as the giver of the Spirit. (Dunn 1980: 142, his emphasis)

Luke's and John's stories of post-resurrection encounters between their Jesus simulacra and various followers are detailed and intimate. Each story addresses the ongoing problem of doubt and faith far more extensively than Matthew's passing remark, "but some doubted" (28:17), and far more positively than the flight and silence of Mark's women (16:8), which raises questions about that story's truthfulness. In Luke's story of the meeting on the Emmaus road and John's story of doubting Thomas, proairetic, hermeneutic, and cultural codes are in play. Initial doubts on the part of one or more disciples give way to statements of faith provoked by direct, personal encounters (the importance of witnesses again) with the risen Jesus, who is explicitly "Lord" and "Christ" (Lk. 24:26, 34, 46; Jn 20:25).[25] John's Thomas simulacrum even calls the resurrected Jesus "God" (20:28, compare Mt. 28:9). Likewise in Mark's longer added ending, which more closely resembles Luke than it does the rest of Mark, Jesus "appeared to the eleven themselves as they sat at table" (16:14), and later in this ending, Jesus is described as "the Lord" (16:19).

Despite the supernatural qualities of their resurrection stories, for both of the gospels of Luke and John, the risen Christ is still fully incarnate; he is no ghost or immaterial spirit. Each of these resurrected Jesus simulacra explicitly has a physical body (Lk. 24:39–43; Jn 20:20, 24–27). In Luke, when the disciples suppose that Jesus is a "spirit," he says, "I am [*egō eimi*],"

25. See Bailey (1963: 104, n.4).

but he also implicitly rejects their supposition by inviting them to touch his body (24:39), as John's Jesus similarly does (20:27). In this regard, the similarities between Lk. 24:36–43 and Jn 20:19–29 and 21:12–13 are especially striking.[26] In contrast, in comparable scenes in Mk 6:49 and Mt. 14:26, which are in effect resurrection scenes prior to the resurrections, the disciples cry out because they think that each of the Jesus simulacra is a ghost (*phantasma*) when they see him walking on the sea. These Jesuses also say, "I am," but they neither reject the disciples' claims nor invite the disciples to touch their bodies. I noted in Chapter 4 that Gilles Deleuze describes the phantasm as a species of simulacrum, "a phenomenon which is formed at a certain moment in the development of surfaces" (1990: 216). Deleuze identifies one type of phantasm as "oneiric": namely, simulacra that "are apt to merge together, to condense and dissipate ... all of the images which correspond to desire or ... dream images" (1990: 276). When Matthew's or Mark's Jesus walks on the water, he is such a dream image.[27]

Hermeneutic and cultural codes are operative here. In the gospel of Mark, the disciples are astonished and unable to understand when Jesus walks on the water. In contrast, although Matthew's walking on the sea story is otherwise similar to the one in Mark, in it Peter even attempts to walk on the water with Jesus, and the disciples "worship" Jesus (14:28–33). Matthew's disciples worship Jesus again after he is resurrected (28:17). According to Deleuze, another type of phantasm is the theological,[28] which are "very far from the objects from which they emanate, and having lost with them any direct connection, they form these grand autonomous figures. ... [O]ne might say that they dance, that they speak, that they modify ad infinitum their tones and gestures" (1990: 275–276). Although the Jesus simulacra of Luke and John are not called phantasms in those gospels, they are indeed "grand autonomous figures." Matthew's walking on the sea story displays that gospel's distinctive blend of the oneiric and

26. See Cribbs (1979: 249–250, 254, n.33), Bultmann (1971: 691–692), and Brown (1970: 1031–1033).
27. See further Aichele (2006: 131–155).
28. According to Deleuze, the phantasm takes one of three forms: theological, oneiric, and erotic (1990: 275–276). The erotic phantasm is "constituted of simulacra issuing from very diverse objects and ... apt to be condensed. ... The image ... is doubtless connected with the actual love object; but, unlike what happens in the case of the other needs, the love object cannot be either absorbed or possessed. The image alone inspires and resuscitates desire, a mirage which no longer signals a consistent reality" (1990: 276). Insofar as there is a Jesus simulacrum in the Revelation of John, it is an erotic phantasm.

the theological phantasm, and Pier Paolo Pasolini's movie version of Matthew captures well many of its more oneiric moments (see Chapter 3).

The word *phantasma* does not appear in John's version of the walking on the sea story (6:16–21), where the disciples say nothing. Nor does it appear in Luke, because the entire episode is absent from that gospel. However, as I noted above, in Luke's story of the resurrection, the disciples are frightened "and supposed that they saw a spirit [*pneuma*]" when Jesus suddenly appears (24:36–37). In all three of the walking on the sea stories and in this story in Luke, the Jesus simulacra respond to the disciples' cry by saying, "it is I [*egō eimi*, 'I am']."[29] Although these responses echo LXX Exod. 3:14 and probably should not be understood simply as affirmations (I am a ghost, I am a spirit), nevertheless the differences between the oneiric-phantasmal Jesuses of Matthew and especially Mark, and the theological-phantasmal Jesuses of Luke and John, are very important. Precisely because they are such "grand autonomous figures," the Jesus simulacra of Luke and John are already on their way to becoming the single theological simulacrum of Jesus Christ.

A Desire for Harmony

As I noted above, explicit harmonizings of the gospels of Luke and John appeared as early as the second century in texts such as the Protevangelium of James or *Epistula Apostolorum*, which blend Luke's birth story with John's incarnation prologue. Both of those texts were very likely written before the New Testament canon was adopted – that is, in a world where there was no Bible as such, and where there was no imperial church. This was roughly the same time at which Tatian produced his harmony of the four biblical gospels, the *Diatesseron*, and like Tatian's book these harmonies of Luke and John may be symptoms of desire for a canon, or even of an emerging virtual Bible. Such texts are also frequently produced in the world today, and they are immensely popular. For example, the gospels of Luke and John are harmonized in the movie, *The Jesus Film* (Sykes and Krisch 1979), which claims to be based on the gospel of Luke but also draws heavily on the gospel of John. As Jeffrey Staley and Richard Walsh say, "The citation of John 3:16–17 in the opening and of John 11:25–26 in the epilogue is indicative of [directors] Sykes and Krisch's Johannine interpretation of Luke's gospel. The camera's descent and ascent also parallels the descending-ascending divine Son of John's gospel" (2007: 95).

29. See Schnackenburg (1980b: 86–89), Brown (1966: 533–538), and Moore (1992: 128, 136).

However, probably the best-known recent example of this harmonizing tendency is Mel Gibson's film, *The Passion of the Christ* (2004), which is discussed further in Chapters 1 and 10. Unlike *The Jesus Film*, Gibson's movie makes no claim to follow a specific gospel. Nevertheless, because the gospels of Luke and John play a specially important role in the canonical simulation of Jesus Christ and in the formation of the Gospel, material from these gospels figures prominently in this movie. Gibson's Satan simulacrum orchestrates Jesus's ordeal with the emphasized assistance of Judas and contrary to the benevolence of Pilate. Similar scenes appear in both Luke and John, but not in either Matthew or Mark. Although the three different biblical accounts of the final words of Jesus are all eventually stated by Gibson's Jesus simulacrum as he hangs on the cross, the bitter last words spoken by both Matthew's and Mark's Jesuses appear first and then give way to the confident last words of Luke's Jesus and finally those of John's Jesus. Sequencing the sayings in this way in the movie does not merely follow the canonical order and Christian tradition ("the seven last words"), but it privileges the stories in Luke and John: it is their "words" which are truly last. The more bitter words from Matthew or Mark are re-contextualized and become nothing more than an initial moment of despair, quickly overcome. In this Gibson follows a common pattern of harmonizing the different passion stories into a single "Passion."

Indeed, if Gibson had not referred at all to either Matthew or Mark in his movie, its larger story would not have been seriously affected. In one curious instance, the infamous words of self-accusation from "all the people" that is unique to Matthew (27:25) are spoken by the crowd that gathers before Pilate to choose a prisoner for release, but no "translation" of the crowd's Aramaic words appears in the movie's subtitles.[30] In Gibson's movie, the spoken dialogue is exclusively in Aramaic or Latin, and this may be the only major instance of non-subtitled dialogue. As a result, only viewers who know Aramaic (a select group indeed!) or are very familiar with Matthew's gospel will understand the self-accusation. For other viewers – the vast majority – these words become meaningless "foreign words," and simply omitting them from the soundtrack would have made no difference. However, it seems that Gibson wants to retain the words but lose their significance altogether. In contrast, in Pier Paolo Pasolini's film, *The Gospel According to Saint Matthew* (1964), the words from Mt. 27:25 are spoken in Italian by a single voice, off screen, and they are subtitled or dubbed in

30. In the making of Gibson's movie, the dialogue was translated into Aramaic or Latin from an English screenplay.

the English versions. While Pasolini evidently wants to minimize the involvement of "the people" at this point, the words are clear.

I do not deny the many differences between the Jesus simulacra of the gospels of Luke and John, some of which have been indicated in previous chapters of this book. Yet despite these important differences, there is a compatibility between these two gospels that neither of them shares with either Matthew or Mark, a "synopsis" of language and meaning quite different and much deeper than the one between Matthew, Mark, and Luke. This compatibility responds well to the reader's desire for a single, harmonious story, and thus it works powerfully within the New Testament's canonical framework. As a result, the intertextual effects described above play an important part in the construction of the Bible's Christ simulacrum. The compatibility between Luke and John is essential to the Gospel of Jesus Christ, and the reality effects that they share or to which they jointly contribute dominate the canonical story of the Gospel.

often quite unconsciously, as do even many scholarly discussions[3] of the life and teachings of Jesus. Many other examples of such seemingly effortless and often probably unconscious blending of the biblical gospels are readily to be found. Pier Paolo Pasolini's film, *The Gospel According to Saint Matthew* (1964), is a striking exception, which yields a non-biblical gospel of Matthew (see Chapter 3).

In the ancient world, harmonizing texts such as the Protevangelium of James performed a function that was valuable precisely because there was as yet no canonical intertext. They provided valuable ways to bridge evident gaps between quite separate texts. In contrast, to produce a harmonizing text in the world today, where Christianity is well established as one of the major world religions and where one form or another of the New Testament canon is officially recognized as authoritative in nearly all Christian churches, is to do something quite different. These modern harmonizations have been produced in a world where there is (and has been now for over 1500 years) a biblical canon supporting the intertextual context of the Gospel of Jesus Christ, through which the many textual disparities are overcome. How can the popularity of these harmonizations be explained?

On one hand, these modern harmonies may imply that the Christian strategy of canonization and the concomitant Gospel of Jesus Christ have been overwhelmingly successful in blending the contents of the four gospels into a single story, to the point that their many differences have become nearly invisible. As I noted in Chapter 2, a great deal of extra-biblical Christian discourse – not only books and sermons, but also practices such as creeds and liturgies and educational curricula – has been and continues to be devoted to developing and reinforcing the concept of the Gospel and its Christ simulation. The Christian churches are still very strong in many parts of the world, and the virtual Bible still has a prominent place in them. In many ways, most Jesus movies (as well as TV shows, novels, and other similar products of popular culture) tend to reflect prevailing ideological positions and therefore reinforce dominant Christian theological understandings of the Bible and of Christianity. They are no different in this regard than the countless other extra-canonical texts (catechisms, creeds, sermons, music, etc.) that serve to supplement the deficiencies of the canon and to proclaim the Gospel of Jesus Christ. Given the mass production and orientation of these highly conventionalized

---

3. See, for example, the ongoing labors of the scholarly Jesus Seminar, sponsored by the Westar Institute, to reconstruct the authentic words and deeds of the historical Jesus.

Beyond Canonical Control

The four biblical gospels contain four distinct stories and describe four distinct Jesuses, but that is unacceptable to Christian ideology, which can only allow one Jesus, who is the Christ. Already in the first century, Paul acknowledges other "gospels" and other Jesuses than his own, but he does so in order to utterly reject them (Gal. 1:8; 2 Cor. 11:4, see further Chapter 2). Indeed, as far as I know, Christians have always rejected any thought that there might be multiple Christs, apart from false ones,[2] perhaps following Paul's lead (see also Mk 13:21–22; Mt. 24:23–24). It is now, and no doubt has been for a long time, very difficult, although not impossible, to think that (for example) the gospels of Matthew and Luke describe two entirely different characters named Jesus.

Most readers tend to encounter the Bible as a single virtuality, an idea that controls the way that they read the actual texts in it. This is true not only for "ordinary people on the street," regardless of whether they are Christian or not, but also for professional biblical scholars, who are usually quite familiar with the contents and structures of the texts. I can "testify" to the constant temptation to treat the four Jesuses as four versions of a single being. The canon of the New Testament pressures readers of all sorts to read the four gospels as chapters of a larger whole, or versions of a single story about a single Jesus, and thus the four different Jesus simulacra that appear within the gospels tend to be read as facets of a single "real" Jesus, who is understood either as an historical or as a theological entity. Although the gospels' Jesus simulacra could not possibly represent four perspectives on or interpretations of a single actual person, that is the way that they have been understood by Christian readers who harmonize them to *create* the "reality" that is constituted by the one Gospel of Jesus Christ.

However, if the canon were working properly, then "external" harmonizings of the gospels, such as are found in most Jesus novels and movies, should not be necessary. Yet such harmonizings are widespread, and very popular. In Chapter 9, I compared the recent harmonizings of the gospels of Luke and John in recent Jesus movies to ancient texts such as the Protevangelium of James or *Epistula Apostolorum*. The comparison is not one of specific content but rather of narrative strategies. Almost all Jesus movies, Jesus novels, and other modern popularizations, including church Christmas and Easter pageants, harmonize the gospels and their simulacra,

---

2. Even Google does not recognize multiple Christs. If you try a Google search on "christs," Google will ask if you meant to write "christ's." There are no specific entries for "christs," except in the generic sense of non-Christian messiahs.

sequence, with prophesies of the Christ to come. This is true even of the Sermon on the Mount, which (along with the visit of the wise men) is perhaps Matthew's most popular feature. If Matthew had been omitted from the New Testament, then the relation of the remaining writings (even Paul's letters, or Hebrews) to the Jewish scriptures would be much less clear, even though they draw heavily upon those scriptures. As Richard Walsh says, "Matthew so thoroughly reconfigures the Hebrew Bible that he prepares the ground for the Christian conception that it is the Old Testament (compare Hebrews 8–10). ... We might aver, then, that the Jews did not create the Old Testament. Matthew did" (2003: 102).

Once the decision is made (in the second century), thanks perhaps to texts such as Matthew, not to accept Marcion's hostile view of the Jewish scriptures and the God of the Jews, the gospel of Matthew serves as a valuable bridge between what eventually become the two Christian canons. As a result, Matthew makes it possible for the Gospel's universal Christ to absorb the specifically Jewish messiah. Otherwise, Matthew's main value in the canon is as a supplement to Luke, whose stories of Christmas, Good Friday, and Easter (among others) are more sentimental and charming, and more popular.

That leaves the christologically difficult gospel of Mark, which has no value at all for the Christian faith or for the Gospel as it is, but instead must be read through a canonical lens, as whoever wrote both the longer and the shorter added endings already anticipated. Indeed, if those endings had not been added, then Mark's fate might well have been the same as the other versions mentioned in the "Secret Gospel of Mark" (Cameron 1982: 69–70). However, Mark might be more dangerous to the Gospel outside of the Bible than it is inside the Bible, thanks both to its remarkable similarities to the theologically more attractive gospels of Matthew and Luke (and hence it may be more insidious than more obviously "heretical" gospels) and also to its disturbing "deficiencies" when compared to either of them or to John (or Paul). Perhaps canonization was even a way to "tame" Mark, to make it safer for Christian consumption. Mark ends up sandwiched between Matthew and the Luke-John-Acts-Paul core of the New Testament, so that its numerous similarities to either Matthew or Luke can be emphasized and its many theologically troublesome bits can be overwhelmed by or absorbed into the emerging orthodoxy. This sequence then firmly supports a canonical Gospel of Jesus Christ as a universal and divine figure, both "negatively," colonizing the Jewish scriptures by way of Matthew and neutralizing the troublesome Mark, and "positively," through the coded affinities of Luke-Acts and John.

beginnings" (1971, especially 31–37) and thus it also connects the Christ simulacrum to another Christian virtuality, the apostolic age, and the apostles' preaching about Christ. The Paul simulacrum of Acts is an especially significant figure in that book's larger story of the God-inspired formation of the Christian church and of its understanding of Christ.

The well-known differences between the Paul simulacrum of Acts and the Paul simulacra who appear in Paul's letters are overcome by the New Testament canon in much the same way as that canon overcomes the differences between the various Jesus simulacra of the gospels and other texts. Instead, the stories about Paul in the Acts of the Apostles serve as a link connecting Paul's message in his various letters to the message of Luke's gospel, and thence also to John, by means of the affinities noted in Chapter 9. Once again, as with Luke and John, some massive theological differences, now between Paul and the Johannine material, must be overcome by the canonical intertext. Nevertheless, the resulting Luke-John-Acts-Paul sequence provides the core New Testament framework through which "Christ the Lord" can be attached to the name of Jesus. Thus the gospels of Luke and John, together with Paul's letters, provide the essential ingredients for the construction of this Jesus Christ simulacrum, and as a result, the Gospel of Jesus Christ stands at the ideological (as well as physical) center of the New Testament.

Although the gospels of Matthew and Mark are also included in the canonical New Testament, they contribute little if anything directly to the canonical Christ simulacrum. The Gospel of Jesus Christ does not require either of these gospels. In other words, if Matthew or Mark were the only gospel(s) in the New Testament, and even if Paul's letters and the rest of the New Testament (including the Acts of the Apostles) remained as they are now, then Christian beliefs about Christ would surely be very different. If that were the case, then the affinities between either of those gospels and other New Testament writings that scholars and other readers now regard as obvious would be much less evident, and it might even be necessary for Christians to create something like the gospel of Luke to mediate between them.

Instead, it may well be the Christ simulacrum of the Gospel that makes it possible for Christians to value the gospels of Matthew or Mark at all. In other words, the intertextual mediation of the New Testament canon allows or even promotes the inclusion of Matthew and Mark. From the standpoint of orthodox christology, Matthew's main value is to connect Jesus to his precursors in the Old Testament – that is, the Christian appropriation of the Jewish scriptures – which themselves conclude, in the revised, Christian

As I noted in Chapter 9, Jesus's death and resurrection are also major ingredients in the complementarity between Luke and John, but those two gospels also each construct Jesus simulacra with stories that include pre-death sayings and actions, and it is these pre-passion stories that eventuate for them in passion, death, and resurrection. By also identifying each of these more developed Jesus simulacra as "Christ the Lord," the gospels of Luke and John crucially supplement Paul's efforts to construct the Gospel. Each of these fully developed Jesuses is not only a Jewish man and the messianic fulfillment of Jewish scriptures, but more importantly, he speaks to all humanity. For both Luke-Acts and John, Jesus is a cosmic figure, God incarnate, and he has been so from his conception or even from the beginning of time. He is the Lord of the entire world.

Both the divinity and imperial universality of Jesus Christ are essential to the Christian Gospel, which is a message not merely for the church but for all humanity. It is something that must be preached throughout the world, and thus it is particularly associated with "the acts of the apostles," as the New Testament book of that name makes clear. Paul also describes himself as:

> an *apostle*, set apart for ... the *gospel* concerning [God's] Son, ... Jesus Christ
> our Lord, through whom we have received grace and *apostleship* to bring
> about the obedience of faith for the sake of his name *among all the nations*.
> (Rom. 1:4–5, emphasis added; see also 1:8, 5:18, 10:12, etc.)

The intertextual reading of the four gospels' Jesus simulacra, when "focused" by Luke and John, produces a "Jesus Christ" who can be quite comfortably fitted to Paul's "Christ Jesus" to become the single "Jesus Christ" of the New Testament and therefore of the virtual Bible. As a result, whenever the four gospels are blended together, as they often are, whether in unconscious reading practices or in more explicit harmonies, the affinities that already exist between Luke and John, and that tie them to Paul's letters, will have a great advantage over anything in either or both of the other two gospels.

Whether by design or accident, the New Testament canonical sequence wedges the gospel of John between Luke and its apparent sequel Acts. This massive textual intercalation further encourages the blending of their stories. The christological juggernaut of Luke-John-Acts is then immediately followed in the New Testament sequence by the letters of Paul, who has already been introduced in stories of the Acts of the Apostles as a pre-eminent Christian apostle. As Robert Wilken argues, the book of Acts plays a particularly important part in establishing a "myth of Christian

Chapter 10

THE VIRTUAL GOSPEL AND THE CANONICAL CONTROL OF MEANING

The poststructuralist critique presents a challenge to all biblical scholars: ultimately we are left with the text; all we have is the text. (Pippin 1992: 26)

One no longer needs to believe in God. We seek rather the "structure," that is, the form which may be filled with beliefs, but the structure has no need to be filled in order to be called "theological." Theology is now the science of nonexisting entities, the manner in which these entities ... animate language and make for it this glorious body. (Deleuze 1990: 281)

The Christ Simulacrum

The gospels of Luke and John continue to play crucial roles in the formation of the Gospel in the modern world. However, Luke and John do not suffice to blend the four gospels' Jesus simulacra into the one Christ simulacrum of the Gospel. The New Testament letters of Paul are far more likely than any of the gospels to conjoin "Jesus" with "Christ" or "the Lord." In Paul's letters, the simulation of Jesus Christ has almost completely absorbed the simulation of Jesus, so much so that Jesus (apart from Christ) can hardly be considered a virtual object in them. This also tends to be the case in the other New Testament writings that are not gospels. Furthermore, Paul's use of the word "gospel" (*euaggelion*), which is one of his favorite terms, comes closer to the theological sense of the Gospel as described in this book than do any of the biblical gospels.[1] Nevertheless, Paul's letters have very little to say about Jesus's life, deeds, or teachings. Simulating Jesus as a living human being is not a high priority for Paul, at least in his letters that have survived. Instead, Paul's concern is with Jesus's death and resurrection as they figure crucially in the theological functioning of Jesus as Lord and Christ. This is "the gospel" for Paul.

---

1. See further Aichele (2006: 96–99).

However, probably the best-known recent example of this harmonizing tendency is Mel Gibson's film, *The Passion of the Christ* (2004), which is discussed further in Chapters 1 and 10. Unlike *The Jesus Film*, Gibson's movie makes no claim to follow a specific gospel. Nevertheless, because the gospels of Luke and John play a specially important role in the canonical simulation of Jesus Christ and in the formation of the Gospel, material from these gospels figures prominently in this movie. Gibson's Satan simulacrum orchestrates Jesus's ordeal with the emphasized assistance of Judas and contrary to the benevolence of Pilate. Similar scenes appear in both Luke and John, but not in either Matthew or Mark. Although the three different biblical accounts of the final words of Jesus are all eventually stated by Gibson's Jesus simulacrum as he hangs on the cross, the bitter last words spoken by both Matthew's and Mark's Jesuses appear first and then give way to the confident last words of Luke's Jesus and finally those of John's Jesus. Sequencing the sayings in this way in the movie does not merely follow the canonical order and Christian tradition ("the seven last words"), but it privileges the stories in Luke and John: it is their "words" which are truly last. The more bitter words from Matthew or Mark are re-contextualized and become nothing more than an initial moment of despair, quickly overcome. In this Gibson follows a common pattern of harmonizing the different passion stories into a single "Passion."

Indeed, if Gibson had not referred at all to either Matthew or Mark in his movie, its larger story would not have been seriously affected. In one curious instance, the infamous words of self-accusation from "all the people" that is unique to Matthew (27:25) are spoken by the crowd that gathers before Pilate to choose a prisoner for release, but no "translation" of the crowd's Aramaic words appears in the movie's subtitles.[30] In Gibson's movie, the spoken dialogue is exclusively in Aramaic or Latin, and this may be the only major instance of non-subtitled dialogue. As a result, only viewers who know Aramaic (a select group indeed!) or are very familiar with Matthew's gospel will understand the self-accusation. For other viewers – the vast majority – these words become meaningless "foreign words," and simply omitting them from the soundtrack would have made no difference. However, it seems that Gibson wants to retain the words but lose their significance altogether. In contrast, in Pier Paolo Pasolini's film, *The Gospel According to Saint Matthew* (1964), the words from Mt. 27:25 are spoken in Italian by a single voice, off screen, and they are subtitled or dubbed in

---

30. In the making of Gibson's movie, the dialogue was translated into Aramaic or Latin from an English screenplay.

the English versions. While Pasolini evidently wants to minimize the involvement of "the people" at this point, the words are clear.

I do not deny the many differences between the Jesus simulacra of the gospels of Luke and John, some of which have been indicated in previous chapters of this book. Yet despite these important differences, there is a compatibility between these two gospels that neither of them shares with either Matthew or Mark, a "synopsis" of language and meaning quite different and much deeper than the one between Matthew, Mark, and Luke. This compatibility responds well to the reader's desire for a single, harmonious story, and thus it works powerfully within the New Testament's canonical framework. As a result, the intertextual effects described above play an important part in the construction of the Bible's Christ simulacrum. The compatibility between Luke and John is essential to the Gospel of Jesus Christ, and the reality effects that they share or to which they jointly contribute dominate the canonical story of the Gospel.

movies – huge production costs require enormous ticket sales – one does not expect especially valuable critical insights from them.

At the same time, and on the other hand, these harmonies may also indicate a fundamental change in the value of the Bible in the modern world – that is, the failing of the canon of the Bible. In today's world of global capitalism, such movies are the products not so much of faith as of marketing and of what Walter Benjamin calls "the work of art in the age of mechanical reproduction" (1968: 217–251) – a process that begins with the printing of books such as the Bible.[4] Indeed, marketing is what evangelism has become in the contemporary, post-Christian world. According to Jeffrey Staley and Richard Walsh, "Advocates for [Sykes and Krisch's *The Jesus Film*] claim that it has been translated into more languages and has been seen by more people than any other Jesus film" (2007: 95). Similarly, Mel Gibson's movie has been seen by many millions of people, including busloads of viewers from local churches. The movies by Gibson and by Peter Sykes and John Krisch have been actively used to promote the cause of Christian evangelism in a post-literate age. As I argued in Chapter 1, Gibson's movie has in effect replaced the biblical gospels, and perhaps the entire Bible, for many of its viewers, at least some of whom had apparently never read a gospel before. Similarly, Staley and Walsh note that *The Jesus Film* has reportedly "been shown to many indigenous people who have never before seen a movie" (2007: 95) – or perhaps never before read a gospel? Among both modern Westerners and "indigenous people," audiences may well be more familiar with movies than they are with books.

As a result, such movies perform quite a different function than that of shoring up the canon. Instead, in each of these cases, a crack appears in the canonical control of meaning. The authoritative, intertextual control of the Bible over the meaning of its component texts is placed in jeopardy, or perhaps even entirely disregarded, as are the written texts themselves. This modern, electronic "marketing" of the Bible and of Christianity effectively demolishes the canon of the Bible, or perhaps it is made possible *by* that demolition, which had begun already 500 years ago with the marketing of printed Bibles. Nevertheless, these movies, like the larger marketing processes to which they contribute, continue to uphold the virtuality of the Gospel. In other words, they affirm the Gospel at the same time that they symptomatize the decline of the biblical canon. As I noted in Chapter 1, although they are closely related, the virtual Bible and the canon are not the same concept.

4. See further Chapter 1, and Aichele (2001: 50–60).

Proliferation of the Simulacra

However, even the virtuality of the Bible, and with it the Gospel of Jesus Christ, may also be starting to fade away. As Benjamin notes:

> the technique of reproduction detaches the reproduced object from the domain of tradition. ... And in permitting the reproduction to meet the beholder or listener in his own particular situation, it reactivates the object reproduced. (1968: 221)

As the canon of the Christian scriptures plays a less and less significant role in the ways that people think about and read biblical texts, for a wide variety of technological and cultural-historical reasons, this will allow a renewed release and proliferation of Jesus simulacra.

The use of a "mass medium" does not necessarily reinforce conventional values.[5] A more radical demolition of the canon appears in Pasolini's film, in which the gospel of Matthew becomes a neo-Marxist story of a people's Jesus, as I noted in Chapter 3. This movie's value for Christian evangelism or other promotion of the Gospel, if any, would be quite limited. *The Gospel According to Saint Matthew* "translates" Matthew quite independently of the rest of the Bible, so that it is no longer "scripture." The quotations of scripture that appear in the movie become simply that, no longer one scripture hijacking another, as happens when the gospel of Matthew is also considered to be scripture. Other cinematic demolitions of the Bible appear in quite different ways in *Jesus of Montreal* (Arcand 1989) and *Monty Python's Life of Brian* (Jones 1979), two other distinctly non-evangelical films, even though both of these movies harmonize the gospels' stories. Not all harmonies support the Gospel.

The change in the Bible's status is not just a matter of the change of medium from printed text to cinema, for comparable ideological effects appear in World Wide Web pages where printed biblical texts have been scanned into digital html or pdf files. All of the Jesus movies mentioned above, as well as other popular culture phenomena in various media, such as novels, TV shows, music, and comic books, are simply the most evident symptoms of that decline, and thus they should not be taken lightly. They are only possible, or desirable, because the Christian canon of the scriptures is crumbling, contrary to massive efforts to maintain it.

In yet other products of popular culture, as I also noted in Chapter 1, texts from the gospels may not be "translated" or even explicitly referenced at all, but very different sorts of cultural play offer radically different

---

5. Again, Deleuze's remarks in (1989: 253–255) are particularly relevant here.

contextualizations of the stories, themes, and images. In such cases, non-conventional and non-Christian ideologies may engage the gospels, and thus they too contribute in various and important, albeit more subtle, ways to the "liberation" of the gospels' semiosis. This pop cultural play with or upon the gospels, even more than in the explicit Jesus movies, also replaces the "source text," but sometimes in a very different way. After all, even if it is not truly a Jesus film,[6] *The Life of Brian* is still recognizable as in some way "about Jesus," but that recognition may be considerably less quick or easy in the case of a text such as Philip Pullman's *The Amber Spyglass* (2000).

In addition, when individual gospels, or parts of them, are read in intertextual tension with recent popular culture products such as films and novels that are not overtly biblical or religious, this results in post-canonical readings for which alternative intertexts control the semiosis of the selected texts. These rewritings also in effect remove the textual bodies from the canon of the scriptures, and "reactivate" (to use Benjamin's word) the possibilities for understanding the gospels' Jesus simulacra and their actions and words entirely apart from the Gospel. In Chapters 5 and 7 I have explored two readings of this sort.[7] The canon of the scriptures has never been entirely effective in controlling the meaning of its texts, and writers, artists, and scholars have played with the semiotic potential of the Bible's texts in many ways for as long as there has been a Bible – or even longer, since the dangers of such play are evident between the biblical texts themselves and may even have been part of the reason that the canon was formed in the first place. Recently scholars have begun to pay more attention to the histories of this play, and as a result we have all become more aware of the limitations of the canon.[8]

Beyond the virtual Bible, there are many different gospels and many different Jesuses, and there is no longer a Gospel and there is no longer a

---

6. Terry Jones's film indicates quite explicitly that it is not strictly speaking a Jesus movie, but it is nevertheless often understood (probably correctly) to be one. In the movie's opening scene, the magi mistakenly bring the traditional gifts to Brian's birth-manger, then discover their error and snatch them back to take them to the stable next door. Later Brian and his mother stand among the audience at a Sermon on the Mount delivered by a very distant and nearly inaudible Jesus simulacrum.

7. For additional examples, see Aichele (2006: 159–221) and essays in Aichele and Walsh (2002).

8. A fine example of such study in regard to a non-gospel text is Sherwood (2000). The Blackwell Bible Commentary series, edited by John Sawyer and others, is among several major contributions to this effort.

single Jesus Christ. In such a world there may be many Jesus Christs, but their relations to the gospels (including Luke or John) will take many different forms, and their plurality will be undeniable. An example of this plurality, although still confined in a single text, may be found in A. J. Langguth's novel, *Jesus Christs* (1968). This book is composed in effect of numerous short stories, each featuring a Jesus Christ, but they are presented continuously, without chapter divisions and as though they were parts of a larger story. As a result, the "series of heterogeneous differences ... call forth their own communication through various signs" (Deleuze 1994: 123). Deleuze is referring to a different novel, Witold Gombrowicz's *Cosmos*, but his comment is relevant nonetheless: Langguth's book allows the reader to understand the multiple Christs as different "incarnations" of a single entity, or as a series of metamorphoses or perhaps resurrections held together by the most tenuous of narrative threads, or as plural, postmodern incompossibilities driven by the "power of the false" (see Deleuze 1989: 126–130).

Still referring to the novel, *Cosmos*, Deleuze says, "Each series tells a story: not different points of view on the same story, ... but completely distinct stories which unfold simultaneously" (1994: 123). This comment from Deleuze applies equally well to the stories in Langguth's novel as to the gospels in the New Testament. If Langguth's novel were read as the Bible usually is, the reader would go mad trying to fuse its various Jesuses into a single Christ. But if the Bible were read as though it were comparable to Langguth's book, the reader would be less quick to assume a single Jesus Christ and more willing to examine its multiple Jesuses.

If one of Langguth's stories were separated from that novel, it would amuse or infuriate or stimulate thought, but it would remain a story taken from that unitary novel. In contrast, the biblical gospels have always been separate stories, bound together despite themselves, as it were. Once freed from canonical captivity and the influence of the Gospel and its Jesus Christ simulacrum, each of them becomes something other than merely a gospel from the Bible – that is, a part of a larger whole. When any of the gospels are read in intertextual tandem with non-canonical texts, differences between them are highlighted even more. The gospels' "heterogeneous differences" then "communicate" in quite other ways, and they are allowed to tell non-synoptic stories of non-biblical Jesuses, as Luke does when read in relation to China Miéville's novel, *King Rat* (see Chapter 5). Although there is again a search for similarities in these readings, it is not primarily for the purpose of arguing historical development, and not exclusive of other readings, as the various modernist solutions to the history behind the texts must exclude one another. Nor is it an attempt to resolve the textual differences into a single "dynamically equivalent" message.

It has sometimes been argued that the multiplicity of gospels and consequently of reality effects in the New Testament is itself a manifestation of something like the postmodern preference for multiplicity and difference. I do not accept that conclusion, but the problem in my view is not the gospels themselves, but rather the canonical structure that constrains the meaning of every text in the Bible to the single "Word of God" or Gospel of Christianity. Through the intertextual, ideological structure that is the Christian canon, semiotic differences between the gospels can be either overlooked or reconciled, questions such as "Which gospel came first?" become crucial, and the texts' reality effects are reduced to fragments of a single true meaning. The virtual Bible is a rejection of difference, a theological unity which may be disturbed by the multiplicity of the gospels but which finally reconciles their differences in the greater unity of the Gospel.

However, when one rejects the virtual Bible's rejection of the gospels' differences, then differences between their reality effects become more evident – more "real." The gospels are then no longer presumed to be different versions of a single story, and readers not only become more aware of important and finally unresolvable differences between their four Jesuses (and the other New Testament Jesuses, especially Paul's "Christ Jesus"), but also of new ways to think about what or who the Jesus simulacrum of each gospel is. Since the range of potential intertextual combinations is unlimited, the tendency is to multiply possible understandings, including incompatible ones. As readers increasingly read the gospel texts apart from the Gospel's control, this will especially benefit Matthew and Mark, for the reasons noted above, but it will also benefit Luke and John (and Paul's letters). Precisely because a much wider range of intertextual contexts is available, the differences between each of these texts becomes more evident. The semiosis of the gospels is unleashed, and Jesus simulacra proliferate without limit.

BIBLIOGRAPHY

Abbott, Edwin A. 1884. *Flatland: a Romance of Many Dimensions*. London: Seely and Co.

Aichele, George. 1997. *Sign, Text, Scripture: Semiotics and the Bible*. Sheffield: Sheffield Academic Press.

Aichele, George. 2001. *The Control of Biblical Meaning: Canon as Semiotic Mechanism*. Harrisburg, PA: Trinity Press International.

Aichele, George. 2005. *The Limits of Story* <http://home.comcast.net/~gcaichele/writings/limits.pdf>, accessed April 27, 2009. Original print publication Society of Biblical Literature, 1985.

Aichele, George. 2006. *The Phantom Messiah: Postmodern Fantasy and the Gospel of Mark*. London: T & T Clark International.

Aichele, George. 2008. "Local Heroes." In David Shepherd (ed.) *Images of the Word: Hollywood's Bible and Beyond*. Atlanta, GA: Society of Biblical Literature.

Aichele, George, and Richard Walsh (eds). 2002. *Screening Scripture: Intertextual Connections Between Scripture and Film*. Harrisburg, PA: Trinity Press International.

Aland, Kurt and Barbara Aland. 1987. *The Text of the New Testament*, Erroll F. Rhodes (trans.). Grand Rapids, MI/Leiden: Eerdmanns/Brill.

Arcand, Denys, director. 1989. *Jesus of Montreal*. Montreal: National Film Board of Canada.

Aristotle. 1967. *Poetics*, Gerald Else (trans.). Ann Arbor, MI: University of Michigan Press.

Badiou, Alain. 1999. *Deleuze: The Clamor of Being*, Louise Burchill (trans.). Minneapolis, MN: University of Minnesota Press.

Bailey, John Amedee. 1963. *The Traditions Common to the Gospels of Luke and John*. Leiden: E. J. Brill.

Barański, Zygmunt G. 1985. "The Texts of *Il Vangelo secondo Matteo*." *The Italianist* 5: 77–106.

Barthes, Roland. 1974. *S/Z*, Richard Miller (trans.). New York: Hill and Wang.

Barthes, Roland. 1975. *The Pleasure of the Text*, Richard Miller (trans.). New York: Hill and Wang.

Barthes, Roland. 1977. "Pasolini's *Salò*: Sade to the Letter." In Paul Willemen (ed.) *Pier Paolo Pasolini*. London: BFI.

Barthes, Roland. 1981. *Camera Lucida*, Richard Howard (trans.). New York: Hill and Wang.

Barthes, Roland. 1982. *Empire of Signs,* Richard Howard (trans.). New York: Hill and Wang.

Barthes, Roland. 1985. *The Responsibility of Forms,* Richard Howard (trans.). Berkeley and Los Angeles, CA: University of California Press.

Barthes, Roland. 1986. *The Rustle of Language,* Richard Howard (trans.). Berkeley and Los Angeles, CA: University of California Press.

Barthes, Roland. 1988. *The Semiotic Challenge,* Richard Howard (trans.). New York: Hill and Wang.

Baudrillard, Jean. 1992. "Strike of Events." *Critical Theory* (<http://www.ctheory.net/ default.asp#Articles>), article 9, excerpt from *L'illusion de la fin,* Charles Dudas (trans.). Accessed September 4, 2004.

Baudrillard, Jean. 1994. *Simulacra and Simulation,* Sheila Faria Glaser (trans.). Ann Arbor MI: University of Michigan Press.

Bauer, Walter. 1957. *A Greek-English Lexicon of the New Testament and Other Early Christian Literature,* William F. Arndt and F. Wilbur Gingrich (trans.). Chicago, IL: University of Chicago and Cambridge: Cambridge University Press.

Beal, Timothy. 2000. "Intertextuality." In A. K. M. Adam (ed.) *Handbook of Postmodern Biblical Interpretation.* St Louis, MO: Chalice Press.

Beal, Timothy. 2002. *Religion and Its Monsters.* New York and London: Routledge.

Beal, Timothy. 2010. *The End of the Word as We Know It.* Orlando, FL: Houghton Mifflin Harcourt.

Belo, Fernando.1981. *A Materialist Reading of the Gospel of Mark,* Matthew J. O'Connell (trans.). Maryknoll, NY: Orbis Books.

Benjamin, Walter. 1968. *Illuminations,* Harry Zohn (trans.). New York: Schocken Books.

Berquist, Jon L. 1996. "Postcolonialism and Imperial Motives for Canonization." *Semeia* 75: 15–35.

Bhabha, Homi K. 1994. *The Location of Culture.* London and New York: Routledge.

Borges, Jorge Luis. 1962. *Ficciones,* Anthony Kerrigan (trans. and ed.). New York: Grove Press, Inc.

Borges, Jorge Luis. 1964. *Labyrinths,* Donald A. Yates and James E. Irby (eds). New York: New Directions.

Borges, Jorge Luis. 2000. "The Homeric Versions." In Eliot Weinberger, Esther Allen and Suzanne Jill Levine (trans.) *Selected Non-Fictions.* New York: Penguin Books.

Boyarin, Daniel. 1994. *A Radical Jew: Paul and the Politics of Identity.* Berkeley and Los Angeles, CA: University of California Press.

Brown, Raymond E. 1966. *The Gospel According to John (I–XII).* The Anchor Bible. Garden City, NY: Doubleday.

Brown, Raymond E. 1970. *The Gospel According to John (XIII–XXI).* The Anchor Bible. Garden City, NY: Doubleday.

Brown, Raymond E. 1993. *The Birth of the Messiah.* New York: Doubleday.

Bultmann, Rudolf. 1971. *The Gospel of John: A Commentary,* G. R. Beasley-Murray, R. W. N. Hoare and J. K. Riches (trans.). Philadelphia, PA: Westminster Press.

Cadwallader, Alan. 2008. "The Markan/Marxist Struggle for the Household." In Roland Boer and Jorunn Økland (eds) *Marxist Feminist Criticism of the Bible,* Sheffield: Sheffield-Phoenix Press.

Cameron, Ron (ed.). 1982. *The Other Gospels.* Philadelphia, PA: The Westminster Press.

Carden, Michael. 2009. *Jottings: Michael Carden's Blog: Reflections on Bible, Religion, Society, Sexuality, Politics.* <http://michaelcardensjottings.blogspot.com/>, accessed May 25, 2009.

Carlson, Thomas A. 2008. *The Indiscrete Image: Infinitude and Creation of the Human.* Chicago, IL: University of Chicago Press.

Carroll, Robert P. 1997. *Wolf in the Sheepfold: the Bible as Problematic for Theology.* London: SCM Press.

Carroll, Robert P. 1998. "Lower Case Bibles: Commodity Culture and the Bible." In J. Cheryl Exum and Stephen D. Moore (eds) *Biblical Studies/Cultural Studies: The Third Sheffield Colloquium,* 46–69. Sheffield: Sheffield Academic Press.

Cartlidge, David R., and David L. Dungan (eds). 1980. *Documents for the Study of the Gospels.* Philadelphia, PA: Fortress Press.

Castaneda, Hector-Neri. 1989. *Thinking, Language, and Experience.* Minneapolis, MN: University of Minnesota Press.

Chatman, Seymour. 1978. *Story and Discourse.* Ithaca, NY: Cornell University Press.

Cribbs, F. Lamar. 1979. "The Agreements that Exist Between Luke and John." In Paul J. Achtemeier (ed.) *SBL Seminar Papers,* 215–261. Missoula, MT: Scholars Press.

Crossan, John Dominic. 1985. *Four Other Gospels.* Minneapolis, MN: Winston Press.

Culpepper, R. Alan. 1983. *Anatomy of the Fourth Gospel.* Philadelphia, PA: Fortress Press.

Daly, Mary. 1978. *Gyn/Ecology.* Boston, MA: Beacon Press.

Davies, Philip R. 1998. "Life of Brian Research." In J. Cheryl Exum and Stephen D. Moore (eds) *Biblical Studies/Cultural Studies: the Third Sheffield Colloquium.* Sheffield: Sheffield Academic Press.

Debray, Régis. 1996. "The Book as Symbolic Object." In Geoffrey Nunberg (ed.) *The Future of the Book.* Berkeley, CA: University of California Press.

Deleuze, Gilles. 1983. *Nietzsche & Philosophy,* Hugh Tomlinson (trans.). New York: Columbia University Press.

Deleuze, Gilles. 1986. *Cinema 1: the Movement-Image,* Hugh Tomlinson and Barbara Habberjam (trans.). Minneapolis, MN: University of Minnesota Press.

Deleuze, Gilles. 1989. *Cinema 2: the Time-Image,* Hugh Tomlinson and Robert Galeta (trans.). London: Continuum.

Deleuze, Gilles. 1990. *The Logic of Sense,* Mark Lester and Charles Stivale (trans.). New York: Columbia University Press.

Deleuze, Gilles. 1994. *Difference and Repetition,* Paul Patton (trans.). New York: Columbia University Press.

Deleuze, Gilles and Claire Parnet. 2007. *Dialogues II,* Hugh Tomlinson and Barbara Habberjam (trans.). New York: Columbia University Press.

Deleuze, Gilles and Félix Guattari. 1983. *Anti-Oedipus,* Robert Hurley, Mark Seem and Helen R. Lane (trans.). Minneapolis, MN:University of Minnesota Press.

Deleuze, Gilles and Félix Guattari. 1987. *A Thousand Plateaus,* Brian Massumi (trans.). Minneapolis, MN: University of Minnesota Press.

Deleuze, Gilles and Félix Guattari. 1994. *What is Philosophy?,* Hugh Tomlinson and Graham Burchell (trans.). New York: Columbia University Press.

de Man, Paul. 1979. *Allegories of Reading.* New Haven, CT: Yale University Press.

de Man, Paul. 1983. *Blindness and Insight.* Minneapolis, MN: University of Minnesota Press.

de Man, Paul. 1986. *The Resistance to Theory*. Minneapolis, MN: University of Minnesota Press.

Derrida, Jacques. 1973. *Speech and Phenomena*, David B. Allison (trans.). Evanston, IL: Northwestern University Press.

Derrida, Jacques. 1976. *Of Grammatology*, Gayatri Chakravorty Spivak (trans.). Baltimore, MD: The Johns Hopkins University Press.

Derrida, Jacques. 1978. *Edmund Husserl's Origin of Geometry: an Introduction*, John P. Leavey, Jr. (trans.). Lincoln, NB: University of Nebraska Press.

Derrida, Jacques. 1981. *Dissemination*, Barbara Johnson (trans.). Chicago, IL: University of Chicago Press.

Derrida, Jacques. 1995. *On the Name*, David Wood, John P. Leavey, Jr. and Ian McLeod (trans.). Stanford, CA: Stanford University Press.

Dick, Philip K. 1982. *Blade Runner*. New York: Ballantine Books. Originally published in 1968 as *Do Androids Dream of Electronic Sheep?*

Dick, Philip K. 1987. *The Philip K. Dick Reader*. New York: Citadel Press.

Docker, John 2001. "In Praise of Polytheism." *Semeia* 88: 149–172.

Ducrot, Oswald and Tzvetan Todorov. 1979. *Encyclopedic Dictionary of the Sciences of Language*. Catherine Porter (trans.). Baltimore, MD: The Johns Hopkins University Press.

Duke, Paul D. 1985. *Irony in the Fourth Gospel*. Atlanta, GA: John Knox Press.

Dunn, James D. G. 1980. *Christology in the Making*. Philadelphia, PA: Westminster Press.

Eco, Umberto. 1976. *A Theory of Semiotics*. Bloomington, IN: Indiana University Press.

Eco, Umberto. 1979. *The Role of the Reader*. Bloomington, IN: Indiana University Press.

Edelstein, David. 2004. "Jesus H. Christ: *The Passion*, Mel Gibson's Bloody Mess." *Slate* (*Washington Post*, February 24, 2004) <http://slate.msn.com/id/2096025/>. Accessed September 8, 2009.

Ehrman, Bart D. 1993. *The Orthodox Corruption of Scripture*. Oxford: Oxford University Press.

Eisenstein, Elizabeth L. 1979. *The Printing Press as an Agent of Change*. 2 volumes. Cambridge: Cambridge University Press.

Farmer, William B. 1993. "The Minor Agreements of Matthew and Luke Against Mark and the Two Gospel Hypothesis." In Georg Strecker (ed.), *Minor Agreements: Symposium Göttingen 1991*, 163–207. Göttingen: Vanderhoeck and Ruprecht.

Farrar, A. M. 1955. "On Dispensing With Q." In D. E. Nineham (ed.) *Studies in the Gospels: Essays in Memory of R. H. Lightfoot*. Oxford: Blackwell.

Feuerbach, Ludwig. 1957. *The Essence of Christianity*, George Eliot (trans.). New York: Harper and Row.

Fowler, Robert M. 1991. *Let the Reader Understand*. Minneapolis, MN: Fortress Press.

Frege, Gottlob. 1952. *Translations From the Writings of Gottlob Frege*, P. T. Geach and M. Black (trans. and ed.). Totowa, NJ: Rowman and Littlefield.

Freud, Sigmund. 1955. "The 'Uncanny,'" Alix Strachey (trans.). In *Complete Psychological Works*, Vol. 17: 219–256. London: The Hogarth Press.

Friedrich, Pia. 1982. *Pier Paolo Pasolini*. Boston, MA: Twain Publishers.

Gaiman, Neil. 2003. *American Gods*. New York: HarperCollins.

Gamble, Harry Y. 1985. *The New Testament Canon: Its Making and Meaning.* Philadelphia, PA: Fortress Press.

Gamble, Harry Y. 1995. *Books and Readers in the Early Church.* New Haven, CT: Yale University Press.

Gibson, Mel, director. 2004. *The Passion of the Christ.* Newmarket Films.

Goodacre, Mark. 2000. *The Case Against Q: Studies in Markan Priority and the Synoptic Problem.* Harrisburg, PA: Trinity Press International.

Goulder, Michael D. 1993. "Luke's Knowledge of Matthew." In Georg Strecker (ed.), *Minor Agreements: Symposium Göttingen 1991,* 143–160. Göttingen: Vanderhoeck and Ruprecht.

Green, Joel B. 1997. *The Gospel of Luke.* Grand Rapids, MI: Wm. B. Eerdmans Publishing Company.

Greene, Naomi. 1990. *Pier Paolo Pasolini: Cinema as Heresy.* Princeton, NJ: Princeton University Press.

Hayles, N. Katherine. 1999. *How We Became Posthuman: Virtual Bodies in Cybernetics, Literature, and Informatics.* Chicago, IL: University of Chicago Press.

Husserl, Edmund. 1978. *The Origin of Geometry,* David Carr, trans. In Jacques Derrida, *Edmund Husserl's Origin of Geometry: an Introduction.* Lincoln, NB: University of Nebraska Press.

Jackson, Peter, director. 2001–2003. *The Lord of the Rings.* Burbank, CA: New Line Productions, Inc.

Jakobson, Roman. 1987. *Language and Literature,* Krystyna Pomorska and Stephen Rudy (eds). Cambridge, MA: Belknap Press of Harvard University.

Johnson, Sherman E. 1960. *A Commentary on the Gospel According to St Mark.* London: A. & C. Black.

Jones, Terry, director. 1979. *Monty Python's Life of Brian.* Orion Pictures (DVD, Criterion, 1999).

Kafka, Franz. 1958. *Parables and Paradoxes.* Various trans. New York: Schocken Books, Inc.

Kelber, Werner. 1983. *The Oral and the Written Gospel.* Philadelphia, PA: Fortress Press.

Kelly, J. N. D. 1960. *Early Christian Doctrines.* New York: Harper & Row.

Kermode, Frank. 1979. *The Genesis of Secrecy.* Cambridge, MA: Harvard University Press.

Kloppenborg, John S. 1987. *The Formation of Q.* Institute for Antiquity and Christianity. Philadelphia, PA: Fortress Press.

Kloppenborg, John S., Marvin W. Meyer, Stephen J. Patterson and Michael G. Steinhauser. 1990. *Q-Thomas Reader.* Sonoma, CA: Polebridge Press.

Kristeva, Julia. 1984. *Revolution in Poetic Language,* Margaret Waller (trans.). New York: Columbia University Press.

Kuhn, Jonas. 2009. "The Pied Piper Homepage" <http://www.ims.uni-stuttgart.de/~jonas/piedpiper.html>, accessed April 27, 2009.

Langguth, A. J. 1968. *Jesus Christs.* New York: Ballantine Books.

Lattimore, Richmond (trans.). 1979. *The Four Gospels and the Revelation.* New York: Dorset Press.

Library of Congress WWW page. 2009. "Freud: Conflict & Culture" <http://lcweb.loc.gov/exhibits/freud/freud02.html#40>, accessed April 27, 2009.

Liddell, Henry George and Scott, Robert (eds). 1996. *A Greek-English Lexicon.* New edition with revised supplement by Henry Stuart Jones and Roderick McKenzie, *et al.* London: Oxford at the Clarendon Press.

Lincoln, Andrew T. 2002. "The Beloved Disciple as Eyewitness and the Fourth Gospel as Witness." *Journal for the Study of the New Testament* 23 (3): 3–26.

Liukkonen, Petri. 2001. "Pier Paolo Pasolini" < http://www.kirjasto.sci.fi/pasolini.htm>, accessed April 27, 2009.

Miéville, China. 1998. *King Rat.* New York: Tom Doherty Associates.

Miéville, China. 2000. *Perdido Street Station.* New York: Ballantine Publishing Group.

Miéville, China. 2002. *The Scar.* New York: Ballantine Publishing Group.

Miéville, China. 2004. *Iron Council.* New York: Del Rey Books.

Miéville, China. 2005. *Looking for Jake.* New York: Del Rey Books.

Mitchell, Stephen (trans.). 1979. *The Book of Job.* New York: HarperCollins.

Moloney, Francis J. 2002. *The Gospel of Mark: A Commentary.* Peabody, MA: Hendrickson Publishers.

Moore, Stephen D. 1992. *Mark & Luke in Poststructuralist Perspectives: Jesus Begins to Write.* New Haven, CT: Yale University Press.

Moore, Stephen D. 1994. *Poststructuralism and the New Testament.* Minneapolis, MN: Fortress Press.

Morgan, Cheryl. 2001. "Interview: China Miéville." *Strange Horizons,* October 1 <http://www.strangehorizons.com/2001/20011001/china.shmtl>. Accessed April 27, 2009.

Myrick, Daniel and Eduardo Sánchez, directors. 1999. *The Blair Witch Project.* Beverley Hills: Haxan Films.

Neirynck, Frans. 1974. *The Minor Agreements of Matthew and Luke Against Mark.* Louvain: Leuven University Press.

Neirynck, Frans. 1993a. "The Minor Agreements and the Two-Source Theory." In Georg Strecker (ed.) *Minor Agreements: Symposium Göttingen 1991,* 25–62. Göttingen: Vanderhoeck and Ruprecht.

Neirynck, Frans. 1993b. "The Minor Agreements in a Horizontal-Line Synopsis." In Georg Strecker (ed.), *Minor Agreements: Symposium Göttingen 1991,* 221–230. Göttingen: Vanderhoeck and Ruprecht.

Nestle, Eberhard, Erwin Nestle, Kurt Aland, *et al.* (eds). 1979. *Novum Testamentum Graece.* 26th edn. In *Greek-English New Testament.* Stuttgart: Deutsche Bibelgesellschaft.

Nida, Eugene, and Charles R. Taber. 1982. *The Theory and Practice of Translation.* Leiden: E. J. Brill.

Nunberg, Geoffrey (ed.). 1996. *The Future of the Book.* Berkeley, CA: University of California Press.

Parker, D. C. 2003. "Through a Screen Darkly: Digital Texts and the New Testament." *Journal for the Study of The New Testament* 25 (4) (June): 395–411.

Parker, Pierson. 1960. "John and John Mark." *Journal of Biblical Literature* 79 (2): 97–110.

Pasolini, Pier Paolo, director. 1964. *The Gospel According to Saint Matthew (Il Vangelo secondo Matteo).* Rome: Arco Film S.r.L. (VHS and DVD, Waterbearer Films 2003).

Patton, Paul and John Protevi (eds). 2003. *Between Deleuze and Derrida.* London: Continuum Books.

Philip K. Dick Trust. 2004. *The Philip K. Dick Official Site*. <http://www.philipkdick.com/>. Accessed April 28, 2009.

Phillips, Marie. 2007. *Gods Behaving Badly*. New York: Little, Brown and Company.

Pippin, Tina. 1992. *Death and Desire: the Rhetoric of Gender in the Apocalypse of John*. Louisville, KY: Westminster/John Knox.

Plato. 1973. *Phaedrus*, Walter Hamilton (trans.). Harmondsworth: Penguin Books.

Pullman, Philip. 1995. *The Golden Compass*. New York: Random House.

Pullman, Philip. 1997. *The Subtle Knife*. New York: Random House.

Pullman, Philip. 2000. *The Amber Spyglass*. New York: Random House.

Pyper, Hugh S. 2005. *An Unsuitable Book: the Bible as Scandalous Text*. Sheffield: Sheffield Phoenix.

Rahlfs, Albert (ed.). 1979. *Septuaginta*. Stuttgart: Deutsche Bibelgesellschaft.

Reinhartz, Adele. 2001. "Jesus in Film: Hollywood Perspectives on the Jewishness of Jesus." *The Journal of Religion and Film* <http://www.unomaha.edu/~jrf/JesusinFilmRein.htm>. Accessed April 27, 2009.

Revised Standard Version. 1971. *The Bible*. New York: Division of Christian Education of the National Council of Churches of Christ in the United States of America.

Robinson, Kim Stanley. 2002. *The Years of Rice and Salt*. New York: Bantam Books.

Sandys-Wunsch, John. 2005. *What Have They Done to the Bible? A History of Modern Biblical Interpretation*. Collegeville, MN: Liturgical Press.

Schaberg, Jane. 1987. *The Illegitimacy of Jesus: a Feminist Theological Interpretation of the Infancy Narratives*. New York: Crossroad Publishing Co.

Schnackenburg, Rudolf. 1980a. *The Gospel According to St John*, Volume 1, Kevin Smyth (trans.). New York: Seabury Press/Crossroad.

Schnackenburg, Rudolf. 1980b. *The Gospel According to St John*, Volume 2, Cecily Hastings, Francis McDonagh, David Smith, and Richard Foley, SJ (trans.). New York: The Crossroad Publishing Company.

Schnackenburg, Rudolf. 1982. *The Gospel According to St John*, Volume 3, David Smith and G. A. Kon (trans.). New York: The Crossroad Publishing Company.

Scott, Ridley, director. 1982. *Blade Runner*. Los Angeles, CA: the Ladd Company, Warner Brothers.

Sherwood, Yvonne. 2000. *A Biblical Text and its Afterlives: the Survival of Jonah in Western Culture*. Cambridge: Cambridge University Press.

Shoemaker, Stephen J. 2001. "Rethinking the 'Gnostic Mary': Mary of Nazareth and Mary of Magdala in Early Christian Tradition." *Journal of Early Christian Studies* 9 (4): 555–595.

Smith, Dwight Moody. 1990. *John Among the Gospels*. Second Edition. Columbia, SC: University of South Carolina Press.

Spielberg, Steven, director. 2002. *Minority Report*. Universal City, CA: Dreamworks/Twentieth Century Fox (DVD).

Staley, Jeffrey Lloyd. 1988. *The Print's First Kiss*. SBL dissertation series #82. Atlanta, GA: Scholars Press.

Staley, Jeffrey Lloyd. 1999. "Disseminations: an Autobiographical Midrash on Fatherhood in John's Gospel." *Semeia* 85: 127–154.

Staley, Jeffrey Lloyd. 2005. "Reading 'This Woman' Back into John 7:1–8:59: *Liar Liar* and the 'Pericope Adulterae' in Intertextual Tango." In George Aichele and Richard Walsh (eds) *Those Outside: Noncanonical Readings of Canonical Gospels*, 85–107. London: Continuum/T&T Clark International.

Staley, Jeffrey L. and Richard Walsh. 2007. *Jesus, the Gospels, and Cinematic Imagination: a Handbook to Jesus on DVD*. Louisville, KY: Westminster John Knox Press.

Sugirtharajah, R. S. 2003. "Loitering With Intent: Biblical Texts in Public Places." *Biblical Interpretation* 11 (3–4): 566–578.

Sykes, Peter, and John Krisch, directors. 1979. *The Jesus Film*. Montreal: Madacy Entertainment.

Taylor, Vincent. 1953. *The Gospel According to Saint Mark*. London: Macmillan & Co., Ltd.

Testa, Bart. 1994. "To Film a Gospel ... and Advent of the Theoretical Stranger." In Patrick Rumble and Bart Testa (eds), *Pier Paolo Pasolini: Contemporary Perspectives*, 180–209. Toronto: University of Toronto Press.

Todorov, Tzvetan. 1973. *The Fantastic*, Richard Howard (trans.). Cleveland, OH: Case Western Reserve University Press.

Tolkien, J. R. R. 1966. "On Fairy-stories." In *The Tolkien Reader*, 33–99. New York: Ballantine Books.

Tolkien, J. R. R. 1994. *The Lord of the Rings*. 3 volumes. New York: Ballantine Books.

Tuckett, Christopher M. 1993. "Minor Agreements and Textual Criticism." In Georg Strecker (ed.), *Minor Agreements: Symposium Göttingen 1991*, 119–141. Göttingen: Vanderhoeck and Ruprecht.

Walsh, Richard. 2003. *Reading the Gospels in the Dark: Portrayals of Jesus in Film*. Harrisburg, PA: Trinity Press International.

Walsh, Richard. 2005. *Finding St Paul in Film*. New York: T&T Clark International.

Wenders, Wim, director. 1987. *Wings of Desire (Der Himmel Über Berlin)*. Berlin: Road Movies Filmproduktion.

Wharton, Thomas. 2001. *Salamander*. New York: Washington Square Press

Williams, James. 2003. *Gilles Deleuze's Difference and Repetition*. Edinburgh: Edinburgh University Press.

Wilken, Robert L. 1971. *The Myth of Christian Beginnings*. Garden City: Doubleday & Co., Inc.

Zefferelli, Franco, director. 1977. *Jesus of Nazareth*. London: ITC.

Ziolkowski, Theodore. 1972. *Fictional Transfigurations of Jesus*. Princeton, NJ: Princeton University Press.

INDEX OF REFERENCES

INDEX OF NAMES

Lightning Source UK Ltd.
Milton Keynes UK

173161UK00002B/1/P